NON SANZ DROICT.

William Shakespeare

The Tragedy of
JULIUS CAESAR

Edited by William and Barbara Rosen

The Signet Classic Shakespeare
GENERAL EDITOR: SYLVAN BARNET

PUBLISHED BY THE NEW AMERICAN LIBRARY, NEW YORK
AND
THE NEW ENGLISH LIBRARY LIMITED, LONDON

Contents

Shakespeare: Prefatory Remarks

Between the record of his baptism in Stratford on 26 April 1564 and the record of his burial in Stratford on 25 April 1616, some forty documents name Shakespeare, and many others name his parents, his children, and his grandchildren. More facts are known about William Shakespeare than about any other playwright of the period except Ben Jonson. The facts should, however, be distinguished from the legends. The latter, inevitably more engaging and better known, tell us that the Stratford boy killed a calf in high style, poached deer and rabbits, and was forced to flee to London, where he held horses outside a playhouse. These traditions are only traditions; they may be true, but no evidence supports them, and it is well to stick to the facts.

Mary Arden, the dramatist's mother, was the daughter of a substantial landowner; about 1557 she married John Shakespeare, who was a glove-maker and trader in various farm commodities. In 1557 John Shakespeare was a member of the Council (the governing body of Stratford), in 1558 a constable of the borough, in 1561 one of the two town chamberlains, in 1565 an alderman (entitling him to the appellation "Mr."), in 1568 high bailiff—the town's highest political office, equivalent to mayor. After 1577, for an unknown reason he drops out of local politics. The birthday of William Shakespeare, the eldest son of this locally prominent man, is unrecorded; but the Stratford parish register records that the infant was baptized on 26 April 1564. (It is quite possible that he was born on 23 April, but this date has probably been assigned by tradition because it is the date on which, fifty-two years later, he died.) The attendance records of the Stratford grammar school of the period are not extant, but it is reasonable to assume that the son of a local official attended the school and received substantial training in Latin. The masters of the school from Shakespeare's seventh to fifteenth years held Oxford degrees; the Elizabethan curriculum excluded mathematics and the natural sciences but taught a good deal of Latin rhetoric, logic, and literature. On 27 November 1582 a marriage license was issued to Shakespeare and Anne Hathaway, eight years his senior. The couple had a child in May, 1583. Perhaps the marriage was necessary, but perhaps the couple had earlier engaged in a formal "troth plight" which would render their children legitimate even if no further ceremony were performed. In 1585 Anne Hathaway bore Shakespeare twins.

That Shakespeare was born is excellent; that he married and had children is pleasant; but that we know nothing about his departure from Stratford to London, or about the beginning of his theatrical career, is lamentable and must be admitted. We would gladly sacrifice details about his children's baptism for details about his earliest days on the stage. Perhaps the poaching episode is true (but it is first reported almost a century after Shakespeare's death), or perhaps he first left Stratford to be a schoolteacher, as another tradition holds; perhaps he was moved by

> Such wind as scatters young men through the world,
> To seek their fortunes further than at home
> Where small experience grows.

In 1592, thanks to the cantankerousness of Robert Greene, a rival playwright and a pamphleteer, we have our first reference, a snarling one, to Shakespeare as an actor and playwright. Greene warns those of his own educated friends who wrote for the theater against an actor who has presumed to turn playwright:

> There is an upstart crow, beautified with our feathers, that with his *tiger's heart wrapped in a player's hide* supposes he

is as well able to bombast out a blank verse as the best of you, and being an absolute Johannes-factotum is in his own conceit the only Shake-scene in a country.

The reference to the player, as well as the allusion to Aesop's crow (who strutted in borrowed plumage, as an actor struts in fine words not his own), makes it clear that by this date Shakespeare had both acted and written. That Shakespeare is meant is indicated not only by "Shake-scene" but by the parody of a line from one of Shakespeare's plays, *3 Henry VI*: "O, tiger's heart wrapped in a woman's hide." If Shakespeare in 1592 was prominent enough to be attacked by an envious dramatist, he probably had served an apprenticeship in the theater for at least a few years.

In any case, by 1592 Shakespeare had acted and written, and there are a number of subsequent references to him as an actor: documents indicate that in 1598 he is a "principal comedian," in 1603 a "principal tragedian," in 1608 he is one of the "men players." The profession of actor was not for a gentleman, and it occasionally drew the scorn of university men who resented writing speeches for persons less educated than themselves, but it was respectable enough: players, if prosperous, were in effect members of the bourgeoisie, and there is nothing to suggest that Stratford considered William Shakespeare less than a solid citizen. When, in 1596, the Shakespeares were granted a coat of arms, the grant was made to Shakespeare's father, but probably William Shakespeare (who the next year bought the second-largest house in town) had arranged the matter on his own behalf. In subsequent transactions he is occasionally styled a gentleman.

Although in 1593 and 1594 Shakespeare published two narrative poems dedicated to the Earl of Southampton, *Venus and Adonis* and *The Rape of Lucrece*, and may well have written most or all of his sonnets in the middle nineties, Shakespeare's literary activity seems to have been almost entirely devoted to the theater. (It may be significant that the two narrative poems were written in years when the plague closed the theaters for several months.) In 1594 he was a charter member of a theatrical company called the

Chamberlain's Men (which in 1603 changed its name to the King's Men); until he retired to Stratford (about 1611, apparently), he was with this remarkably stable company. From 1599 the company acted primarily at the Globe Theatre, in which Shakespeare held a one-tenth interest. Other Elizabethan dramatists are known to have acted, but no other is known also to have been entitled to a share in the profits of the playhouse.

Shakespeare's first eight published plays did not have his name on them, but this is not remarkable; the most popular play of the sixteenth century, Thomas Kyd's *The Spanish Tragedy*, went through many editions without naming Kyd, and Kyd's authorship is known only because a book on the profession of acting happens to quote (and attribute to Kyd) some lines on the interest of Roman emperors in the drama. What is remarkable is that after 1598 Shakespeare's name commonly appears on printed plays—some of which are not his. Another indication of his popularity comes from Francis Meres, author of *Palladis Tamia: Wit's Treasury* (1598): in this anthology of snippets accompanied by an essay on literature, many playwrights are mentioned, but Shakespeare's name occurs more often than any other, and Shakespeare is the only playwright whose plays are listed.

From his acting, playwriting, and share in a theater, Shakespeare seems to have made considerable money. He put it to work, making substantial investments in Stratford real estate. When he made his will (less than a month before he died), he sought to leave his property intact to his descendants. Of small bequests to relatives and to friends (including three actors, Richard Burbage, John Heminges, and Henry Condell), that to his wife of the second-best bed has provoked the most comment; perhaps it was the bed the couple had slept in, the best being reserved for visitors. In any case, had Shakespeare not excepted it, the bed would have gone (with the rest of his household possessions) to his daughter and her husband. On 25 April 1616 he was buried within the chancel of the church at Stratford. An unattractive monument to his memory, placed on a wall near the grave, says he died on 23 April. Over the grave itself are the lines, perhaps by Shakespeare, that (more than his literary fame) have kept his bones undisturbed in the crowded burial ground where old bones were often dislodged to make way for new:

> Good friend, for Jesus' sake forbear
> To dig the dust enclosèd here.
> Blessed be the man that spares these stones
> And cursed be he that moves my bones.

Thirty-seven plays, as well as some nondramatic poems, are held to constitute the Shakespeare canon. The dates of composition of most of the works are highly uncertain, but there is often evidence of a *terminus a quo* (starting point) and/or a *terminus ad quem* (terminal point) that provides a framework for intelligent guessing. For example, *Richard II* cannot be earlier than 1595, the publication date of some material to which it is indebted; *The Merchant of Venice* cannot be later than 1598, the year Francis Meres mentioned it. Sometimes arguments for a date hang on an alleged topical allusion, such as the lines about the unseasonable weather in *A Midsummer Night's Dream*, II.i.81–87, but such an allusion (if indeed it is an allusion) can be variously interpreted, and in any case there is always the possibility that a topical allusion was inserted during a revision, years after the composition of a play. Dates are often attributed on the basis of style, and although conjectures about style usually rest on other conjectures, sooner or later one must rely on one's literary sense. There is no real proof, for example, that *Othello* is not as early as *Romeo and Juliet*, but one feels *Othello* is later, and because the first record of its performance is 1604, one is glad enough to set its composition at that date and not push it back into Shakespeare's early years. The following chronology, then, is as much indebted to informed guesswork and sensitivity as it is to fact. The dates, necessarily imprecise, indicate something like a scholarly consensus.

PLAYS

1588–93	*The Comedy of Errors*
1588–94	*Love's Labor's Lost*

1590–91	*2 Henry VI*
1590–91	*3 Henry VI*
1591–92	*1 Henry VI*
1592–93	*Richard III*
1592–94	*Titus Andronicus*
1593–94	*The Taming of the Shrew*
1593–95	*The Two Gentlemen of Verona*
1594–96	*Romeo and Juliet*
1595	*Richard II*
1594–96	*A Midsummer Night's Dream*
1596–97	*King John*
1596–97	*The Merchant of Venice*
1597	*1 Henry IV*
1597–98	*2 Henry IV*
1598–1600	*Much Ado About Nothing*
1598–99	*Henry V*
1599	*Julius Caesar*
1599–1600	*As You Like It*
1599–1600	*Twelfth Night*
1600–01	*Hamlet*
1597–1601	*The Merry Wives of Windsor*
1601–02	*Troilus and Cressida*
1602–04	*All's Well That Ends Well*
1603–04	*Othello*
1604	*Measure for Measure*
1605–06	*King Lear*
1605–06	*Macbeth*
1606–07	*Antony and Cleopatra*
1605–08	*Timon of Athens*
1607–09	*Coriolanus*
1608–09	*Pericles*
1609–10	*Cymbeline*
1610–11	*The Winter's Tale*
1611–12	*The Tempest*
1612–13	*Henry VIII*

POEMS

| 1592 | *Venus and Adonis* |
| 1593–94 | *The Rape of Lucrece* |

1593–1600 *Sonnets*
1600–01   *The Phoenix and the Turtle*

Shakespeare's Theater

In Shakespeare's infancy, Elizabethan actors performed wherever they could—in great halls, at court, in the courtyards of inns. The innyards must have made rather unsatisfactory theaters: on some days they were unavailable because carters bringing goods to London used them as depots; when available, they had to be rented from the innkeeper; perhaps most important, London inns were subject to the Common Council of London, which was not well disposed toward theatricals. In 1574 the Common Council required that plays and playing places in London be licensed. It asserted that

> sundry great disorders and inconveniences have been found to ensue to this city by the inordinate haunting of great multitudes of people, specially youth, to plays, interludes, and shows, namely occasion of frays and quarrels, evil practices of incontinency in great inns having chambers and secret places adjoining to their open stages and galleries,

and ordered that innkeepers who wished licenses to hold performances put up a bond and make contributions to the poor.

The requirement that plays and innyard theaters be licensed, along with the other drawbacks of playing at inns, probably drove James Burbage (a carpenter-turned-actor) to rent in 1576 a plot of land northeast of the city walls and to build here—on property outside the jurisdiction of the city—England's first permanent construction designed for plays. He called it simply the Theatre. About all that is known of its construction is that it was wood. It soon had imitators, the most famous being the Globe (1599), built across the Thames (again outside the city's jurisdiction), out of timbers of the Theatre, which had been dismantled when Burbage's lease ran out.

There are three important sources of information about the structure of Elizabethan playhouses—drawings, a contract, and stage directions in plays. Of drawings, only the so-called De Witt drawing (c. 1596) of the Swan—really a friend's copy of De Witt's drawing—is of much significance. It shows a building of three tiers, with a stage jutting from a wall into the yard or center of the building. The tiers are roofed, and part of the stage is covered by a roof that projects from the rear and is supported at its front on two posts, but the groundlings, who paid a penny to stand in front of the stage, were exposed to the sky. (Performances in such a playhouse were held only in the daytime; artificial illumination was not used.) At the rear of the stage are two doors; above the stage is a gallery. The second major source of information, the contract for the Fortune, specifies that although the Globe is to be the model, the Fortune is to be square, eighty feet outside and fifty-five inside. The stage is to be forty-three feet broad, and is to extend into the middle of the yard (i.e., it is twenty-seven and a half feet deep). For patrons willing to pay more than the general admission charged of the groundlings, there were to be three galleries provided with seats. From the third chief source, stage directions, one learns that entrance to the stage was by doors, presumably spaced widely apart at the rear ("Enter one citizen at one door, and another at the other"), and that in addition to the platform stage there was occasionally some sort of curtained booth or alcove allowing for "discovery" scenes, and some sort of playing space "aloft" or "above" to represent (for example) the top of a city's walls or a room above the street. Doubtless each theater had its own peculiarities, but perhaps we can talk about a "typical" Elizabethan theater if we realize that no theater need exactly have fit the description, just as no father is the typical father with 3.7 children. This hypothetical theater is wooden, round or polygonal (in *Henry V* Shakespeare calls it a "wooden O"), capable of holding some eight hundred spectators standing in the yard around the projecting elevated stage and some fifteen hundred additional spectators seated in the three roofed galleries. The stage, protected by a "shadow" or "heavens" or roof, is entered by two doors; behind the doors is the "tiring house" (attiring house, i.e., dressing room), and above the doors is some sort of gallery that may sometimes hold spectators but that can be used (for example) as the bedroom from which Romeo—according to a stage direction in one text—"goeth down." Some evidence suggests that a throne can be lowered onto the platform stage, perhaps from the "shadow"; certainly characters can descend from the stage through a trap or traps into the cellar or "hell." Sometimes this space beneath the platform accommodates a sound-effects man or musician (in *Antony and Cleopatra* "music of the hautboys is under the stage") or an actor (in *Hamlet* the "Ghost cries under the stage"). Most characters simply walk on and off, but because there is no curtain in front of the platform, corpses will have to be carried off (Hamlet must lug Polonius' guts into the neighbor room), or will have to fall at the rear, where the curtain on the alcove or booth can be drawn to conceal them.

Such may have been the so-called "public theater." Another kind of theater, called the "private theater" because its much greater admission charge limited its audience to the wealthy or the prodigal, must be briefly mentioned. The private theater was basically a large room, entirely roofed and therefore artificially illuminated, with a stage at one end. In 1576 one such theater was established in Blackfriars, a Dominican priory in London that had been suppressed in 1538 and confiscated by the Crown and thus was not under the city's jurisdiction. All the actors in the Blackfriars theater were boys about eight to thirteen years old (in the public theaters similar boys played female parts; a boy Lady Macbeth played to a man Macbeth). This private theater had a precarious existence, and ceased operations in 1584. In 1596 James Burbage, who had already made theatrical history by building the Theatre, began to construct a second Blackfriars theater. He died in 1597, and for several years this second Blackfriars theater was used by a troupe of boys, but in 1608 two of Burbage's sons and five other actors (including Shakespeare) became joint operators of the theater, using it in the winter when the open-air Globe was unsuitable. Perhaps such a smaller theater, roofed, artificially illuminated, and with a tradition of a courtly audience, exerted an influence on Shakespeare's late plays.

Performances in the private theaters may well have had intermissions during which music was played, but in the public theaters the action was probably uninterrupted, flowing from scene to scene almost without a break. Actors would enter, speak, exit, and others would immediately enter and establish (if necessary) the new locale by a few properties and by words and gestures. Here are some samples of Shakespeare's scene painting:

> This is Illyria, lady.

> Well, this is the Forest of Arden.

> This castle hath a pleasant seat; the air
> Nimbly and sweetly recommends itself
> Unto our gentle senses.

On the other hand, it is a mistake to conceive of the Elizabethan stage as bare. Although Shakespeare's Chorus in *Henry V* calls the stage an "unworthy scaffold" and urges the spectators to "eke out our performance with your mind," there was considerable spectacle. The last act of *Macbeth*, for example, has five stage directions calling for "drum and colors," and another sort of appeal to the eye is indicated by the stage direction "Enter Macduff, with Macbeth's head." Some scenery and properties may have been substantial; doubtless a throne was used, and in one play of the period we encounter this direction: "Hector takes up a great piece of rock and casts at Ajax, who tears up a young tree by the roots and assails Hector." The matter is of some importance, and will be glanced at again in the next section.

The Texts of Shakespeare

Though eighteen of his plays were published during his lifetime, Shakespeare seems never to have supervised their publication. There is nothing unusual here; when a play-wright sold a play to a theatrical company he surrendered his ownership of it. Normally a company would not publish the play, because to publish it meant to allow competitors to acquire the piece. Some plays, however, did get published: apparently treacherous actors sometimes pieced together a play for a publisher, sometimes a company in need of money sold a play, and sometimes a company allowed a play to be published that no longer drew audiences. That Shakespeare did not concern himself with publication, then, is scarcely remarkable; of his contemporaries only Ben Jonson carefully supervised the publication of his own plays. In 1623, seven years after Shakespeare's death, John Hem-inges and Henry Condell (two senior members of Shake-speare's company, who had performed with him for about twenty years) collected his plays—published and unpub-lished—into a large volume, commonly called the First Folio. (A folio is a volume consisting of sheets that have been folded once, each sheet thus making two leaves, or four pages. The eighteen plays published during Shakespeare's lifetime had been issued one play per volume in small books called quartos. Each sheet in a quarto has been folded twice, making four leaves, or eight pages.) The First Folio contains thirty-six plays; a thirty-seventh, *Pericles*, though not in the Folio, is regarded as canonical. Heminges and Condell suggest in an address "To the great variety of readers" that the republished plays are presented in better form than in the quartos: "Before you were abused with diverse stolen and surreptitious copies, maimed and de-formed by the frauds and stealths of injurious impostors that exposed them; even those, are now offered to your view cured and perfect of their limbs, and all the rest absolute in their numbers, as he [i.e., Shakespeare] conceived them."

Whoever was assigned to prepare the texts for publication in the First Folio seems to have taken his job seriously and yet not to have performed it with uniform care. The sources of the texts seem to have been, in general, good unpublished copies or the best published copies. The first play in the collection, *The Tempest*, is divided into acts and scenes, has unusually full stage directions and descriptions of spectacle, and concludes with a list of the characters, but the editor was not able (or willing) to present all of the succeeding texts so fully dressed. Later texts occasionally show signs of carelessness: in one scene of *Much Ado About Nothing* the names of actors, instead of characters, appear as speech prefixes, as they had in the quarto, which the Folio reprints; proofreading throughout the Folio is spotty and apparently was done without reference to the printer's copy; the pagination of *Hamlet* jumps from 156 to 257.

A modern editor of Shakespeare must first select his copy; no problem if the play exists only in the Folio, but a considerable problem if the relationship between a quarto and the Folio—or an early quarto and a later one—is unclear. When an editor has chosen what seems to him to be the most authoritative text or texts for his copy, he has not done with making decisions. First of all, he must reckon with Elizabethan spelling. If he is not producing a facsimile, he probably modernizes it, but ought he to preserve the old form of words that apparently were pronounced quite unlike their modern forms—"lanthorn" "alablaster"? If he preserves these forms, is he really preserving Shakespeare's forms or perhaps those of a compositor in the printing house? What is one to do when one finds "lanthorn" and "lantern" in adjacent lines? (The editors of this series in general, but not invariably, assume that words should be spelled in their modern form.) Elizabethan punctuation, too, presents problems. For example in the First Folio, the only text for the play, Macbeth rejects his wife's idea that he can wash the blood from his hand:

> no: this my Hand will rather
> The multitudinous Seas incarnardine,
> Making the Greene one, Red.

Obviously an editor will remove the superfluous capitals, and he will probably alter the spelling to "incarnadine," but will he leave the comma before "red," letting Macbeth speak of the sea as "the green one," or will he (like most modern editors) remove the comma and thus have Macbeth say that his hand will make the ocean *uniformly* red?

An editor will sometimes have to change more than spelling or punctuation. Macbeth says to his wife:

> I dare do all that may become a man,
> Who dares no more, is none.

For two centuries editors have agreed that the second line is unsatisfactory, and have emended "no" to "do": "Who dares do more is none." But when in the same play Ross says that fearful persons

> floate vpon a wilde and violent Sea
> Each way, and moue,

need "move" be emended to "none," as it often is, on the hunch that the compositor misread the manuscript? The editors of the Signet Classic Shakespeare have restrained themselves from making abundant emendations. In their minds they hear Dr. Johnson on the dangers of emending: "I have adopted the Roman sentiment, that it is more honorable to save a citizen than to kill an enemy." Some departures (in addition to spelling, punctuation, and lineation) from the copy text have of course been made, but the original readings are listed in a note following the play, so that the reader can evaluate them for himself.

The editors of the Signet Classic Shakespeare, following tradition, have added line numbers and in many cases act and scene divisions as well as indications of locale at the beginning of scenes. The Folio divided most of the plays into acts and some into scenes. Early eighteenth-century editors increased the divisions. These divisions, which provide a convenient way of referring to passages in the plays, have been retained, but when not in the text chosen as the basis for the Signet Classic text they are enclosed in square brackets [ ] to indicate that they are editorial additions. Similarly, although no play of Shakespeare's published during his lifetime was equipped with indications of locale at the heads of scene divisions, locales have here been added in square brackets for the convenience of the reader, who lacks the information afforded to spectators by costumes, properties, and gestures. The spectator can tell at a glance he is in the throne room, but without an editorial indication the reader may be puzzled for a while. It should be mentioned, incidentally, that there are a few authentic stage directions—perhaps Shakespeare's, perhaps a prompter's—that suggest locales: for example, "Enter Brutus in his orchard," and "They go up into the Senate house." It is hoped that the bracketed additions provide the reader with the sort of help provided in these two authentic directions, but it is equally hoped that the reader will remember that the stage was not loaded with scenery.

No editor during the course of his work can fail to recollect some words Heminges and Condell prefixed to the Folio:

> It had been a thing, we confess, worthy to have been wished, that the author himself had lived to have set forth and overseen his own writings. But since it hath been ordained otherwise, and he by death departed from that right, we pray you do not envy his friends the office of their care and pain to have collected and published them.

Nor can an editor, after he has done his best, forget Heminges and Condell's final words: "And so we leave you to other of his friends, whom if you need can be your guides. If you need them not, you can lead yourselves, and others. And such readers we wish him."

SYLVAN BARNET
Tufts University

Introduction

Thomas Platter, a Swiss traveler to England, recorded his visit of September 21, 1599, to a London theater: at about two o'clock, after lunch, he and his party crossed the river, and in a house with a thatched roof saw an excellent performance of the tragedy of the first Emperor Julius Caesar. (Platter was mistaken in giving to Caesar the title of "Emperor," either because he was weak in history or because he was impressed by the imperious portrayal of the title role.) He went on to note that there was a cast of about fifteen, and that after the play, according to custom, there was a most elegant and curious dance, two participants being dressed in men's clothes, and two in women's.

The dance that Platter saw was the jig, and the play was undoubtedly Shakespeare's *The Tragedy of Julius Caesar*, performed at the newly constructed Globe Theatre. It is quite probable that Shakespeare wrote the play early in 1599, and it marks an important stage in his development. His previous work, *Henry V* (1599), was the last of a long series of English history plays; and while attention shifts to Roman times in *Julius Caesar*, Shakespeare incorporates those ideas of history that grew through the English plays. Starting as a chronicle of wars and bloody events, the histories progressively move toward a recognition of tragedy through historical process. As the histories unfold, Shakespeare's horror of civil war becomes increasingly apparent; and as the focus narrows to individual rulers, we see the development of his intense belief in the divine quality of kingship as the only possible safeguard against civil dissension.

In *Julius Caesar* Shakespeare continues to explore the drama of power politics and personal conscience; only now, as if to gain perspective on the great issues of the histories, he moves the setting to a more distant time. The shift to ancient history would have sharpened rather than blunted the play's contemporary relevance because of the acknowledged Elizabethan habit of viewing history as a series of object lessons for present conduct.

We must not forget how widespread was the longing for unshakable rule and how overwhelming was the dread of civil war at the time *Julius Caesar* was first performed. Elizabeth I had come to the throne in 1558 when the country was in such a state of rebellion and confusion that it seemed likely to slip back into the horrors of the Wars of the Roses. Elizabeth had given her subjects peace, and the nation had prospered; for many years she had been a strong ruler, despite the repeated Catholic claims that she was illegitimate and therefore not a true successor. Attempts at assassination had been many. By 1599 she was old and visibly failing. She had no direct heir; there was no one whose claim to the throne after her was beyond dispute. Childless like Caesar, she could pass on the office only by naming an heir, and this she refused to do, perhaps in order to prevent the growth of factions. The shadow of war and dissension grew ominous. In such circumstances, we see first among the issues of *Julius Caesar* the very topical and concrete problem of a disputed succession, and the more abstract problem of killing—and replacing—the ruler.

Even without Machiavelli many Elizabethans knew that the moral problems of government are not necessarily the same as the moral problems of men. It was precisely because Elizabeth had compromised her personal beliefs whenever the public interest demanded it that she had been so successful a ruler; indeed, in many cases it is still impossible to know what she as a private person believed. Mary Tudor, who had tried to rule in accordance with religious principles, had brought about years of bloodshed. The theory of divine grace accorded to the public actions of a duly appointed ruler was not childish authoritarianism but a philosophical way of resolving the well-perceived gap between what the man might believe and what the ruler must do.

When we view *Julius Caesar* in the light of the political considerations of its own time, many of the difficulties of the play, which are discussed in critical articles in this volume, can be seen in perspective. Caesar *is* proud, and destined for the punishment of *hubris;* he is, nonetheless, "the ruler" by ability as well as power, as Plutarch himself suggests in *The Life of Julius Caesar*, a primary source for Shakespeare's work:

> ... the Romans, inclining to Caesar's prosperity and taking the bit in the mouth, supposing that to be ruled by one man alone, it would be a good mean for them to take breath a little, after so many troubles and miseries as they had abidden in these civil wars, they chose him perpetual Dictator. ... And now for himself, after he had ended his civil wars, he did so honorably behave himself, that there was no fault to be found in him. ...

Plutarch goes on to list Caesar's achievements and enterprises, and suggests that his only failing is a desire to be *called* king. However, Caesar's personal faults have no bearing upon his public abilities.

Brutus is high-minded and disinterested, even though his love of political liberty leads him to transgress the rules of allegiance to a ruler and gratitude to a benefactor. His personal virtues, however, have no bearing upon his public abilities. He is naïve enough to believe that a republic needs no power structure, that the removal of Caesar will simply allow power to flow back to the officers of the republic. But of course events prove otherwise, and he and Cassius are forced in their turn to assume power against those who would "destroy the revolution." Neither Brutus nor Cassius has the ability—or the right—to rule, and both are defeated. Yet the man who ultimately replaces them is not the man who roused the public against them, but the one whose impersonal manner from the beginning marks him as the next possessor of the power to rule—Octavius Caesar.

Brutus, Octavius, and Antony all become guilty as men. Brutus kills his friend; Octavius joins the others of the Triumvirate in condemning innocent men to death; Antony deliberately rouses a mob and turns it loose to do what mischief it will. What they do, however, does not matter in considering the fitness of each to rule. Personal innocence or guilt is not in question, and we are not asked to feel that one man or another is "right." We are asked to see that while a just man in private life is to be praised, a just man in public life may very well bring about catastrophe. The wicked—or, like Caesar, the conceited and superstitious— may be the genius as a ruler. Man's worth as a private individual does not necessarily ensure his value as a public ruler. Less sentimental than many of his critics, Shakespeare sees that a morally repulsive act may at times be a politically desirable one; that a man who acts from the highest of motives may be too busy keeping his conscience clean to lead well; that a man who once does evil in the expectation that good will be the final result may be forced more deeply into self-deception and impotence than a man who acts simply from expediency. But he also sees that the pursuit of expediency and lack of scruple do not in themselves guarantee ability to govern—else why not, ultimately, an Antony in command?

There is a natural inclination to desire unequivocal answers and absolute judgments, to simplify events until they can be seen as black or white; and we are naturally bewildered when forced into a position that requires us to judge but forbids us the use of simple terms of reference. It is not surprising, therefore, that we may be confounded by *Julius Caesar*, for often we confront situations in which personalities and actions are neither wholly right nor wholly wrong. We cannot feel unreserved hate or love for any character; each seems to call for a different response as he reacts to the seemingly irreconcilable demands of public and private life. Caesar is deaf, aging, subject to epileptic fits, inclined to superstition, warmhearted to his friends in private yet inflexible in public. But if we can believe Antony at all, Caesar has a genuine love of his country. His fault is a kind of ecstasy that the exercise of his office brings upon him. As a private individual he shows many weaknesses; as a public institution he sees himself superior to all ordinary dangers, and believes that his office is a power that must not be opposed. Indeed, Caesar constantly uses his name to speak of his alter ego, the Dictator, and in an early speech to Antony, in which he reveals his distrust of Cassius, he sums up the two views of himself as he unwittingly contrasts two attitudes: the public office that is perfect, and the private individual who is defective. It is as though his public self is quite dissociated from his personal weaknesses:

> I rather tell thee what is to be feared
> Than what I fear; for always I am Caesar.
> Come on my right hand, for this ear is deaf,
> And tell me truly what thou think'st of him.

> (I.ii.211–14)

Caesar may have a number of weaknesses, but none of the personal defects impair the spirit of Caesar—the capacity to rule. The play vividly demonstrates that there is more stability, freedom, and justice in Rome with Caesar alive than with Caesar dead.

We may be far more sympathetic to the personality of Brutus; yet we must admit that neither he nor Cassius has any specific charges that would warrant the killing of Caesar. Cassius derides Caesar's weaknesses. His attacks are the result of personal envy—why should the fact that Caesar failed in a swimming contest, or suffered from fever, make him contemptible as a ruler? And Brutus admits that he has no immediate cause for indicting his friend. His soliloquy at the beginning of Act II is an agonized attempt to reconcile the idea of tyranny with the personal Caesar he knows. He begins his analysis of the situation with the conclusion—"It must be by his death"—and then, unable to find anything concrete for which Caesar deserves death, he has to resort to possibilities and probabilities: "He would be crowned./How that might change his nature, there's the question." In the end he convinces himself of the necessity of murder by thinking not of what is but what might be, by imagining the future abuse of power, and finally, by employing false analogy:

> And therefore think him as a serpent's egg
> Which hatched, would as his kind grow mischievous,
> And kill him in the shell.
>
> (II.i.32–34)

But Caesar is a man, not a serpent's egg; and Brutus is no less mistaken when he tries to kill the spirit of Caesar by doing away with the man. He only succeeds in killing the man, not his spirit—and this is forcefully dramatized when, after the assassination, the people are eager to transfer their allegiance to Brutus, just as they had abandoned Pompey for Caesar:

> *Third Plebeian.* Let him be Caesar.
> *Fourth Plebeian.*   Caesar's better parts
>   Shall be crowned in Brutus.
>
> (III.ii.52–53)

It is not only Brutus' misfortune but his fault that his achievements turn out, ironically, to be the reverse of his best intentions. He brings to Rome anarchy and the horrors of civil war, not "Peace, freedom, and liberty."

In dramatizing the complex issues of power politics, *Julius Caesar* offers no easy solution to problems that are no less baffling to our own age. Many will find that this work is one of Shakespeare's most perplexing, for it is disconcerting when a play—or history itself—appeals to man's earnest desire to judge actions in terms of simple, personal standards of right and wrong and then betrays and mocks his deepest convictions by suggesting that Power is better than Virtue, that efficiency may be preferable to goodness, or that conscience may be dangerously inadequate in determining political action.

An individual's scrupulous concern for morality may, indeed, be disastrously impolitic. Cassius leads Brutus to an abhorrent deed, but when the consequences involve Brutus in the exercise of power, Brutus continues to think and act in accordance with private morality. His scruples about killing Antony or about unjustly raising money hinder the success of the conspiracy. His wish to fight a pitched battle, to decide the matter once and for all, instead of following stratagems and winning by attrition, is also the decision of a man who refuses to take on the role of politician. It is noteworthy that Cassius, after his initial victory, consistently defers to Brutus' moral scruples; knowing him to be wrong in his strategy, he is still swayed by the very image of nobility for which Brutus was chosen as the figurehead of the conspiracy. The irony is unmistakable: the politic man sets up an image of virtue, dissociated from politics, to serve his own purposes, to endear him to the populace; but once that image is established, his freedom to act without it is curbed, and he is hampered in the achievement of his political ends by the very image he has fostered.

The spirit of Caesar that dominates the play is to be associated, finally, with the exercise of supreme power. When Caesar dies, power is without a master, and as such, indiscriminately destructive. Each man in his turn tries to grasp the lightning that has been set free, and is fearfully transformed, until finally it comes to rest upon the man who alone, by gift of personality and legitimate succession, may wield it unscathed.

Shakespeare fully delineates the intriguing pattern of shifting power as an old Caesar is succeeded by a young one. The politic Cassius gives in to an impolitic Brutus and both fail as a result. Antony, Octavius, and Lepidus begin with complete ruthlessness; however, this does not guarantee them power or even win the battle for them—their opponents defeat themselves through mistakes. Lepidus, the "straw man," is first burdened with responsibility, then eliminated; and afterward, effortlessly, Antony, the ruthless and emotional partner, is displaced by the man without a temperament, the personification of impersonal rule.

The transfer of power from Antony to Octavius is subtly and swiftly dramatized in Act V, Scene i, when Octavius suddenly opposes Antony's command and leads his troops in his own way—"I do not cross you," he tells Antony, "but I will do so." From this point Antony refers to his partner as "Caesar," whereas until that moment he had called him only "Octavius." Even when Octavius asks for advice immediately after he has asserted his independence (V.i.23), Antony calls him "Caesar" before bidding him "Make forth." And soon afterward Octavius is seen as the one who is beginning to prevail; it is he who gives directions: "Come, Antony; away!" In the last scene of the play Octavius is in total charge of the action, while Antony is returned to his first prominent role, that of funeral orator. Antony may deliver the wonderful eulogy for Brutus, but Octavius, in businesslike fashion, gives the orders for burial, and without consulting or mentioning Antony, says to his former adversaries: "All that served Brutus, I will entertain them," as if he were in sole command. Finally, Octavius renders the play's concluding speech, which is conventionally given by the person of highest rank, whose task is to restore order to the state.

In portraying Octavius and describing his rise to power, Shakespeare departs from his primary source, Plutarch's *Lives*, and his changes are important for our understanding of the play. Plutarch's Octavius is not an exceptional soldier but an outwardly pleasant person of charm and wit, the very opposite of Shakespeare's characterization. And whereas Shakespeare's Octavius gains stature at the battle of Philippi, in Plutarch's *The Life of Marcus Antonius* he is sick at this time, and Antony "had the chiefest glory of all this victory." In Plutarch's *Life of Marcus Brutus* it is further reported that Octavius was absent from the battle; he had himself carried from his camp because of a friend's ominous dream, "and no man could tell what became of Octavius Caesar after he was carried out of his camp."

Shakespeare's independent treatment of Octavius reveals his conception of the kind of man who can wield power in the spirit of Caesar. Brutus, Cassius, and Antony grasp at power and are unable to retain it, perhaps because in exercising it they are more swayed by personal passions than Caesar. Octavius had no part in the murder; he is the only person in the play as free of the passions of love or hate as Caesar claimed to be. In his speech at the beginning of Act V he identifies himself with the spirit of Caesar, makes himself spiritually his heir, and assumes the duty of revenge:

Look,
I draw a sword against conspirators.
When think you that the sword goes up again?
Never, till Caesar's three and thirty wounds
Be well avenged; or till another Caesar
Have added slaughter to the sword of traitors.

(V.i.50–55)

At the close of the play we are meant to feel that the exercise of power necessary for these times has once more been placed in adequate hands. The spirit of Caesar, for good or ill, has not been put to rest.

WILLIAM ROSEN
BARBARA ROSEN
University of Connecticut

The Tragedy of
JULIUS CAESAR

[*Dramatis Personae*

Julius Caesar
Octavius Caesar   } triumvirs after
Marcus Antonius   the death of Julius Caesar
M. Aemilius Lepidus }
Cicero   }
Publius   } senators
Popilius Lena }
Marcus Brutus
Cassius
Casca
Trebonius
Ligarius   } conspirators against Julius Caesar
Decius Brutus
Metellus Cimber
Cinna
Flavius   } tribunes
Marullus }
Artemidorus of Cnidos, a teacher of rhetoric
A Soothsayer
Cinna, a poet
Another Poet
Lucilius
Titinius
Messala   } friends to Brutus and Cassius
Young Cato
Volumnius
Varro
Clitus
Claudius   } servants to Brutus
Strato
Lucius
Dardanius
Pindarus, servant to Cassius
Calphurnia, wife to Caesar
Portia, wife to Brutus
Senators, Citizens, Guards, Attendants, &c.

Scene: During most of the play, at Rome;
afterward near Sardis, and near Philippi]

The Tragedy of Julius Caesar

ACT I

Scene I. [*Rome. A street.*]

*Enter Flavius, Marullus, and certain Commoners over the
stage.*

Flavius. Hence! Home, you idle creatures, get you home!
　Is this a holiday? What, know you not,
　Being mechanical,°1 you ought not walk
　Upon a laboring day without the sign
　Of your profession?° Speak, what trade art thou?　　　5

Carpenter. Why, sir, a carpenter.

Marullus. Where is thy leather apron and thy rule?
　What dost thou with thy best apparel on?
　You, sir, what trade are you?

Cobbler. Truly, sir, in respect of a fine° workman, I am　　10
　but, as you would say, a cobbler.°

Marullus. But what trade art thou? Answer me directly.°

Cobbler. A trade, sir, that, I hope, I may use with a

---

1 The degree sign (°) indicates a footnote, which is keyed to the text by
line number. Text references are printed in *italic* type; the annotation
follows in roman type.
I.i.3 *mechanical* of the working class　4–5 *sign/Of your profession*
mark of your trade, i.e., working clothes　10 *in respect of a fine* in
comparison with a skilled　11 *cobbler* (1) shoemaker (2) bungler
12 *directly* straightforwardly

15 safe conscience, which is indeed, sir, a mender of bad
soles.°

Flavius. What trade, thou knave? Thou naughty° knave,
what trade?

Cobbler. Nay, I beseech you, sir, be not out° with me:
yet, if you be out,° sir, I can mend you.°

20 *Marullus.* What mean'st thou by that? Mend me, thou
saucy fellow?

Cobbler. Why, sir, cobble you.

Flavius. Thou art a cobbler, art thou?

Cobbler. Truly, sir, all that I live by is with the awl: I
25 meddle with no tradesman's matters, nor women's
matters; but withal,° I am indeed, sir, a surgeon to
old shoes: when they are in great danger, I recover°
them. As proper men as ever trod upon neat's
leather° have gone upon my handiwork.

30 *Flavius.* But wherefore art not in thy shop today?
Why dost thou lead these men about the streets?

Cobbler. Truly, sir, to wear out their shoes, to get
myself into more work. But indeed, sir, we make
holiday to see Caesar and to rejoice in his triumph.°

Marullus. Wherefore rejoice? What conquest brings he
35 home?
What tributaries° follow him to Rome,
To grace in captive bonds his chariot wheels?
You blocks, you stones, you worse than senseless
things!
O you hard hearts, you cruel men of Rome,
40 Knew you not Pompey?° Many a time and oft
Have you climbed up to walls and battlements,
To tow'rs and windows, yea, to chimney tops,

15 *soles* (pun on "souls")   16 *naughty* worthless   18 *out* angry
19 *be out* i.e., have worn-out shoes   19 *mend you* (1) mend your
shoes (2) improve your character   26 *withal* (1) nevertheless (2) with
awl (3) with all   27 *recover* (1) resole (2) cure   28–29 *neat's leather*
cattle's hide   34 *triumph* triumphal celebration   36 *tributaries* captives   40 *Pompey* (defeated by Caesar in 48 B.C., later murdered)

Your infants in your arms, and there have sat
The livelong day, with patient expectation,
To see great Pompey pass the streets of Rome.   45
And when you saw his chariot but appear,
Have you not made an universal shout,
That Tiber trembled underneath her banks
To hear the replication° of your sounds
Made in her concave shores?°   50
And do you now put on your best attire?
And do you now cull out a holiday?
And do you now strew flowers in his way
That comes in triumph over Pompey's blood?°
Be gone!   55
Run to your houses, fall upon your knees,
Pray to the gods to intermit° the plague
That needs must light on this ingratitude.

Flavius. Go, go, good countrymen, and, for this fault,
Assemble all the poor men of your sort;   60
Draw them to Tiber banks and weep your tears
Into the channel, till the lowest stream
Do kiss the most exalted shores of all.°
                        Exeunt all the Commoners.
See, whe'r° their basest mettle° be not moved;
They vanish tongue-tied in their guiltiness.   65
Go you down that way towards the Capitol;
This way will I. Disrobe the images,
If you do find them decked with ceremonies.°

Marullus. May we do so?
You know it is the feast of Lupercal.°   70

Flavius. It is no matter; let no images
Be hung with Caesar's trophies. I'll about

---

49 *replication* echo   50 *concave shores* hollowed-out banks   54 *in triumph over Pompey's blood* as the conqueror of Pompey's sons   57 *intermit* hold back   63 *most exalted shores of all* highest water mark   64 *whe'r* whether   64 *mettle* (1) substance (2) disposition   68 *ceremonies* robes (or ornaments)   70 *Lupercal* (fertility festival held on February 15; Caesar's triumph really took place in the preceding October, but Shakespeare combines events and shortens time spans for dramatic effect)

And drive away the vulgar° from the streets;
So do you too, where you perceive them thick.
75 These growing feathers plucked from Caesar's wing
Will make him fly an ordinary pitch,°
Who else would soar above the view of men
And keep us all in servile fearfulness.   *Exeunt.*

[Scene II. *A public place.*]

*Enter Caesar, Antony (for the course), Calphurnia, Portia,
Decius, Cicero, Brutus, Cassius, Casca, a Soothsayer;
after them, Marullus and Flavius.*

Caesar. Calphurnia!

Casca.   Peace, ho! Caesar speaks.

Caesar.   Calphurnia!

Calphurnia. Here, my lord.

Caesar. Stand you directly in Antonius' way
     When he doth run his course. Antonius!

5 *Antony.* Caesar, my lord?

Caesar. Forget not in your speed, Antonius,
     To touch Calphurnia; for our elders say
     The barren, touchèd in this holy chase,
     Shake off their sterile curse.

Antony.   I shall remember:
10   When Caesar says "Do this," it is performed.

Caesar. Set on, and leave no ceremony out.

Soothsayer. Caesar!

Caesar. Ha! Who calls?

73 *vulgar* common people   76 *pitch* height

Casca. Bid every noise be still; peace yet again!

Caesar. Who is it in the press° that calls on me?   15
  I hear a tongue, shriller than all the music,
  Cry "Caesar." Speak; Caesar is turned to hear.

Soothsayer. Beware the ides of March.°

Caesar.   What man is that?

Brutus. A soothsayer bids you beware the ides of March.

Caesar. Set him before me; let me see his face.   20

Cassius. Fellow, come from the throng; look upon
  Caesar.

Caesar. What say'st thou to me now? Speak once again.

Soothsayer. Beware the ides of March.

Caesar. He is a dreamer, let us leave him. Pass.
        Sennet.° Exeunt. Mane[n]t° Brutus and Cassius.

Cassius. Will you go see the order of the course?°   25

Brutus. Not I.

Cassius. I pray you do.

Brutus. I am not gamesome:° I do lack some part
  Of that quick spirit° that is in Antony.
  Let me not hinder, Cassius, your desires;   30
  I'll leave you.

Cassius. Brutus, I do observe you now of late;
  I have not from your eyes that gentleness
  And show of love as I was wont° to have;
  You bear too stubborn and too strange a hand°   35
  Over your friend that loves you.

I.ii.15 *press* crowd   18 *ides of March* March 15   24 s.d. *Sennet* flourish of trumpets marking ceremonial entrance or exit   24 s.d. *Mane[n]t* (they) remain   25 *order of the course* progress of the race   28 *gamesome* (1) fond of sport (2) merry   29 *quick spirit* (1) lively nature (2) prompt obedience   34 *wont* accustomed   35 *bear . . . hand* treat too haughtily and distantly, keep at arm's length (the metaphor is from horsemanship)

Brutus.   Cassius,
Be not deceived: if I have veiled my look,
I turn the trouble of my countenance
Merely upon myself.° Vexèd I am
40   Of late with passions of some difference,°
Conceptions only proper to myself,°
Which give some soil,° perhaps, to my behaviors;
But let not therefore my good friends be grieved
(Among which number, Cassius, be you one)
45   Nor construe° any further my neglect
Than that poor Brutus, with himself at war,
Forgets the shows° of love to other men.

Cassius. Then, Brutus, I have much mistook your
          passion;°
By means whereof° this breast of mine hath buried
50   Thoughts of great value, worthy cogitations.
Tell me, good Brutus, can you see your face?

Brutus. No, Cassius; for the eye sees not itself
But by reflection, by some other things.

Cassius. 'Tis just:°
55   And it is very much lamented, Brutus,
That you have no such mirrors as will turn
Your hidden worthiness into your eye,
That you might see your shadow.° I have heard
Where many of the best respect° in Rome
60   (Except immortal Caesar), speaking of Brutus,
And groaning underneath this age's yoke,
Have wished that noble Brutus had his eyes.

Brutus. Into what dangers would you lead me, Cassius,
That you would have me seek into myself
65   For that which is not in me?

37–39 *if I have . . . upon myself* i.e., if I have seemed withdrawn, it is because I am displeased with myself and no one else (*Merely* = wholly)
40 *passions of some difference* conflicting emotions   41 *Conceptions
. . . myself* ideas concerning me only   42 *soil* blemish   45 *construe* in-
terpret   47 *shows* manifestations   48 *passion* feelings   49 *By means
whereof* as a consequence of which   54 *just* true   58 *shadow* reflection, i.e., yourself as others see you   59 *best respect* highest reputation

Cassius. Therefore, good Brutus, be prepared to hear;
    And since you know you cannot see yourself
    So well as by reflection, I, your glass°
    Will modestly discover to yourself
    That of yourself which you yet know not of.   70
    And be not jealous on° me, gentle Brutus:
    Were I a common laughter,° or did use
    To stale with ordinary oaths my love
    To every new protester;° if you know
    That I do fawn on men and hug them hard,   75
    And after scandal° them; or if you know
    That I profess myself° in banqueting
    To all the rout,° then hold me dangerous.
                                    Flourish° and shout.

Brutus. What means this shouting? I do fear the people
    Choose Caesar for their king.

Cassius.   Ay, do you fear it?   80
    Then must I think you would not have it so.

Brutus. I would not, Cassius, yet I love him well.
    But wherefore do you hold me here so long?
    What is it that you would impart to me?
    If it be aught toward the general good,°   85
    Set honor in one eye and death i' th' other,
    And I will look on both indifferently;°
    For let the gods so speed me,° as I love
    The name of honor more than I fear death.

Cassius. I know that virtue to be in you, Brutus,   90
    As well as I do know your outward favor.°
    Well, honor is the subject of my story.
    I cannot tell what you and other men
    Think of this life, but for my single self,

68 *glass* mirror   71 *jealous on* suspicious of   72 *laughter* object of
mockery   72–74 *did use . . . protester* were accustomed to make cheap
with glib and frequent avowals to every new promiser of friendship
(*ordinary* = [1] tavern [2] everyday)   76 *scandal* slander   77 *profess
myself* declare my friendship   78 *rout* vulgar crowd   78 s.d. *Flourish*
ceremonial sounding of trumpets   85 *general good* public welfare
87 *indifferently* impartially   88 *speed me* make me prosper   91 *favor*
appearance

95   I had as lief not be,° as live to be
In awe of such a thing as I myself.°
I was born free as Caesar; so were you:
We both have fed as well, and we can both
Endure the winter's cold as well as he:
100   For once, upon a raw and gusty day,
The troubled Tiber chafing with° her shores,
Caesar said to me "Dar'st thou, Cassius, now
Leap in with me into this angry flood,
And swim to yonder point?" Upon the word,
105   Accout'red° as I was, I plungèd in
And bade him follow: so indeed he did.
The torrent roared, and we did buffet it
With lusty sinews, throwing it aside
And stemming it with hearts of controversy.°
110   But ere we could arrive the point proposed,
Caesar cried "Help me, Cassius, or I sink!"
I, as Aeneas,° our great ancestor,
Did from the flames of Troy upon his shoulder
The old Anchises bear, so from the waves of Tiber
115   Did I the tired Caesar. And this man
Is now become a god, and Cassius is
A wretched creature, and must bend his body
If Caesar carelessly but nod on him.
He had a fever when he was in Spain,
120   And when the fit was on him, I did mark
How he did shake; 'tis true, this god did shake.
His coward lips did from their color fly,°
And that same eye whose bend° doth awe the world
Did lose his° luster; I did hear him groan;
125   Ay, and that tongue of his, that bade the Romans
Mark him and write his speeches in their books,
Alas, it cried, "Give me some drink, Titinius,"

95 *as lief not be* just as soon not exist   96 *such a thing as I myself* i.e.,
another human being (Caesar)   101 *chafing with* raging against
105 *Accout'red* fully armed   109 *stemming . . . controversy* moving
forward against it (1) aggressively (2) in rivalry   112 *Aeneas* (legendary founder of the Roman state, and hero of Vergil's *Aeneid*. Anchises
was his feeble father)   122 *His coward . . . fly* the color fled from his
lips like a deserter fleeing from his banner in battle (*color* = [1] hue
[2] banner)   123 *bend* glance   124 *his* its

As a sick girl. Ye gods! It doth amaze me,
A man of such a feeble temper° should
So get the start of° the majestic world,   *130*
And bear the palm° alone.   *Shout. Flourish.*

Brutus. Another general shout?
   I do believe that these applauses are
   For some new honors that are heaped on Caesar.

Cassius. Why, man, he doth bestride the narrow world   *135*
   Like a Colossus,° and we petty men
   Walk under his huge legs and peep about
   To find ourselves dishonorable° graves.
   Men at some time are masters of their fates:
   The fault, dear Brutus, is not in our stars,°   *140*
   But in ourselves, that we are underlings.
   Brutus and Caesar: what should be in that "Caesar"?
   Why should that name be sounded° more than yours?
   Write them together, yours is as fair a name;
   Sound them, it doth become the mouth as well;   *145*
   Weigh them, it is as heavy; conjure with 'em,
   "Brutus" will start° a spirit as soon as "Caesar."
   Now, in the names of all the gods at once,
   Upon what meat doth this our Caesar feed,
   That he is grown so great? Age, thou art shamed!   *150*
   Rome, thou hast lost the breed of noble bloods!
   When went there by an age, since the great flood,°
   But it was famed with° more than with one man?
   When could they say (till now) that talked of Rome,
   That her wide walks encompassed but one man?   *155*
   Now is it Rome indeed, and room° enough,

---

129 *feeble temper* weak constitution   130 *get the start of* outdistance
131 *bear the palm* carry off the victor's prize   136 *Colossus* (an im-
mense statue of Apollo, said to straddle the entrance to the harbor of
Rhodes so that ships sailed under its legs)   138 *dishonorable* (because
we are dominated by Caesar)   140 *stars* destinies (in Shakespeare's
day one's temperament, and therefore one's actions and course of life,
were thought to be largely determined by the position of the planets at
one's birth)   143 *sounded* (1) spoken (2) proclaimed by trumpet
147 *start* raise   152 *great flood* (classical story told of the drowning of
all mankind except Deucalion and his wife Pyrrha, spared by Zeus because of their virtue)   153 *But it was famed with* without the age being
made famous by   156 *Rome . . . room* (homonyms, hence a pun)

When there is in it but one only man.
O, you and I have heard our fathers say,
There was a Brutus° once that would have brooked°
160   Th' eternal devil to keep his state in Rome
As easily as a king.

Brutus. That you do love me, I am nothing jealous;°
What you would work me to,° I have some aim;°
How I have thought of this, and of these times,
165   I shall recount hereafter. For this present,
I would not so (with love I might entreat you)
Be any further moved. What you have said
I will consider; what you have to say
I will with patience hear, and find a time
170   Both meet° to hear and answer such high things.
Till then, my noble friend, chew° upon this:
Brutus had rather be a villager
Than to repute himself a son of Rome
Under these hard conditions as this time
Is like to lay upon us.

175   *Cassius.*   I am glad
That my weak words have struck but thus much show
Of fire from Brutus.

Enter Caesar and his Train.°

Brutus. The games are done, and Caesar is returning.

Cassius. As they pass by, pluck Casca by the sleeve,
180   And he will (after his sour fashion) tell you
What hath proceeded worthy note today.

Brutus. I will do so. But look you, Cassius,
The angry spot doth glow on Caesar's brow,
And all the rest look like a chidden train:
185   Calphurnia's cheek is pale, and Cicero

---

159 *a Brutus* (Lucius Junius Brutus helped expel the Tarquins and
found the Republic in 509 B.C.)   159 *brooked* tolerated   162 *nothing
jealous* not at all doubtful   163 *work me to* persuade me of   163 *aim*
idea   170 *meet* suitable   171 *chew* reflect   177 s.d. *Train* retinue

    Looks with such ferret° and such fiery eyes
    As we have seen him in the Capitol,
    Being crossed in conference° by some senators.

Cassius. Casca will tell us what the matter is.

Caesar. Antonius.   190

Antony. Caesar?

Caesar. Let me have men about me that are fat,
    Sleek-headed men, and such as sleep a-nights.
    Yond Cassius has a lean and hungry look;
    He thinks too much: such men are dangerous.   195

Antony. Fear him not, Caesar, he's not dangerous;
    He is a noble Roman, and well given.°

Caesar. Would he were fatter! But I fear him not.
    Yet if my name were liable to fear,°
    I do not know the man I should avoid   200
    So soon as that spare Cassius. He reads much,
    He is a great observer, and he looks
    Quite through the deeds° of men. He loves no plays,
    As thou dost, Antony; he hears no music;°
    Seldom he smiles, and smiles in such a sort°   205
    As if he mocked himself, and scorned his spirit
    That could be moved to smile at anything.
    Such men as he be never at heart's ease
    Whiles they behold a greater than themselves,
    And therefore are they very dangerous.   210
    I rather tell thee what is to be feared
    Than what I fear; for always I am Caesar.
    Come on my right hand, for this ear is deaf,

---

186 *ferret* ferretlike (a ferret is a vicious, weasel-like animal with red eyes)   188 *conference* debate   197 *given* disposed   199 *if my name . . . to fear* i.e., if the idea of fear could ever be associated with me   203 *through the deeds* i.e., to the hidden motives of actions   204 *hears no music* (cf. *Merchant of Venice*, V.i.83ff: "The man that hath no music in himself,/Nor is not moved with concord of sweet sounds,/Is fit for treasons. . . . Let no such man be trusted")   205 *sort* manner

And tell me truly what thou think'st of him.
            Sennet. Exeunt Caesar and his Train.

Casca. You pulled me by the cloak; would you speak
215   with me?

Brutus. Ay, Casca; tell us what hath chanced today,
That Caesar looks so sad.°

Casca. Why, you were with him, were you not?

Brutus. I should not then ask Casca what had chanced.

220   *Casca.* Why, there was a crown offered him; and being
offered him, he put it by° with the back of his hand,
thus; and then the people fell a-shouting.

Brutus. What was the second noise for?

Casca. Why, for that too.

225   *Cassius.* They shouted thrice; what was the last cry for?

Casca. Why, for that too.

Brutus. Was the crown offered him thrice?

Casca. Ay, marry,° was't, and he put it by thrice, every
time gentler than other; and at every putting-by mine
230   honest neighbors shouted.

Cassius. Who offered him the crown?

Casca. Why, Antony.

Brutus. Tell us the manner of it, gentle Casca.

Casca. I can as well be hanged as tell the manner of it:
235   it was mere foolery; I did not mark it. I saw Mark
Antony offer him a crown—yet 'twas not a crown
neither, 'twas one of these coronets°—and, as I told
you, he put it by once; but for all that, to my thinking, he would fain° have had it. Then he offered it to
240   him again; then he put it by again; but to my thinking, he was very loath to lay his fingers off it. And

217 *sad* serious   221 *put it by* pushed it aside   228 *marry* truly (originally an oath, "By the Virgin Mary")   237 *coronets* small crowns
239 *fain* gladly

then he offered it the third time. He put it the third
time by; and still° as he refused it, the rabblement
hooted, and clapped their chopt° hands, and threw
up their sweaty nightcaps,° and uttered such a deal   245
of stinking breath because Caesar refused the crown,
that it had, almost, choked Caesar; for he swounded°
and fell down at it. And for mine own part, I durst
not laugh, for fear of opening my lips and receiving
the bad air.   250

Cassius. But, soft,° I pray you; what, did Caesar
    swound?

Casca. He fell down in the market place, and foamed
    at mouth, and was speechless.

Brutus. 'Tis very like he hath the falling-sickness.°

Cassius. No, Caesar hath it not; but you, and I,   255
    And honest Casca, we have the falling-sickness.°

Casca. I know not what you mean by that, but I am
    sure Caesar fell down. If the tag-rag people° did not
    clap him and hiss him, according as he pleased and
    displeased them, as they use° to do the players in the   260
    theater, I am no true man.

Brutus. What said he when he came unto himself?

Casca. Marry, before he fell down, when he perceived
    the common herd was glad he refused the crown, he
    plucked me ope his doublet° and offered them his   265
    throat to cut. An I had been a man of any occupation,°
    if I would not have taken him at a word, I would I
    might go to hell among the rogues. And so he fell.
    When he came to himself again, he said, if he had

---

243 *still* every time   244 *chopt* rough, chapped   245 *nightcaps* (contemptuous term for workingmen's caps)   247 *swounded* fainted   251
soft slowly, "wait a minute"   254 *falling-sickness* epilepsy   256 *we
have the falling-sickness* i.e., we are becoming powerless and are
declining under Caesar's rule   258 *tag-rag people* ragged mob
260 *use* are accustomed   265 *ope his doublet* open his jacket   266 *man
of any occupation* (1) workingman, i.e., one of those to whom Caesar's
speech was addressed (2) "man of action"

270 done or said anything amiss, he desired their wor-
ships to think it was his infirmity. Three or four
wenches, where I stood, cried "Alas, good soul!" and
forgave him with all their hearts; but there's no heed
to be taken of them; if Caesar had stabbed their
275 mothers, they would have done no less.

Brutus. And after that, he came thus sad away?

Casca. Ay.

Cassius. Did Cicero say anything?

Casca. Ay, he spoke Greek.

280 *Cassius.* To what effect?

Casca. Nay, an I tell you that, I'll ne'er look you i' th'
face again. But those that understood him smiled at
one another and shook their heads; but for mine own
part, it was Greek to me. I could tell you more news
285 too: Marullus and Flavius, for pulling scarfs off
Caesar's images, are put to silence.° Fare you well.
There was more foolery yet, if I could remember it.

Cassius. Will you sup with me tonight, Casca?

Casca. No, I am promised forth.°

290 *Cassius.* Will you dine with me tomorrow?

Casca. Ay, if I be alive, and your mind hold,° and
your dinner worth the eating.

Cassius. Good; I will expect you.

Casca. Do so. Farewell, both.   *Exit.*

295 *Brutus.* What a blunt fellow is this grown to be!
He was quick mettle° when he went to school.

Cassius. So is he now in execution
Of any bold or noble enterprise,

---

286 *put to silence* silenced (by being stripped of their tribuneships, and
perhaps exiled or executed)   289 *am promised forth* have a previous
engagement   291 *hold* does not change   296 *quick mettle* of a lively
disposition

However he puts on this tardy form.°
This rudeness is a sauce to his good wit,°   300
Which gives men stomach° to disgest° his words
With better appetite.

Brutus. And so it is. For this time I will leave you.
Tomorrow, if you please to speak with me,
I will come home to you; or if you will,   305
Come home to me, and I will wait for you.

Cassius. I will do so. Till then, think of the world.°

Exit Brutus.

Well, Brutus, thou art noble; yet I see
Thy honorable mettle° may be wrought
From that it is disposed;° therefore it is meet°   310
That noble minds keep ever with their likes;
For who so firm that cannot be seduced?
Caesar doth bear me hard,° but he loves Brutus.
If I were Brutus now, and he were Cassius,
He should not humor° me. I will this night,   315
In several hands,° in at his windows throw,
As if they came from several citizens,
Writings, all tending to° the great opinion
That Rome holds of his name; wherein obscurely
Caesar's ambition shall be glancèd at.°   320
And after this, let Caesar seat him sure;°
For we will shake him, or worse days endure.   *Exit.*

---

299 *tardy form* sluggish appearance   300 *wit* intelligence   301 *stomach* appetite   301 *disgest* digest   307 *the world* i.e., the current state of affairs   309 *mettle* (1) disposition (2) metal   309–10 *wrought . . . disposed* shaped (like iron) contrary to its natural form   310 *meet* fitting   313 *bear me hard* hold a grudge against me   315 *humor* cajole, influence by flattery   316 *several hands* different handwritings   318 *tending to* bearing on   320 *glancèd at* indirectly touched upon   321 *seat him sure* make his position secure

[Scene III. *A street.*]

Thunder and lightning. Enter [from opposite sides,]
Casca and Cicero.

Cicero. Good even, Casca; brought you Caesar home?
  Why are you breathless? And why stare you so?

Casca. Are not you moved, when all the sway of earth°
  Shakes like a thing unfirm? O Cicero,
5   I have seen tempests, when the scolding winds
  Have rived° the knotty oaks, and I have seen
  Th' ambitious ocean swell and rage and foam,
  To be exalted with° the threat'ning clouds;
  But never till tonight, never till now,
10   Did I go through a tempest dropping fire.
  Either there is a civil strife in heaven,
  Or else the world, too saucy° with the gods,
  Incenses them to send destruction.

Cicero. Why, saw you anything more wonderful?

15 *Casca.* A common slave—you know him well by sight—
  Held up his left hand, which did flame and burn
  Like twenty torches joined, and yet his hand,
  Not sensible of° fire, remained unscorched.
  Besides—I ha' not since put up my sword—
20   Against° the Capitol I met a lion,
  Who glazed° upon me and went surly by
  Without annoying me. And there were drawn
  Upon a heap° a hundred ghastly° women,

I.iii.3 *all the sway of earth* i.e., the whole scheme of things (*sway:* ruling
principle)   6 *rived* split   8 *exalted with* elevated to   12 *saucy* pre-
sumptuous   18 *sensible of* sensitive to   20 *Against* directly opposite
(?) near (?)   21 *glazed* stared   22–23 *drawn/Upon a heap* huddled together   23 *ghastly* white as ghosts

Transformèd with their fear, who swore they saw
Men, all in fire, walk up and down the streets.   25
And yesterday the bird of night° did sit
Even at noonday upon the market place,
Hooting and shrieking. When these prodigies°
Do so conjointly meet,° let not men say,
"These are their reasons, they are natural,"   30
For I believe they are portentous things
Unto the climate° that they point upon.

Cicero. Indeed, it is a strange-disposèd° time:
But men may construe things after their fashion,°
Clean from the purpose° of the things themselves.   35
Comes Caesar to the Capitol tomorrow?

Casca. He doth; for he did bid Antonius
Send word to you he would be there tomorrow.

Cicero. Good night then, Casca; this disturbèd sky
Is not to walk in.

Casca.   Farewell, Cicero.   *Exit Cicero.* 40

                    Enter Cassius.

Cassius. Who's there?

Casca.   A Roman.

Cassius.   Casca, by your voice.

Casca. Your ear is good. Cassius, what night is this?

Cassius. A very pleasing night to honest men.

Casca. Who ever knew the heavens menace so?

Cassius. Those that have known the earth so full of
    faults.   45
For my part, I have walked about the streets,
Submitting me unto the perilous night,

26 *bird of night* owl (a bird of ill omen)   28 *prodigies* unnatural events
29 *conjointly meet* coincide   32 *climate* region   33 *strange-disposèd*
abnormal   34 *after their fashion* in their own way   35 *Clean from
the purpose* quite contrary to the real meaning

And thus unbracèd,° Casca, as you see,
Have bared my bosom to the thunder-stone;°
50 And when the cross° blue lightning seemed to open
The breast of heaven, I did present myself
Even in the aim and very flash of it.

Casca. But wherefore did you so much tempt the
    heavens?
It is the part° of men to fear and tremble
55 When the most mighty gods by tokens° send
Such dreadful heralds to astonish° us.

Cassius. You are dull, Casca, and those sparks of life
That should be in a Roman you do want,°
Or else you use not. You look pale, and gaze,
60 And put on° fear, and cast yourself in wonder,°
To see the strange impatience of the heavens;
But if you would consider the true cause
Why all these fires, why all these gliding ghosts,
Why birds and beasts from quality and kind,°
65 Why old men,° fools, and children calculate,°
Why all these things change from their ordinance,°
Their natures and preformèd faculties,°
To monstrous quality,° why, you shall find
That heaven hath infused them with these spirits°
70 To make them instruments of fear and warning
Unto some monstrous state.°
Now could I, Casca, name to thee a man
Most like this dreadful night,
That thunders, lightens, opens graves, and roars
75 As doth the lion in the Capitol;
A man no mightier than thyself, or me,

---

48 *unbracèd* with doublet unfastened   49 *thunder-stone* lightning bolt
50 *cross* jagged   54 *part* role   55 *tokens* prophetic signs   56 *astonish*
stun   58 *want* lack   60 *put on* display   60 *cast yourself in wonder* are
amazed   64 *from quality and kind* (act) against their natures   65 *old
men* i.e., the senile, in second childhood   65 *calculate* make predictions (cf. proverb, "Fools and children often do prophesy")   66 *ordinance* natural order of behavior   67 *preformèd faculties* innate qualities   68 *monstrous quality* unnatural condition   69 *spirits* super-
natural powers   71 *monstrous state* abnormal state of affairs

In personal action, yet prodigious° grown
And fearful,° as these strange eruptions° are.

Casca. 'Tis Caesar that you mean, is it not, Cassius?

Cassius. Let it be who it is; for Romans now   80
Have thews° and limbs like to their ancestors;
But, woe the while!° Our fathers' minds are dead,
And we are governed with our mothers' spirits;
Our yoke and sufferance° show us womanish.

Casca. Indeed, they say the senators tomorrow   85
Mean to establish Caesar as a king;
And he shall wear his crown by sea and land,
In every place save here in Italy.

Cassius. I know where I will wear this dagger then;
Cassius from bondage will deliver Cassius.   90
Therein,° ye gods, you make the weak most strong;
Therein, ye gods, you tyrants do defeat.
Nor stony tower, nor walls of beaten brass,
Nor airless dungeon, nor strong links of iron,
Can be retentive to° the strength of spirit;   95
But life, being weary of these worldly bars,
Never lacks power to dismiss itself.
If I know this, know all the world besides,
That part of tyranny that I do bear
I can shake off at pleasure.   *Thunder still.*

Casca.   So can I;   100
So every bondman in his own hand bears
The power to cancel his captivity.

Cassius. And why should Caesar be a tyrant then?
Poor man, I know he would not be a wolf
But that he sees the Romans are but sheep;   105
He were no lion, were not Romans hinds.°

---

77 *prodigious* ominous   78 *fearful* causing fear   78 *eruptions* dis-
turbances of nature   81 *thews* sinews   82 *woe the while* alas for the
times   84 *yoke and sufferance* servitude and the meek endurance of it
91 *Therein* i.e., in suicide   95 *be retentive to* hold in   106 *hinds*
(1) female deer (2) peasants (3) servants

Those that with haste will make a mighty fire
Begin it with weak straws. What trash is Rome,
What rubbish and what offal, when it serves
110   For the base matter to illuminate
So vile a thing as Caesar! But, O grief,
Where hast thou led me? I, perhaps, speak this
Before a willing bondman; then I know
My answer must be made.° But I am armed,
115   And dangers are to me indifferent.°

Casca. You speak to Casca, and to such a man
That is no fleering° tell-tale. Hold, my hand.
Be factious° for redress of all these griefs,
And I will set this foot of mine as far
As who goes farthest.   [*They clasp hands.*]

120   *Cassius.*   There's a bargain made.
Now know you, Casca, I have moved already
Some certain of the noblest-minded Romans
To undergo° with me an enterprise
Of honorable dangerous consequence;
125   And I do know, by this° they stay for me
In Pompey's porch;° for now, this fearful night,
There is no stir or walking in the streets,
And the complexion of the element°
In favor's like° the work we have in hand,
130   Most bloody, fiery, and most terrible.

Enter Cinna.

Casca. Stand close° awhile, for here comes one in haste.

Cassius. 'Tis Cinna; I do know him by his gait;
He is a friend. Cinna, where haste you so?

114 *My answer must be made* I shall have to answer for my words
115 *indifferent* unimportant   117 *fleering* flattering   118 *factious* ac-
tive in forming a political party   123 *undergo* undertake   125 *by this*
by this time   126 *Pompey's porch* portico of Pompey's Theater
128 *complexion of the element* condition of the sky   129 *In favor's
like* in appearance is like   131 *close* hidden

Cinna. To find out you. Who's that? Metellus Cimber?

Cassius. No, it is Casca, one incorporate   135
  To° our attempts. Am I not stayed° for, Cinna?

Cinna. I am glad on't.° What a fearful night is this!
  There's two or three of us have seen strange sights.

Cassius. Am I not stayed for? Tell me.

Cinna.   Yes, you are.
  O Cassius, if you could   140
  But win the noble Brutus to our party—

Cassius. Be you content. Good Cinna, take this paper,
  And look you lay it in the praetor's chair,°
  Where Brutus may but find it;° and throw this
  In at his window; set this up with wax   145
  Upon old Brutus'° statue. All this done,
  Repair° to Pompey's porch, where you shall find us.
  Is Decius° Brutus and Trebonius there?

Cinna. All but Metellus Cimber, and he's gone
  To seek you at your house. Well, I will hie,°   150
  And so bestow these papers as you bade me.

Cassius. That done, repair to Pompey's Theater.
                                     Exit Cinna.
  Come, Casca, you and I will yet ere day
  See Brutus at his house; three parts of him
  Is ours already, and the man entire   155
  Upon the next encounter yields him ours.

135–36 *incorporate/To* intimately bound up with   136 *stayed* waited
137 *on't* of it (i.e., that Casca has joined the conspiracy)   143 *praetor's
chair* official chair in which Brutus would sit as chief magistrate, an
office next in rank to consul   144 *Where Brutus may but find it* where
only Brutus may find it   146 *old Brutus* (Lucius Junius Brutus, founder
of the Roman Republic)   147 *Repair* go   148 *Decius* (actually
Decimus, a kinsman of Marcus Brutus; the error is found in North's
Plutarch)   150 *hie* hurry

Casca. O, he sits high in all the people's hearts;
   And that which would appear offense in us,
   His countenance,° like richest alchemy,°
160   Will change to virtue and to worthiness.

Cassius. Him, and his worth, and our great need of him,
   You have right well conceited.° Let us go,
   For it is after midnight, and ere day
   We will awake him and be sure of him.   *Exeunt.*

159 *countenance* support   159 *alchemy* (the "science" by which many experimenters tried to turn base metals into gold)   162 *conceited* (1) understood (2) described in an elaborate simile

ACT II

[Scene I. *Rome.*]

Enter Brutus in his orchard.°

Brutus. What, Lucius, ho!
  I cannot, by the progress of the stars,
  Give guess how near to day. Lucius, I say!
  I would it were my fault to sleep so soundly.
  When, Lucius, when? Awake, I say! What, Lucius!   5

Enter Lucius.

Lucius. Called you, my lord?

Brutus. Get me a taper° in my study, Lucius.
  When it is lighted, come and call me here.

Lucius. I will, my lord.   *Exit.*

Brutus. It must be by his death; and for my part,   10
  I know no personal cause to spurn at° him,
  But for the general.° He would be crowned.
  How that might change his nature, there's the question.
  It is the bright day that brings forth the adder,
  And that craves° wary walking. Crown him that,   15
  And then I grant we put a sting in him

II.i.s.d. *orchard* garden   7 *taper* candle   11 *spurn at*   rebel (literally
"kick") against   12 *general* public welfare   15 *craves* demands

That at his will he may do danger° with.
Th' abuse of greatness is when it disjoins
Remorse° from power; and, to speak truth of Caesar,
20 I have not known when his affections swayed°
More than his reason. But 'tis a common proof°
That lowliness° is young ambition's ladder,
Whereto the climber upward turns his face;
But when he once attains the upmost round,°
25 He then unto the ladder turns his back,
Looks in the clouds, scorning the base degrees°
By which he did ascend. So Caesar may;
Then lest he may, prevent.° And, since the quarrel°
Will bear no color° for the thing he is,
30 Fashion it° thus: that what he is, augmented,
Would run to these and these extremities;°
And therefore think him as a serpent's egg
Which hatched, would as his kind° grow mischievous,
And kill him in the shell.

Enter Lucius.

35 *Lucius.* The taper burneth in your closet,° sir.
Searching the window for a flint, I found
This paper thus sealed up, and I am sure
It did not lie there when I went to bed.

Gives him the letter.

Brutus. Get you to bed again; it is not day.
40 Is not tomorrow, boy, the ides of March?

Lucius. I know not, sir.

Brutus. Look in the calendar and bring me word.

Lucius. I will, sir.   *Exit.*

---

17 *danger* harm   18–19 *disjoins/Remorse* separates mercy   20 *affections swayed* emotions ruled   21 *common proof* matter of common experience   22 *lowliness* humility   24 *round* rung   26 *base degrees* (1) low steps of the ladder (2) less important grades of office (3) common people   28 *prevent* take action to forestall   28 *quarrel* cause of complaint   29 *bear no color* have no excuse   30 *Fashion it* construct the case   31 *these and these extremities* such and such extremes (of tyranny)   33 *as his kind* according to its nature   35 *closet* study

Brutus. The exhalations° whizzing in the air
    Give so much light that I may read by them.   45
                        Opens the letter and reads.

    "Brutus, thou sleep'st; awake, and see thyself.
    Shall Rome, &c.° Speak, strike, redress.
    Brutus, thou sleep'st; awake."

Such instigations have been often dropped
Where I have took them up.   50
"Shall Rome, &c." Thus must I piece it out:°
Shall Rome stand under one man's awe?° What,
    Rome?
My ancestors did from the streets of Rome
The Tarquin drive, when he was called a king.
"Speak, strike, redress." Am I entreated   55
To speak and strike? O Rome, I make thee promise,
If the redress will follow, thou receivest
Thy full petition at the hand of° Brutus!

                Enter Lucius.

Lucius. Sir, March is wasted fifteen days. *Knock within.*

Brutus. 'Tis good. Go to the gate; somebody knocks.   60
                        [Exit Lucius.]
Since Cassius first did whet° me against Caesar,
I have not slept.
Between the acting of a dreadful thing
And the first motion,° all the interim is
Like a phantasma,° or a hideous dream.   65
The genius° and the mortal instruments°
Are then in council, and the state of a man,
Like to a little kingdom, suffers then
The nature of an insurrection.°

---

44 *exhalations* meteors   47, 51 *&c.* (read "et cetera")   51 *piece it out*
develop the meaning   52 *under one man's awe* in awe of one man
58 *Thy full . . . hand of* all you ask from   61 *whet* incite   64 *motion*
prompting   65 *phantasma* hallucination   66 *genius* guardian spirit
(?) reasoning spirit (?)   66 *mortal instruments* the emotions and physical powers (which should be ruled and guided by reason)   69 *nature of
an insurrection* a kind of insurrection

Enter Lucius.

70 *Lucius.* Sir, 'tis your brother° Cassius at the door,
    Who doth desire to see you.

Brutus.   Is he alone?

Lucius. No, sir, there are moe° with him.

Brutus.   Do you know them?

Lucius. No, sir; their hats are plucked about their ears,
    And half their faces buried in their cloaks,
75 That by no means I may discover° them
    By any mark of favor.°

Brutus.   Let 'em enter. [*Exit Lucius.*]
    They are the faction. O conspiracy,
    Sham'st thou to show thy dang'rous brow by night,
    When evils are most free?° O, then by day
80 Where wilt thou find a cavern dark enough
    To mask thy monstrous visage? Seek none, con-
        spiracy;
    Hide it in smiles and affability:
    For if thou path,° thy native semblance° on,
    Not Erebus° itself were dim enough
85 To hide thee from prevention.°

Enter the conspirators, Cassius, Casca, Decius, Cinna,
    Metellus [Cimber], and Trebonius.

Cassius. I think we are too bold upon° your rest.
    Good morrow, Brutus; do we trouble you?

Brutus. I have been up this hour, awake all night.
    Know I these men that come along with you?

90 *Cassius.* Yes, every man of them; and no man here
    But honors you; and every one doth wish

---

70 *brother* i.e., brother-in-law (Cassius was married to Brutus' sister)
72 *moe* more   75 *discover* recognize   76 *favor* appearance   79 *evils
are most free* evil things roam most freely   83 *path* walk (verb)
83 *native semblance* true appearance   84 *Erebus* dark region between
earth and Hades   85 *from prevention* from being forestalled and hindered   86 *upon* in intruding on

You had but that opinion of yourself
Which every noble Roman bears of you.
This is Trebonius.

Brutus.   He is welcome hither.

Cassius. This, Decius Brutus.

Brutus.   He is welcome too.   95

Cassius. This, Casca; this, Cinna; and this, Metellus
    Cimber.

Brutus. They are all welcome.
    What watchful cares° do interpose themselves
    Betwixt your eyes and night?

Cassius. Shall I entreat a word?   *They whisper.*   100

Decius. Here lies the east; doth not the day break here?

Casca. No.

Cinna. O, pardon, sir, it doth; and yon gray lines
    That fret° the clouds are messengers of day.

Casca. You shall confess that you are both deceived.   105
    Here, as I point my sword, the sun arises,
    Which is a great way growing on° the south,
    Weighing° the youthful season of the year.
    Some two months hence, up higher toward the north
    He first presents his fire; and the high° east   110
    Stands as the Capitol, directly here.

Brutus. Give me your hands all over, one by one.

Cassius. And let us swear our resolution.

Brutus. No, not an oath. If not the face of men,°
    The sufferance° of our souls, the time's abuse°—   115

---

98 *watchful cares* cares that keep you awake   104 *fret* pattern, inter-
lace   107 *growing on* tending toward   108 *Weighing* considering
110 *high* due   114 *the face of men* i.e., the sincere and resolute appearance of the conspirators, which should not be distrusted   115 *sufferance* patient endurance   115 *time's abuse* corruption of the age
(i.e., Caesar's assumption of unconstitutional powers)

If these be motives weak, break off betimes,°
And every man hence to his idle bed.
So let high-sighted° tyranny range° on
Till each man drop by lottery.° But if these
120 (As I am sure they do) bear fire enough
To kindle cowards and to steel with valor
The melting spirits of women, then, countrymen,
What need we any spur but our own cause
To prick° us to redress? What other bond
125 Than secret Romans° that have spoke the word,
And will not palter?° And what other oath
Than honesty° to honesty engaged°
That this shall be, or we will fall for it?
Swear° priests and cowards and men cautelous,°
130 Old feeble carrions° and such suffering souls
That welcome wrongs; unto bad causes swear
Such creatures as men doubt; but do not stain
The even° virtue of our enterprise,
Nor th' insuppressive mettle° of our spirits,
135 To think that or our cause or° our performance
Did need an oath; when every drop of blood
That every Roman bears, and nobly bears,
Is guilty of a several bastardy°
If he do break the smallest particle
140 Of any promise that hath passed from him.

Cassius. But what of Cicero? Shall we sound him?
  I think he will stand very strong with us.

Casca. Let us not leave him out.

Cinna.   No, by no means.

Metellus. O, let us have him, for his silver hairs

---

116 *betimes* immediately   118 *high-sighted* arrogant (viewing widely
from on high, like a falcon ready to swoop on prey)   118 *range* rove
or fly in search of prey   119 *by lottery* by chance, i.e., at the tyrant's
whim   124 *prick* urge   125 *secret Romans* the fact that we are
Romans capable of maintaining secrecy   126 *palter* equivocate
127 *honesty* personal honor   127 *engaged* pledged   129 *Swear* bind
by oath   129 *cautelous* deceitful   130 *carrions* wretches almost dead
and rotting   133 *even* unblemished, perfect   134 *insuppressive mettle*
indomitable temper   135 *or . . . or* either . . . or   138 *guilty . . .
bastardy* i.e., guilty of an act not truly Roman

Will purchase us a good opinion,°   145
And buy men's voices to commend our deeds.
It shall be said his judgment ruled our hands;
Our youths and wildness shall no whit° appear,
But all be buried in his gravity.°

Brutus. O, name him not! Let us not break with him;°   150
For he will never follow anything
That other men begin.

Cassius.   Then leave him out.

Casca. Indeed, he is not fit.

Decius. Shall no man else be touched but only Caesar?

Cassius. Decius, well urged.° I think it is not meet   155
Mark Antony, so well beloved of Caesar,
Should outlive Caesar; we shall find of° him
A shrewd contriver;° and you know, his means;
If he improve° them, may well stretch so far
As to annoy° us all; which to prevent,°   160
Let Antony and Caesar fall together.

Brutus. Our course will seem too bloody, Caius Cassius,
To cut the head off and then hack the limbs,
Like wrath in death and envy° afterwards;
For Antony is but a limb of Caesar.   165
Let's be sacrificers, but not butchers, Caius.
We all stand up against the spirit of Caesar,°
And in the spirit of men there is no blood.
O, that we then could come by° Caesar's spirit,
And not dismember Caesar! But, alas,   170
Caesar must bleed for it. And, gentle° friends,
Let's kill him boldly, but not wrathfully;

---

145 *opinion* reputation   148 *no whit* not in the slightest   149 *gravity* sobriety and stability (Latin *gravitas*)   150 *break with him* divulge our plan to him   155 *urged* suggested   157 *of* in   158 *shrewd contriver* cunning and malicious plotter   159 *improve* make good use of   160 *annoy* harm   160 *prevent* forestall   164 *envy* malice, i.e., as though we were killing Caesar for personal spite and hatred   167 *the spirit of Caesar* the principles (of tyranny) for which Caesar stands   169 *come by* get possession of   171 *gentle* noble

Let's carve him as a dish fit for the gods,
Not hew him as a carcass fit for hounds.
175 And let our hearts, as subtle masters do,
Stir up their servants° to an act of rage,
And after seem to chide 'em. This shall make
Our purpose necessary, and not envious;°
Which so appearing to the common eyes,
180 We shall be called purgers,° not murderers.
And for Mark Antony, think not of him;
For he can do no more than Caesar's arm
When Caesar's head is off.

Cassius.   Yet I fear him;
For in the ingrafted° love he bears to Caesar——

185 *Brutus.* Alas, good Cassius, do not think of him.
If he love Caesar, all that he can do
Is to himself—take thought° and die for Caesar.
And that were much he should,° for he is given
To sports, to wildness, and much company.

190 *Trebonius.* There is no fear° in him; let him not die,
For he will live and laugh at this hereafter.

                                        Clock strikes.

Brutus. Peace! Count the clock.

Cassius.   The clock hath stricken three.

Trebonius. 'Tis time to part.

Cassius.   But it is doubtful yet
Whether Caesar will come forth today or no;
195 For he is superstitious grown of late,
Quite from the main° opinion he held once
Of fantasy, of dreams, and ceremonies.°
It may be these apparent prodigies,°
The unaccustomed terror of this night,

176 *servants* (1) the hands (2) the passions   178 *envious* malicious
180 *purgers* healers   184 *ingrafted* firmly rooted   187 *take thought*
grow melancholy with brooding   188 *that were much he should* that
would be too much to expect of him   190 *no fear* nothing to fear
196 *Quite from the main* at variance with the strong   197 *ceremonies*
omens   198 *apparent prodigies* obvious signs of disaster

And the persuasion of his augurers°   200
May hold him from the Capitol today.

Decius. Never fear that. If he be so resolved,
  I can o'ersway him;° for he loves to hear
  That unicorns may be betrayed with trees,°
  And bears with glasses,° elephants with holes,°   205
  Lions with toils,° and men with flatterers;
  But when I tell him he hates flatterers,
  He says he does, being then most flatterèd.
  Let me work;
  For I can give his humor° the true bent,°   210
  And I will bring him to the Capitol.

Cassius. Nay, we will all of us be there to fetch him.

Brutus. By the eighth hour; is that the uttermost?°

Cinna. Be that the uttermost, and fail not then.

Metellus. Caius Ligarius doth bear Caesar hard,°   215
  Who rated° him for speaking well of Pompey.
  I wonder none of you have thought of him.

Brutus. Now, good Metellus, go along by him.°
  He loves me well, and I have given him reasons;
  Send him but hither, and I'll fashion° him.   220

Cassius. The morning comes upon 's; we'll leave you,
        Brutus.
  And, friends, disperse yourselves; but all remember
  What you have said, and show yourselves true
        Romans.

Brutus. Good gentlemen, look fresh and merrily.
  Let not our looks put on° our purposes,   225

200 *augurers* augurs (priests who foretold, from omens, the future)
203 *o'ersway him* persuade him to change his mind   204 *betrayed with
trees* i.e., tricked into running at a tree (at the last moment its prey
steps aside so that the horn is deeply embedded and the unicorn is
helpless)   205 *glasses* mirrors   205 *holes* pitfalls   206 *toils* nets,
snares   210 *humor* temperament   210 *bent* direction   213 *uttermost*
latest   215 *bear Caesar hard* has a grudge against Caesar   216 *rated*
berated   218 *him* his house   220 *fashion* shape (to our designs)
225 *put on* display

But bear it° as our Roman actors do,
With untired spirits and formal constancy.°
And so good morrow to you every one.

                          Exeunt. Manet° Brutus.

Boy! Lucius! Fast asleep? It is no matter;
230 Enjoy the honey-heavy dew° of slumber.
Thou hast no figures nor no fantasies°
Which busy care draws in the brains of men;
Therefore thou sleep'st so sound.

                 Enter Portia.

Portia.   Brutus, my lord.

Brutus. Portia, what mean you? Wherefore rise you now?
235   It is not for your health thus to commit
Your weak condition to the raw cold morning.

Portia. Nor for yours neither. Y'have ungently,° Brutus,
Stole from my bed; and yesternight at supper
You suddenly arose and walked about,
240 Musing and sighing, with your arms across;°
And when I asked you what the matter was,
You stared upon me with ungentle looks.
I urged you further; then you scratched your head,
And too impatiently stamped with your foot.
245 Yet I insisted, yet you answered not,
But with an angry wafter° of your hand
Gave sign for me to leave you. So I did,
Fearing to strengthen that impatience
Which seemed too much enkindled, and withal°
250 Hoping it was but an effect of humor,°
Which sometime hath his° hour with every man.
It will not let you eat, nor talk, nor sleep,
And could it work so much upon your shape

---

226 *bear it* play our parts   227 *formal constancy* consistent decorum
228s.d. *Manet* remains   230 *dew* i.e., refreshment   231 *figures . . .
fantasies* (both words specify figments of the imagination)   237 *ungently* discourteously   240 *across* folded (a sign of melancholy)
246 *wafter* waving   249 *withal* also   250 *effect of humor* i.e., sign of a
temporary mood   251 *his* its

As it hath much prevailed on your condition,°
I should not know you° Brutus. Dear my lord,   255
Make me acquainted with your cause of grief.

Brutus. I am not well in health, and that is all.

Portia. Brutus is wise and, were he not in health,
He would embrace the means to come by it.

Brutus. Why, so I do. Good Portia, go to bed.   260

Portia. Is Brutus sick, and is it physical°
To walk unbracèd° and suck up the humors°
Of the dank morning? What, is Brutus sick,
And will he steal out of his wholesome bed,
To dare the vile contagion of the night,°   265
And tempt the rheumy and unpurgèd air°
To add unto his sickness? No, my Brutus;
You have some sick offense° within your mind,
Which by the right and virtue of my place°
I ought to know of; and upon my knees   270
I charm° you, by my once commended beauty,
By all your vows of love, and that great vow
Which did incorporate° and make us one,
That you unfold to me, your self, your half,
Why you are heavy,° and what men tonight   275
Have had resort to you; for here have been
Some six or seven, who did hide their faces
Even from darkness.

Brutus.   Kneel not, gentle Portia.

Portia. I should not need, if you were gentle Brutus.
Within the bond of marriage, tell me, Brutus,   280
Is it excepted° I should know no secrets
That appertain to you? Am I your self

254 *condition* disposition   255 *know you* recognize you as   261 *physical* healthy   262 *unbracèd* with doublet unfastened   262 *humors* dampness, mist   265 *night* (night air was thought to be harmful, even poisonous)   266 *tempt . . . air* risk the damp and unpurified (by the sun) air   268 *sick offense* sickness that harms   269 *place* situation (as wife)   271 *charm* entreat   273 *incorporate* make us one flesh (cf. Matthew 19:5, "they twain shall be one flesh")   275 *heavy* dejected   281 *excepted* made an exception that

But, as it were, in sort or limitation,°
To keep with you at meals, comfort your bed,
And talk to you sometimes? Dwell I but in the
285   suburbs°
Of your good pleasure? If it be no more,
Portia is Brutus' harlot, not his wife.

Brutus. You are my true and honorable wife,
As dear to me as are the ruddy drops
290   That visit my sad heart.

Portia. If this were true, then should I know this secret.
I grant I am a woman; but withal°
A woman that Lord Brutus took to wife.
I grant I am a woman; but withal
295   A woman well reputed, Cato's daughter.°
Think you I am no stronger than my sex,
Being so fathered and so husbanded?
Tell me your counsels,° I will not disclose 'em.
I have made strong proof of my constancy,°
300   Giving myself a voluntary wound
Here in the thigh; can I bear that with patience,
And not my husband's secrets?

Brutus.   O ye gods,
Render me worthy of this noble wife!   *Knock.*
Hark, hark! One knocks. Portia, go in a while,
305   And by and by thy bosom shall partake
The secrets of my heart.
All my engagements° I will construe° to thee,
All the charactery of° my sad brows.
Leave me with haste.   *Exit Portia.*

---

283 *in sort or limitation* after a fashion or within a certain restriction
(legal terms)   285 *suburbs* outlying districts (where the brothels and
least respectable taverns were found)   292 *withal* at the same time
295 *Cato's daughter* (Marcus Porcius Cato was famous for his integrity; he joined Pompey against Caesar and killed himself at Utica
in 46 B.C. to avoid capture; he was Brutus' uncle as well as father-in-
law)   298 *counsels* secrets   299 *proof of my constancy* trial of my
resolution   307 *engagements* commitments   307 *construe* explain
308 *charactery of* writing upon, i.e., wrinkles of grief and worry

Enter Lucius and [Caius] Ligarius.

                    Lucius, who's that knocks?

Lucius. Here is a sick man that would speak with you.   *310*

Brutus. Caius Ligarius, that Metellus spake of.
   Boy, stand aside. Caius Ligarius! How?°

Caius. Vouchsafe° good morrow from a feeble tongue.

Brutus. O, what a time have you chose out, brave° Caius,
   To wear a kerchief!° Would you were not sick!   *315*

Caius. I am not sick, if Brutus have in hand
   Any exploit worthy the name of honor.

Brutus. Such an exploit have I in hand, Ligarius,
   Had you a healthful ear to hear of it.

Caius. By all the gods that Romans bow before,   *320*
   I here discard my sickness! Soul of Rome,
   Brave son, derived from honorable loins,°
   Thou, like an exorcist,° hast conjured up
   My mortifièd° spirit. Now bid me run,
   And I will strive with things impossible,   *325*
   Yea, get the better of them. What's to do?

Brutus. A piece of work that will make sick men whole.°

Caius. But are not some whole that we must make sick?

Brutus. That must we also. What it is, my Caius,
   I shall unfold to thee, as we are going   *330*
   To whom° it must be done.

Caius.   Set on° your foot,
   And with a heart new-fired I follow you,

---

312 *How* how are you   313 *Vouchsafe* please accept   314 *brave* noble
315 *To wear a kerchief* (as a protection against drafts), i.e., to be sick
322 *from honorable loins* i.e., descent from Lucius Junius Brutus,
founder of the Roman Republic   323 *exorcist* conjurer   324 *morti-*
fièd deadened   327 *whole* healthy   331 *To whom* to the house of him
to whom   331 *Set on* advance

To do I know not what; but it sufficeth
That Brutus leads me on.   *Thunder.*

Brutus.   Follow me, then.   *Exeunt.*

[Scene II. *Caesar's house.*]

Thunder and lightning. Enter Julius Caesar in his
nightgown.°

Caesar. Nor heaven nor earth have been at peace
     tonight:
Thrice hath Calphurnia in her sleep cried out,
"Help, ho! They murder Caesar!" Who's within?

Enter a Servant.

Servant. My lord?

5 *Caesar.* Go bid the priests do present° sacrifice,
And bring me their opinions of success.°

Servant. I will, my lord.   *Exit.*

Enter Calphurnia.

Calphurnia. What mean you, Caesar? Think you to walk
     forth?
You shall not stir out of your house today.

Caesar. Caesar shall forth. The things that threatened
10   me
Ne'er looked but on my back; when they shall see
The face of Caesar, they are vanishèd.

Calphurnia. Caesar, I never stood on ceremonies,°
Yet now they fright me. There is one within,
15   Besides the things that we have heard and seen,
Recounts most horrid sights seen by the watch.°

II.ii.s.d. *nightgown* dressing gown   5 *present* immediate   6 *opinions*
of success judgment as to the future course of events   13 *stood on*
ceremonies paid attention to omens   16 *watch* nightwatchmen

A lioness hath whelpèd in the streets,
And graves have yawned, and yielded up their dead;
Fierce fiery warriors fought upon the clouds
In ranks and squadrons and right form° of war,   20
Which drizzled blood upon the Capitol;
The noise of battle hurtled° in the air,
Horses did neigh and dying men did groan,
And ghosts did shriek and squeal about the streets.
O Caesar, these things are beyond all use,°   25
And I do fear them.

Caesar.   What can be avoided
Whose end is purposed by the mighty gods?
Yet Caesar shall go forth; for these predictions
Are to° the world in general as to Caesar.

Calphurnia. When beggars die, there are no comets seen;   30
   The heavens themselves blaze forth° the death of
   princes.

Caesar. Cowards die many times before their deaths;
   The valiant never taste of death but once.
   Of all the wonders that I yet have heard,
   It seems to me most strange that men should fear,   35
   Seeing that death, a necessary end,
   Will come when it will come.

                    Enter a Servant.

                              What say the augurers?

Servant. They would not have you to stir forth today.
   Plucking the entrails of an offering forth,
   They could not find a heart within the beast.   40

Caesar. The gods do this in shame of cowardice:
   Caesar should° be a beast without a heart°
   If he should stay at home today for fear.
   No, Caesar shall not; Danger knows full well
   That Caesar is more dangerous than he.   45

20 *right form* proper military formation   22 *hurtled* clashed   25 *use*
normal experience   29 *Are to* apply to   31 *blaze forth* i.e., proclaim
(by comets and meteors)   42 *should* would   42 *heart* (the organ of
courage)

We are two lions littered in one day,
And I the elder and more terrible,
And Caesar shall go forth.

Calphurnia.   Alas, my lord,
Your wisdom is consumed in confidence.°
50 Do not go forth today. Call it my fear
That keeps you in the house and not your own.
We'll send Mark Antony to the Senate House,
And he shall say you are not well today.
Let me, upon my knee, prevail in this.

55 *Caesar.* Mark Antony shall say I am not well,
And for thy humor,° I will stay at home.

Enter Decius.

Here's Decius Brutus, he shall tell them so.

Decius. Caesar, all hail! Good morrow, worthy Caesar;
I come to fetch° you to the Senate House.

60 *Caesar.* And you are come in very happy time°
To bear my greeting to the senators,
And tell them that I will not come today.
Cannot, is false; and that I dare not, falser:
I will not come today. Tell them so, Decius.

Calphurnia. Say he is sick.

65 *Caesar.*   Shall Caesar send a lie?
Have I in conquest stretched mine arm so far
To be afeard to tell graybeards the truth?
Decius, go tell them Caesar will not come.

Decius. Most mighty Caesar, let me know some cause,
70 Lest I be laughed at when I tell them so.

Caesar. The cause is in my will: I will not come.
That is enough to satisfy the Senate.
But for your private satisfaction,
Because I love you, I will let you know.

---

49 *consumed in confidence* destroyed by too much confidence   56 *humor* whim   59 *fetch* escort   60 *happy time* favorable time (i.e., just at the right moment)

Calphurnia here, my wife, stays° me at home.   75
She dreamt tonight° she saw my statue,°
Which, like a fountain with an hundred spouts,
Did run pure blood, and many lusty Romans
Came smiling and did bathe their hands in it.
And these does she apply for° warnings and portents°   80
And evils imminent, and on her knee
Hath begged that I will stay at home today.

Decius. This dream is all amiss interpreted;
   It was a vision fair and fortunate:
   Your statue spouting blood in many pipes,   85
   In which so many smiling Romans bathed,
   Signifies that from you great Rome shall suck
   Reviving blood, and that great men shall press
   For tinctures, stains, relics, and cognizance.°
   This by Calphurnia's dream is signified.   90

Caesar. And this way have you well expounded it.

Decius. I have, when you have heard what I can say;
   And know it now, the Senate have concluded
   To give this day a crown to mighty Caesar.
   If you shall send them word you will not come,   95
   Their minds may change. Besides, it were a mock
   Apt to be rendered,° for someone to say
   "Break up the Senate till another time,
   When Caesar's wife shall meet with better dreams."
   If Caesar hide himself, shall they not whisper   100
   "Lo, Caesar is afraid"?
   Pardon me, Caesar, for my dear dear love
   To your proceeding° bids me tell you this,
   And reason to my love is liable.°

75 *stays* keeps   76 *tonight* i.e., last night   76 *statue* (trisyllabic; pronounced "stat-u-a")   80 *apply for* explain as   80 *portents* (accent on
last syllable)   89 *tinctures . . . cognizance* (Samuel Johnson para-
phrases the line: "The Romans, says Decius, all come to you, as to a
saint, for relics; as to a prince, for honors")   *tinctures* (1) alchemical
elixirs (2) colors, metals, etc. used in explain as   *stains* colors in a coat
of arms   *relics* venerated property of a martyr   *cognizance* mark of
identification worn by a nobleman's followers   96–97 *mock . . . rendered* jeering remark likely to be made   103 *proceeding* advancement
104 *reason . . . liable* i.e., my affection proves stronger than my judgment (of impropriety) in telling you this (*liable* = subordinate)

Caesar. How foolish do your fears seem now,

105   Calphurnia!

     I am ashamèd I did yield to them.

     Give me my robe,° for I will go.

*Enter Brutus, Ligarius, Metellus [Cimber], Casca,
Trebonius, Cinna, and Publius.*

     And look where Publius is come to fetch me.

Publius. Good morrow, Caesar.

Caesar.   Welcome, Publius.

110   What, Brutus, are you stirred so early too?

     Good morrow, Casca. Caius Ligarius,

     Caesar was ne'er so much your enemy°

     As that same ague which hath made you lean.

     What is't o'clock?

Brutus.   Caesar, 'tis strucken eight.

115 *Caesar.* I thank you for your pains and courtesy.

                 Enter Antony.

     See! Antony, that revels long a-nights,

     Is notwithstanding up. Good morrow, Antony.

Antony. So to most noble Caesar.

Caesar.   Bid them prepare° within.

     I am to blame to be thus waited for.

120   Now, Cinna; now, Metellus; what, Trebonius,

     I have an hour's talk in store for you;

     Remember that you call on me today;

     Be near me, that I may remember you.

Trebonius. Caesar, I will [*aside*] and so near will I be,

125   That your best friends shall wish I had been further.

Caesar. Good friends, go in and taste some wine with
     me,

107 *robe* toga 112 *enemy* (Ligarius had supported Pompey against
Caesar in the Civil War and had recently been pardoned by Caesar)
118 *prepare* i.e., set out the wine mentioned in line 126

And we (like friends) will straightway go together.

Brutus. [*Aside*] That every like is not the same,° O Caesar,
　The heart of Brutus earns° to think upon.　　*Exeunt.*

　　　　[Scene III. *A street near the Capitol, close to
　　　　　　　Brutus' house.*]

　　　　Enter Artemidorus [*reading a paper*].

[*Artemidorus.*] "Caesar, beware of Brutus; take heed of
　Cassius; come not near Casca; have an eye to Cinna;
　trust not Trebonius; mark well Metellus Cimber;
　Decius Brutus loves thee not; thou hast wronged
　Caius Ligarius. There is but one mind in all these　　5
　men, and it is bent° against Caesar. If thou beest not
　immortal, look about you: security gives way to
　conspiracy.° The mighty gods defend thee!
　　　　　　　　　Thy lover,° ARTEMIDORUS."
　Here will I stand till Caesar pass along,　　　　　　　10
　And as a suitor° will I give him this.
　My heart laments that virtue cannot live
　Out of the teeth of emulation.°
　If thou read this, O Caesar, thou mayest live;
　If not, the Fates with traitors do contrive.°　　*Exit.*　　15

128 *That every like is not the same* i.e., what a pity that those who
appear like friends may actually be enemies　129 *earns* grieves
II.iii.6 *bent* directed　7–8 *security gives way to conspiracy* overcon-
fidence gives conspiracy its opportunity　9 *lover* devoted friend
11 *as a suitor* like a petitioner　13 *Out of the teeth of emulation*
beyond the reach of envious rivalry　15 *contrive* conspire

[Scene IV. *Another part of the street.*]

Enter Portia and Lucius.

Portia. I prithee, boy, run to the Senate House;
   Stay not to answer me, but get thee gone.
   Why dost thou stay?

Lucius.   To know my errand, madam.

Portia. I would have had thee there and here again
5   Ere I can tell thee what thou shouldst do there.
   O constancy,° be strong upon my side;
   Set a huge mountain 'tween my heart and tongue!
   I have a man's mind, but a woman's might.°
   How hard it is for women to keep counsel!°
   Art thou here yet?

10   *Lucius.*   Madam, what should I do?
   Run to the Capitol, and nothing else?
   And so return to you, and nothing else?

Portia. Yes, bring me word, boy, if thy lord look well,
   For he went sickly forth; and take good note
15   What Caesar doth, what suitors press to him.
   Hark, boy, what noise is that?

Lucius. I hear none, madam.

Portia.   Prithee, listen well.
   I heard a bustling rumor like a fray,°
   And the wind brings it from the Capitol.

20   *Lucius.* Sooth,° madam, I hear nothing.

II.iv.6 *constancy* resolution   8 *might* physical strength   9 *counsel*
secret (Brutus has obviously told her of the conspiracy, though "stage
time" has allowed no opportunity for this; the inconsistency is not
noticeable during a performance)   18 *bustling rumor like a fray* confused noise as of battle   20 *Sooth* truly

Enter the Soothsayer.

Portia. Come hither, fellow. Which way hast thou been?

Soothsayer. At mine own house, good lady.

Portia. What is't o'clock?

Soothsayer.   About the ninth hour, lady.

Portia. Is Caesar yet gone to the Capitol?

Soothsayer. Madam, not yet; I go to take my stand,   25
    To see him pass on to the Capitol.

Portia. Thou hast some suit to Caesar, hast thou not?

Soothsayer. That I have, lady; if it will please Caesar
    To be so good to Caesar as to hear me,
    I shall beseech him to befriend himself.   30

Portia. Why, know'st thou any harm's intended towards
    him?

Soothsayer. None that I know will be, much that I fear
    may chance.°
    Good morrow to you. Here the street is narrow;
    The throng that follows Caesar at the heels,
    Of senators, of praetors, common suitors,   35
    Will crowd a feeble man almost to death.
    I'll get me to a place more void,° and there
    Speak to great Caesar as he comes along.   *Exit.*

Portia. I must go in. Ay me, how weak a thing
    The heart of woman is! O Brutus,   40
    The heavens speed° thee in thine enterprise!
    Sure, the boy heard me—Brutus hath a suit
    That Caesar will not grant—O, I grow faint.
    Run, Lucius, and commend me° to my lord;
    Say I am merry;° come to me again,   45
    And bring me word what he doth say to thee.
                              Exeunt [severally].

32 *chance* happen   37 *more void* more empty (less crowded)   41
speed prosper   44 *commend me* give my love   45 *merry* cheerful

ACT III

[Scene I. *Rome. Before the Capitol.*]

Flourish. Enter Caesar, Brutus, Cassius, Casca,
Decius, Metellus [Cimber], Trebonius, Cinna,
Antony, Lepidus, Artemidorus, Publius, [Popilius,]
and the Soothsayer.

Caesar. The ides of March are come.

Soothsayer. Ay, Caesar, but not gone.

Artemidorus. Hail, Caesar! Read this schedule.°

Decius. Trebonius doth desire you to o'er-read,
5 At your best leisure, this his humble suit.

Artemidorus. O Caesar, read mine first; for mine's a suit
That touches° Caesar nearer. Read it, great Caesar.

Caesar. What touches us ourself shall be last served.

Artemidorus. Delay not, Caesar; read it instantly.

Caesar. What, is the fellow mad?

10 *Publius.*   Sirrah, give place.°

Cassius. What, urge you your petitions in the street?
Come to the Capitol.

III.i.3 *schedule* scroll 7 *touches* concerns 10 *Sirrah, give place*
fellow, get out of the way

[*Caesar goes to the Capitol, the rest following.*]

Popilius. I wish your enterprise today may thrive.

Cassius. What enterprise, Popilius?

Popilius.   Fare you well.
                              [*Advances to Caesar.*]

Brutus. What said Popilius Lena?   15

Cassius. He wished today our enterprise might thrive.
I fear our purpose is discoverèd.

Brutus. Look how he makes to° Caesar; mark him.

Cassius. Casca, be sudden,° for we fear prevention.°
Brutus, what shall be done? If this be known,   20
Cassius or Caesar never shall turn back,°
For I will slay myself.

Brutus.   Cassius, be constant.°
Popilius Lena speaks not of our purposes;
For look, he smiles, and Caesar doth not change.°

Cassius. Trebonius knows his time; for look you, Brutus,   25
He draws Mark Antony out of the way.
                              [*Exeunt Antony and Trebonius.*]

Decius. Where is Metellus Cimber? Let him go
And presently prefer° his suit to Caesar.

Brutus. He is addressed.° Press near and second him.

Cinna. Casca, you are the first that rears your hand.   30

Caesar. Are we all ready? What is now amiss
That Caesar and his Senate must redress?

Metellus. Most high, most mighty, and most puissant°
    Caesar,
Metellus Cimber throws before thy seat
An humble heart.   [*Kneeling.*]

---

18 *makes to* heads for   19 *sudden* swift   19 *prevention* being forestalled   21 *turn back* i.e., return alive   22 *constant* calm   24 *change*
change his expression   28 *presently prefer* immediately present   29
addressed ready   33 *puissant* powerful

35 *Caesar.*　　　　　　I must prevent thee, Cimber.
These couchings° and these lowly courtesies°
Might fire the blood of ordinary men,
And turn preordinance and first decree°
Into the law of children. Be not fond°
40 To think that Caesar bears such rebel blood°
That will be thawed from the true quality°
With that° which melteth fools—I mean sweet words,
Low-crookèd curtsies, and base spaniel° fawning.
Thy brother by decree is banishèd.
45 If thou dost bend and pray and fawn for him,
I spurn thee like a cur out of my way.
Know, Caesar doth not wrong, nor without cause
Will he be satisfied.

Metellus. Is there no voice more worthy than my own,
50 To sound more sweetly in great Caesar's ear
For the repealing° of my banished brother?

Brutus. I kiss thy hand, but not in flattery, Caesar,
Desiring thee that Publius Cimber may
Have an immediate freedom of repeal.°

Caesar. What, Brutus?

55 *Cassius.*　　　　　　Pardon, Caesar; Caesar, pardon!
As low as to thy foot doth Cassius fall
To beg enfranchisement° for Publius Cimber.

Caesar. I could be well moved, if I were as you;
If I could pray to move,° prayers would move me;
60 But I am constant as the Northern Star,°
Of whose true-fixed and resting° quality

36 *couchings* low bowings　36 *lowly courtesies* humble obeisances
38 *preordinance and first decree* customs and laws established from an-
tiquity　39 *fond* so foolish as　40 *bears such rebel blood* has such un-
controlled emotions　41 *true quality* proper quality (i.e., firmness)
42 *With that* by those things　43 *spaniel* doglike, cringing　51 *repeal-
ing* recalling　54 *freedom of repeal* permission to be recalled from
exile　57 *enfranchisement* recall, freedom　59 *pray to move* i.e., beg
others to change their minds　60 *constant as the Northern Star* un-
changing as the polestar　61 *resting* changeless

There is no fellow° in the firmament.
The skies are painted with unnumb'red° sparks,
They are all fire and every one doth shine;
But there's but one in all doth hold° his place.   65
So in the world; 'tis furnished well with men,
And men are flesh and blood, and apprehensive;°
Yet in the number I do know but one
That unassailable holds on his rank,°
Unshaked of motion;° and that I am he,   70
Let me a little show it, even in this—
That I was constant° Cimber should be banished,
And constant do remain to keep him so.

Cinna. O Caesar——

Caesar.   Hence! Wilt thou lift up Olympus?°

Decius. Great Caesar——

Caesar.   Doth not Brutus bootless° kneel?   75

Casca. Speak hands for me!   *They stab Caesar.*

Caesar. Et tu, Brutè?° Then fall Caesar.   *Dies.*

Cinna. Liberty! Freedom! Tyranny is dead!
    Run hence, proclaim, cry it about the streets.

Cassius. Some to the common pulpits,° and cry out   80
    "Liberty, freedom, and enfranchisement!"

Brutus. People, and senators, be not affrighted.
    Fly not; stand still; ambition's debt is paid.°

Casca. Go to the pulpit, Brutus.

Decius.   And Cassius too.

---

62 *fellow* equal   63 *unnumb'red* innumerable   65 *hold* keep   67 *apprehensive* capable of reason   69 *holds on his rank* maintains his position   70 *Unshaked of motion* i.e., unmoved by internal or external forces   72 *constant* firmly determined   74 *Olympus* a mountain in Greece where the gods lived and held court   75 *bootless* in vain   77 *Et tu, Brutè* and you (too), Brutus   80 *pulpits* platforms for public speakers   83 *ambition's debt is paid* ambition has received what was due to it

85 *Brutus.* Where's Publius?°

Cinna. Here, quite confounded with this mutiny.°

Metellus. Stand fast together, lest some friend of Caesar's
    Should chance——

Brutus. Talk not of standing.° Publius, good cheer;
90 There is no harm intended to your person,
    Nor to no Roman else. So tell them, Publius.

Cassius. And leave us, Publius, lest that the people
    Rushing on us should do your age some mischief.

Brutus. Do so; and let no man abide° this deed
95 But we the doers.

Enter Trebonius.

Cassius. Where is Antony?

Trebonius.   Fled to his house amazed.°
    Men, wives, and children stare, cry out and run,
    As° it were doomsday.

Brutus.   Fates, we will know your pleasures.
    That we shall die, we know; 'tis but the time,
100 And drawing days out, that men stand upon.°

Casca. Why, he that cuts off twenty years of life
    Cuts off so many years of fearing death.

Brutus. Grant that, and then is death a benefit.
    So are we Caesar's friends, that have abridged
105 His time of fearing death. Stoop, Romans, stoop,
    And let us bathe our hands in Caesar's blood
    Up to the elbows, and besmear our swords.
    Then walk we forth, even to the market place,°
    And waving our red weapons o'er our heads,

85 *Publius* an old senator, too infirm to flee   86 *confounded with this mutiny* overwhelmed by this uproar   89 *Talk not of standing* i.e., don't worry about making a stand, organizing resistance   94 *abide* bear the consequences of   96 *amazed* utterly confused   98 *As* as if   100 *drawing . . . upon* (hope of) prolonging life, that men are concerned about   108 *the market place* the Roman Forum, center of business and public affairs

Let's all cry "Peace, freedom, and liberty!"   110

Cassius. Stoop then, and wash. How many ages hence
  Shall this our lofty scene be acted over
  In states unborn and accents yet unknown!

Brutus. How many times shall Caesar bleed in sport,°
  That now on Pompey's basis° lies along°   115
  No worthier than the dust!

Cassius.   So oft as that shall be,
  So often shall the knot° of us be called
  The men that gave their country liberty.

Decius. What, shall we forth?

Cassius.   Ay, every man away.
  Brutus shall lead, and we will grace° his heels   120
  With the most boldest and best hearts of Rome.

                Enter a Servant.

Brutus. Soft,° who comes here? A friend of Antony's.

Servant. Thus, Brutus, did my master bid me kneel;
  Thus did Mark Antony bid me fall down;
  And, being prostrate, thus he bade me say: 125
  Brutus is noble, wise, valiant, and honest;°
  Caesar was mighty, bold, royal,° and loving.
  Say I love Brutus and I honor him;
  Say I feared Caesar, honored him, and loved him.
  If Brutus will vouchsafe that Antony   130
  May safely come to him and be resolved°
  How Caesar hath deserved to lie in death,
  Mark Antony shall not love Caesar dead
  So well as Brutus living; but will follow
  The fortunes and affairs of noble Brutus   135
  Thorough° the hazards of this untrod state°

---

114 *in sport* for entertainment, i.e., as part of a play   115 *basis*
pedestal of statue   115 *along* stretched out   117 *knot* closely bound
group   120 *grace* do honor to   122 *Soft* wait a moment   126 *honest*
honorable   127 *royal* of princely generosity   131 *be resolved* have it
explained to his satisfaction   136 *Thorough* through   136 *untrod*
state new and uncertain state of affairs

With all true faith. So says my master Antony.

Brutus. Thy master is a wise and valiant Roman;
  I never thought him worse.
140   Tell him, so° please him come unto this place,
  He shall be satisfied and, by my honor,
  Depart untouched.

Servant.   I'll fetch him presently.°

                        Exit Servant.

Brutus. I know that we shall have him well to friend.°

Cassius. I wish we may. But yet have I a mind
145   That fears him much; and my misgiving still
  Falls shrewdly to the purpose.°

             Enter Antony.

Brutus. But here comes Antony. Welcome, Mark
  Antony.

Antony. O mighty Caesar! Dost thou lie so low?
  Are all thy conquests, glories, triumphs, spoils,
150   Shrunk to this little measure? Fare thee well.
  I know not, gentlemen, what you intend,
  Who else must be let blood,° who else is rank.°
  If I myself, there is no hour so fit
  As Caesar's death's hour, nor no instrument
155   Of half that worth as those your swords, made rich
  With the most noble blood of all this world.
  I do beseech ye, if you bear me hard,°
  Now, whilst your purpled° hands do reek and smoke,°
  Fulfill your pleasure. Live° a thousand years,
160   I shall not find myself so apt° to die;

---

140 *so* if it should   142 *presently* immediately   143 *well to friend* as a
good friend   145–46 *misgiving . . . purpose* my forebodings always
turn out to be justified   152 *let blood* (1) bled, purged (common
Elizabethan practice of drawing blood to cure those swollen with disease) (2) put to death   152 *rank* (1) swollen with disease (2) over-
grown, i.e., too powerful   157 *bear me hard* have a grudge against me
158 *purpled* (1) made scarlet (with blood) (2) made royal (?)   158 *reek
and smoke* i.e., steam (with freshly shed warm blood)   159 *Live*
though I live   160 *apt* prepared

No place will please me so, no mean° of death,
As here by Caesar, and by you cut off,
The choice and master spirits of this age.

Brutus. O Antony, beg not your death of us!
Though now we must appear bloody and cruel,   165
As by our hands and this our present act
You see we do, yet see you but our hands
And this the bleeding business they have done.
Our hearts you see not; they are pitiful;°
And pity to the general wrong of Rome—   170
As fire drives out fire, so pity pity°—
Hath done this deed on Caesar. For your part,
To you our swords have leaden° points, Mark An-
     tony:
Our arms in strength of malice, and our hearts
Of brothers' temper,° do receive you in   175
With all kind love, good thoughts, and reverence.

Cassius. Your voice° shall be as strong as any man's
In the disposing of new dignities.°

Brutus. Only be patient till we have appeased
The multitude, beside themselves with fear,   180
And then we will deliver° you the cause
Why I, that did love Caesar when I struck him,
Have thus proceeded.

Antony.   I doubt not of your wisdom.
Let each man render me his bloody hand.
First, Marcus Brutus, will I shake with you;   185
Next, Caius Cassius, do I take your hand;
Now, Decius Brutus, yours; now yours, Metellus;
Yours, Cinna; and, my valiant Casca, yours;
Though last, not least in love, yours, good Trebonius.
Gentlemen all—alas, what shall I say?   190
My credit° now stands on such slippery ground

161 *mean* manner   169 *pitiful* full of pity   171 *pity pity* pity for
Rome's subjection drove out pity for Caesar   173 *leaden* blunt   174–
75 *Our arms . . . temper* our arms, strong with the might inspired by
enmity, and our hearts, full of brotherly feeling   177 *voice* vote   178
dignities offices   181 *deliver* communicate to   191 *credit* reputation

That one of two bad ways you must conceit° me,
Either a coward or a flatterer.
That I did love thee, Caesar, O, 'tis true!
195 If then thy spirit look upon us now,
Shall it not grieve thee dearer° than thy death
To see thy Antony making his peace,
Shaking the bloody fingers of thy foes,
Most noble, in the presence of thy corse?°
200 Had I as many eyes as thou hast wounds,
Weeping as fast as they stream forth thy blood,
It would become me better than to close°
In terms of friendship with thine enemies.
Pardon me, Julius! Here wast thou bayed,° brave
      hart;°
205 Here didst thou fall, and here thy hunters stand,
Signed in thy spoil° and crimsoned in thy lethe.°
O world, thou wast the forest to this hart;
And this indeed, O world, the heart of thee.
How like a deer, stroken° by many princes,
210 Dost thou here lie!

Cassius. Mark Antony——

Antony.   Pardon me, Caius Cassius.
The enemies of Caesar shall say this;
Then, in a friend, it is cold modesty.°

Cassius. I blame you not for praising Caesar so;
215 But what compact mean you to have with us?
Will you be pricked in number° of our friends,
Or shall we on,° and not depend on you?

---

192 *conceit* judge   196 *dearer* more deeply   199 *corse* corpse
202 *close* make an agreement   204 *bayed* brought to bay   204 *hart*
(1) deer (2) heart   206 *Signed in thy spoil* marked with the signs of
your slaughter   206 *lethe* (dissyllabic; the river of oblivion from which
the dead drank in Hades; here, by extension, "stream of death," or
"lifeblood")   209 *stroken* struck down   213 *modesty* moderation
216 *pricked in number* marked down (the modern "ticks off names";
the Roman made small holes in his wax-covered tablets)   217 *on* proceed

Antony. Therefore I took your hands, but was indeed
    Swayed from the point by looking down on Caesar.
    Friends am I with you all, and love you all,   220
    Upon this hope, that you shall give me reasons
    Why, and wherein, Caesar was dangerous.

Brutus. Or else were this a savage spectacle.
    Our reasons are so full of good regard°
    That were you, Antony, the son of Caesar,   225
    You should be satisfied.

Antony.   That's all I seek;
    And am moreover suitor that I may
    Produce° his body to the market place,
    And in the pulpit, as becomes a friend,
    Speak in the order° of his funeral.   230

Brutus. You shall, Mark Antony.

Cassius.   Brutus, a word with you.
    [*Aside to Brutus*] You know not what you do; do not
        consent
    That Antony speak in his funeral.
    Know you how much the people may be moved
    By that which he will utter?

Brutus.   By your pardon: 235
    I will myself into the pulpit first,
    And show the reason of our Caesar's death.
    What Antony shall speak, I will protest°
    He speaks by leave and by permission,
    And that we are contented Caesar shall   240
    Have all true° rites and lawful ceremonies.
    It shall advantage° more than do us wrong.°

Cassius. I know not what may fall;° I like it not.

Brutus. Mark Antony, here, take you Caesar's body.
    You shall not in your funeral speech blame us,   245
    But speak all good you can devise of Caesar,
    And say you do't by our permission;

224 *good regard* sound considerations   228 *Produce* bring forth
230 *order* course of ceremonies   238 *protest* declare   241 *true* proper
242 *advantage* benefit   242 *wrong* harm   243 *fall* happen

Else shall you not have any hand at all
About his funeral. And you shall speak
250 In the same pulpit whereto I am going,
After my speech is ended.

Antony.   Be it so;
I do desire no more.

Brutus. Prepare the body then, and follow us.
                    Exeunt. Manet Antony.

Antony. O pardon me, thou bleeding piece of earth,
255 That I am meek and gentle with these butchers!
Thou art the ruins of the noblest man
That ever livèd in the tide of times.°
Woe to the hand that shed this costly blood!
Over thy wounds now do I prophesy
260 (Which like dumb mouths do ope their ruby lips
To beg the voice and utterance of my tongue),
A curse shall light upon the limbs of men;
Domestic fury and fierce civil strife
Shall cumber° all the parts of Italy;
265 Blood and destruction shall be so in use,°
And dreadful objects so familiar,
That mothers shall but smile when they behold
Their infants quartered with the hands of war,
All pity choked with custom of fell deeds;°
270 And Caesar's spirit, ranging° for revenge,
With Atè° by his side come hot from hell,
Shall in these confines° with a monarch's voice
Cry "Havoc,"° and let slip° the dogs of war,
That this foul deed shall smell above the earth
275 With carrion° men, groaning for burial.

                    Enter Octavius' Servant.

You serve Octavius Caesar, do you not?

---

257 *tide of times* course (ebb and flow) of history   264 *cumber* burden,
oppress   265 *in use* customary   269 *custom of fell deeds* habituation
to cruel acts   270 *ranging* roving widely in search of prey   271 *Atè*
Greek goddess of discord and vengeance   272 *confines* boundaries,
regions   273 *Cry "Havoc"* give the signal for unrestricted slaughter
and looting   273 *let slip* unleash   275 *carrion* dead and rotting

Servant. I do, Mark Antony.

Antony. Caesar did write for him to come to Rome.

Servant. He did receive his letters and is coming,
    And bid me say to you by word of mouth—
    O Caesar!   [*Seeing the body.*]   280

Antony. Thy heart is big;° get thee apart and weep.
    Passion,° I see, is catching, for mine eyes,
    Seeing those beads of sorrow stand in thine,
    Began to water. Is thy master coming?   285

Servant. He lies tonight within seven leagues of Rome.

Antony. Post° back with speed, and tell him what hath
    chanced.°
    Here is a mourning Rome, a dangerous Rome,
    No Rome° of safety for Octavius yet.
    Hie° hence and tell him so. Yet stay awhile;   290
    Thou shalt not back till I have borne this corse
    Into the market place; there shall I try°
    In my oration how the people take
    The cruel issue° of these bloody men;
    According to the which, thou shalt discourse   295
    To young Octavius of the state of things.
    Lend me your hand.   *Exeunt.*

282 *big* swollen (with grief)   283 *Passion* intense emotion, grief
287 *Post* ride post (with relays of horses), hasten   287 *chanced* happened   289 *Rome* (another play on the pronunciation "room"; cf. I.ii.156)   290 *Hie* hurry   292 *try* test   294 *cruel issue* outcome of the cruelty

[Scene II. *The Forum.*]

Enter Brutus and goes into the pulpit, and Cassius,
with the Plebeians.

Plebeians. We will be satisfied!° Let us be satisfied!

Brutus. Then follow me, and give me audience, friends.
Cassius, go you into the other street
And part the numbers.°
5   Those that will hear me speak, let 'em stay here;
Those that will follow Cassius, go with him;
And public reasons shall be renderèd
Of Caesar's death.

First Plebeian.   I will hear Brutus speak.

Second Plebeian. I will hear Cassius, and compare their
reasons,
10   When severally° we hear them renderèd.
         [*Exit Cassius, with some of the Plebeians.*]

Third Plebeian. The noble Brutus is ascended. Silence!

Brutus. Be patient till the last.°
Romans, countrymen, and lovers,° hear me for my
cause, and be silent, that you may hear. Believe me
15   for mine honor, and have respect° to mine honor,
that you may believe. Censure° me in your wisdom,
and awake your senses,° that you may the better
judge. If there be any in this assembly, any dear friend
of Caesar's, to him I say that Brutus' love to Caesar
20   was no less than his. If then that friend demand why

III.ii.1 *will be satisfied* want a full explanation   4 *part the numbers* divide the crowd   10 *severally* separately   12 *last* conclusion (of my
speech)   13 *lovers* dear friends   15 *respect* regard   16 *Censure* judge
17 *senses* powers of understanding, reason

Brutus rose against Caesar, this is my answer: Not
that I loved Caesar less, but that I loved Rome more.
Had you rather Caesar were living, and die all slaves,
than that Caesar were dead, to live all free men? As
Caesar loved me, I weep for him; as he was fortunate,   25
I rejoice at it; as he was valiant, I honor him; but,
as he was ambitious, I slew him. There is tears, for
his love; joy, for his fortune; honor, for his valor;
and death, for his ambition. Who is here so base,
that would be a bondman?° If any, speak; for him   30
have I offended. Who is here so rude,° that would not
be a Roman? If any, speak; for him have I offended.
Who is here so vile, that will not love his country?
If any, speak; for him have I offended. I pause for a
reply.   35

All. None, Brutus, none!

Brutus. Then none have I offended. I have done no
  more to Caesar than you shall do° to Brutus. The
  question of his death is enrolled° in the Capitol; his
  glory not extenuated,° wherein he was worthy, nor   40
  his offenses enforced,° for which he suffered death.

            Enter Mark Antony, with Caesar's body.

Here comes his body, mourned by Mark Antony,
who, though he had no hand in his death, shall receive
the benefit of his dying, a place° in the commonwealth, as which of you shall not? With this I depart,   45
that, as I slew my best lover° for the good of Rome,
I have the same dagger for myself, when it shall
please my country to need my death.

All. Live, Brutus! Live, live!

First Plebeian. Bring him with triumph home unto his
    house.   50

---

30 *bondman* slave   31 *rude* barbarous   38 *shall do* i.e., if I should
become equally tyrannical   38–39 *The question . . . enrolled* the considerations that made necessary his death are recorded   40 *extenuated*
depreciated   41 *enforced* exaggerated   44 *place* i.e., as a free citizen
46 *lover* friend

Second Plebeian. Give him a statue with his ancestors.

Third Plebeian. Let him be Caesar.

Fourth Plebeian.   Caesar's better parts°
Shall be crowned in Brutus.

First Plebeian. We'll bring him to his house with shouts
and clamors.

Brutus. My countrymen——

55 *Second Plebeian.*   Peace! Silence! Brutus speaks.

First Plebeian. Peace, ho!
Brutus. Good countrymen, let me depart alone,
And, for my sake, stay here with Antony.
Do grace to Caesar's corpse, and grace his speech°
60 Tending° to Caesar's glories, which Mark Antony
By our permission, is allowed to make.
I do entreat you, not a man depart,
Save I alone, till Antony have spoke.   *Exit.*

First Plebeian. Stay, ho! And let us hear Mark Antony.

65 *Third Plebeian.* Let him go up into the public chair;°
We'll hear him. Noble Antony, go up.

Antony. For Brutus' sake, I am beholding° to you.

Fourth Plebeian. What does he say of Brutus?

Third Plebeian.   He says, for Brutus' sake,
He finds himself beholding to us all.

Fourth Plebeian. 'Twere best he speak no harm of Brutus
70 here!

First Plebeian. This Caesar was a tyrant.

Third Plebeian.   Nay, that's certain.
We are blest that Rome is rid of him.

---

52 *parts* qualities   59 *Do . . . speech* show respect to dead Caesar and
listen respectfully to Antony's speech   60 *Tending* relating   65 *public chair* pulpit, rostrum   67 *beholding* beholden, indebted

Second Plebeian. Peace! Let us hear what Antony can
    say.

Antony. You gentle Romans——

All.   Peace, ho! Let us hear him.

Antony. Friends, Romans, countrymen, lend me your
    ears;   75
  I come to bury Caesar, not to praise him.
  The evil that men do lives after them,
  The good is oft interrèd with their bones;
  So let it be with Caesar. The noble Brutus
  Hath told you Caesar was ambitious.   80
  If it were so, it was a grievous fault,
  And grievously hath Caesar answered° it.
  Here, under leave of Brutus and the rest
  (For Brutus is an honorable man,
  So are they all, all honorable men),   85
  Come I to speak in Caesar's funeral.
  He was my friend, faithful and just to me;
  But Brutus says he was ambitious,
  And Brutus is an honorable man.
  He hath brought many captives home to Rome,   90
  Whose ransoms did the general coffers° fill;
  Did this in Caesar seem ambitious?
  When that the poor have cried, Caesar hath wept;
  Ambition should be made of sterner stuff.
  Yet Brutus says he was ambitious;   95
  And Brutus is an honorable man.
  You all did see that on the Lupercal
  I thrice presented him a kingly crown,
  Which he did thrice refuse. Was this ambition?
  Yet Brutus says he was ambitious;   100
  And sure he is an honorable man.
  I speak not to disprove what Brutus spoke,
  But here I am to speak what I do know.
  You all did love him once, not without cause;
  What cause withholds you then to mourn for him?   105
  O judgment, thou art fled to brutish beasts,

82 *answered* paid the penalty for   91 *general coffers* public treasury

And men have lost their reason! Bear with me;
My heart is in the coffin there with Caesar,
And I must pause till it come back to me.

First Plebeian. Methinks there is much reason in his
110   sayings.

Second Plebeian. If thou consider rightly of the matter,
Caesar has had great wrong.

Third Plebeian.   Has he, masters?
I fear there will a worse come in his place.

Fourth Plebeian. Marked ye his words? He would not
take the crown,
115   Therefore 'tis certain he was not ambitious.

First Plebeian. If it be found so, some will dear abide it.°

Second Plebeian. Poor soul, his eyes are red as fire with
weeping.

Third Plebeian. There's not a nobler man in Rome than
Antony.

Fourth Plebeian. Now mark him, he begins again to
speak.

120 *Antony.* But yesterday the word of Caesar might
Have stood against the world; now lies he there,
And none so poor to° do him reverence.
O masters! If I were disposed to stir
Your hearts and minds to mutiny and rage,
125   I should do Brutus wrong and Cassius wrong,
Who, you all know, are honorable men.
I will not do them wrong; I rather choose
To wrong the dead, to wrong myself and you,
Than I will wrong such honorable men.
130   But here's a parchment with the seal of Caesar;
I found it in his closet;° 'tis his will.
Let but the commons° hear this testament,
Which, pardon me, I do not mean to read,

116 *dear abide it* pay dearly for it   122 *so poor to* so low in rank as to
131 *closet* study (?) desk (?)   132 *commons* plebeians

And they would go and kiss dead Caesar's wounds,
And dip their napkins° in his sacred blood;   *135*
Yea, beg a hair of him for memory,
And dying, mention it within their wills,
Bequeathing it as a rich legacy
Unto their issue.°

Fourth Plebeian. We'll hear the will; read it, Mark
    Antony.   *140*

All. The will, the will! We will hear Caesar's will!

Antony. Have patience, gentle friends, I must not read it.
    It is not meet° you know how Caesar loved you.
    You are not wood, you are not stones, but men;
    And being men, hearing the will of Caesar,   *145*
    It will inflame you, it will make you mad.
    'Tis good you know not that you are his heirs;
    For if you should, O, what would come of it?

Fourth Plebeian. Read the will! We'll hear it, Antony!
    You shall read us the will, Caesar's will!   *150*

Antony. Will you be patient? Will you stay° awhile?
    I have o'ershot myself° to tell you of it.
    I fear I wrong the honorable men
    Whose daggers have stabbed Caesar; I do fear it.

Fourth Plebeian. They were traitors. Honorable men!   *155*

All. The will! The testament!

Second Plebeian. They were villains, murderers! The
    will! Read the will!

Antony. You will compel me then to read the will?
    Then make a ring about the corpse of Caesar,   *160*
    And let me show you him that made the will.
    Shall I descend? And will you give me leave?

All. Come down.

Second Plebeian. Descend.   [*Antony comes down.*]

135 *napkins* handkerchiefs   139 *issue* heirs   143 *meet* fitting   151
stay wait   152 *o'ershot myself* gone further than I intended

165 *Third Plebeian.* You shall have leave.

Fourth Plebeian. A ring! Stand round.

First Plebeian. Stand from the hearse, stand from the body!

Second Plebeian. Room for Antony, most noble Antony!

Antony. Nay, press not so upon me; stand far° off.

170 *All.* Stand back! Room! Bear back.

Antony. If you have tears, prepare to shed them now.
  You all do know this mantle;° I remember
  The first time ever Caesar put it on:
  'Twas on a summer's evening, in his tent,
175 That day he overcame the Nervii.°
  Look, in this place ran Cassius' dagger through;
  See what a rent the envious° Casca made;
  Through this the well-belovèd Brutus stabbed,
  And as he plucked his cursèd steel away,
180 Mark how the blood of Caesar followed it,
  As° rushing out of doors, to be resolved°
  If Brutus so unkindly° knocked, or no;
  For Brutus, as you know, was Caesar's angel.°
  Judge, O you gods, how dearly Caesar loved him!
185 This was the most unkindest° cut of all;
  For when the noble Caesar saw him stab,
  Ingratitude, more strong than traitors' arms,
  Quite vanquished him. Then burst his mighty heart;
  And, in his mantle muffling up his face,
190 Even at the base° of Pompey's statue°
  (Which all the while ran blood) great Caesar fell.
  O, what a fall was there, my countrymen!
  Then I, and you, and all of us fell down,
  Whilst bloody treason flourished° over us.

169 *far* farther   172 *mantle* cloak (here, the toga)   175 *Nervii* (a fierce
tribe decisively conquered by Caesar in 57 B.C.)   177 *envious* spiteful
181 *As* as though   181 *to be resolved* to learn for certain   182 *un-
kindly* (1) cruelly (2) unnaturally   183 *angel* favorite (i.e., considered
incapable of evil)   185 *most unkindest* most cruel and unnatural
190 *base* pedestal   190 *statue* (pronounced "stat-u-a")   194 *flour-
ished* (1) swaggered (2) brandished a sword in triumph

O, now you weep, and I perceive you feel   195
The dint° of pity; these are gracious drops.
Kind souls, what° weep you when you but behold
Our Caesar's vesture° wounded? Look you here,
Here is himself, marred° as you see with° traitors.

First Plebeian. O piteous spectacle!   200

Second Plebeian. O noble Caesar!

Third Plebeian. O woeful day!

Fourth Plebeian. O traitors, villains!

First Plebeian. O most bloody sight!

Second Plebeian. We will be revenged.   205

[*All.*] Revenge! About!° Seek! Burn! Fire! Kill! Slay!
Let not a traitor live!

Antony. Stay, countrymen.

First Plebeian. Peace there! Hear the noble Antony.

Second Plebeian. We'll hear him, we'll follow him, we'll   210
die with him!

Antony. Good friends, sweet friends, let me not stir you
up
To such a sudden flood of mutiny.
They that have done this deed are honorable.
What private griefs° they have, alas, I know not,   215
That made them do it. They are wise and honorable,
And will, no doubt, with reasons answer you.
I come not, friends, to steal away your hearts;
I am no orator, as Brutus is;
But (as you know me all) a plain blunt man   220
That love my friend, and that they know full well
That gave me public leave to speak° of him.
For I have neither writ, nor words, nor worth,

196 *dint* stroke   197 *what* why   198 *vesture* clothing   199 *marred*
mangled   199 *with* by   206 *About* let's go   215 *private griefs* personal grievances   222 *public leave to speak* permission to speak in
public

Action, nor utterance,° nor the power of speech
225 To stir men's blood; I only speak right on.°
I tell you that which you yourselves do know,
Show you sweet Caesar's wounds, poor poor dumb
     mouths,
And bid them speak for me. But were I Brutus,
And Brutus Antony, there were an Antony
230 Would ruffle up° your spirits, and put a tongue
In every wound of Caesar that should move
The stones of Rome to rise and mutiny.

All. We'll mutiny.

First Plebeian.   We'll burn the house of Brutus.

Third Plebeian. Away, then! Come, seek the conspirators.

235 *Antony.* Yet hear me, countrymen. Yet hear me speak.

All. Peace, ho! Hear Antony, most noble Antony!

Antony. Why, friends, you go to do you know not what:
Wherein hath Caesar thus deserved your loves?
Alas, you know not; I must tell you then:
240 You have forgot the will I told you of.

All. Most true, the will! Let's stay and hear the will.

Antony. Here is the will, and under Caesar's seal.
To every Roman citizen he gives,
To every several° man, seventy-five drachmas.

Second Plebeian. Most noble Caesar! We'll revenge his
245 death!

Third Plebeian. O royal° Caesar!

Antony. Hear me with patience.

All. Peace, ho!

223–24 *neither . . . utterance* neither a written speech, nor fluency, nor
reputation, nor (an orator's) gestures, nor good delivery (perhaps *writ*
should be emended to *wit*, "intellectual cleverness")   225 *right on*
directly, without premeditation   230 *ruffle up* incite to rage   244 *several* individual   246 *royal* nobly generous

Antony. Moreover, he hath left you all his walks,°
 His private arbors, and new-planted orchards,°   *250*
 On this side Tiber; he hath left them you,
 And to your heirs forever: common pleasures,°
 To walk abroad and recreate yourselves.
 Here was a Caesar! When comes such another?

First Plebeian. Never, never! Come, away, away! *255*
 We'll burn his body in the holy place,
 And with the brands fire the traitors' houses.
 Take up the body.

Second Plebeian. Go fetch fire.

Third Plebeian. Pluck down benches.   *260*

Fourth Plebeian. Pluck down forms, windows,° anything!   *Exeunt Plebeians* [*with the body*].

Antony. Now let it work:° Mischief, thou art afoot,
 Take thou what course thou wilt.

     Enter Servant.

        How now, fellow?

Servant. Sir, Octavius is already come to Rome. *265*

Antony. Where is he?

Servant. He and Lepidus are at Caesar's house.

Antony. And thither will I straight° to visit him;
 He comes upon a wish.° Fortune is merry,
 And in this mood will give us anything.   *270*

Servant. I heard him say, Brutus and Cassius
 Are rid° like madmen through the gates of Rome.

Antony. Belike° they had some notice of° the people,
 How I had moved them. Bring me to Octavius.
          Exeunt.

---

249 *walks* parks 250 *orchards* gardens 252 *common pleasures* public
places of recreation 261 *forms, windows* long benches (and) shutters
263 *work* (1) ferment (as yeast) (2) work itself out 268 *will I straight*
will I (go) at once 269 *upon a wish* just as I wished 272 *Are rid* have
ridden 273 *Belike* probably 273 *notice of* news about

[Scene III. *A street.*]

Enter Cinna the Poet, and after him the Plebeians.

Cinna. I dreamt tonight° that I did feast with Caesar,
And things unluckily charge my fantasy.°
I have no will to wander forth° of doors,
Yet something leads me forth.

5 *First Plebeian.* What is your name?

Second Plebeian. Whither are you going?

Third Plebeian. Where do you dwell?

Fourth Plebeian. Are you a married man or a bachelor?

Second Plebeian. Answer every man directly.°

10 *First Plebeian.* Ay, and briefly.

Fourth Plebeian. Ay, and wisely.

Third Plebeian. Ay, and truly, you were best.

Cinna. What is my name? Whither am I going? Where
do I dwell? Am I a married man or a bachelor? Then,
15 to answer every man directly and briefly, wisely and
truly: wisely I say, I am a bachelor.

Second Plebeian. That's as much as to say, they are
fools that marry; you'll bear me a bang° for that, I
fear. Proceed directly.

20 *Cinna.* Directly, I am going to Caesar's funeral.

First Plebeian. As a friend or an enemy?

III.iii.1 *tonight* last night   2 *things . . . fantasy* events give ominous
weight to my imaginings   3 *forth* out   9 *directly* straightforwardly
18 *bear me a bang* get a blow from me

Cinna. As a friend.

Second Plebeian. That matter is answered directly.

Fourth Plebeian. For your dwelling, briefly.

Cinna. Briefly, I dwell by the Capitol.   25

Third Plebeian. Your name, sir, truly.

Cinna. Truly, my name is Cinna.

First Plebeian. Tear him to pieces! He's a conspirator.

Cinna. I am Cinna the poet! I am Cinna the poet!

Fourth Plebeian. Tear him for his bad verses! Tear him   30
     for his bad verses!

Cinna. I am not Cinna the conspirator.

Fourth Plebeian. It is no matter, his name's Cinna;
     pluck but his name out of his heart, and turn him
     going.°   35

Third Plebeian. Tear him, tear him! [*They attack him.*]
     Come, brands, ho! Firebrands! To Brutus', to Cas-
     sius'! Burn all! Some to Decius' house, and some to
     Casca's; some to Ligarius'! Away, go!
                         Exeunt all the Plebeians [*with Cinna*].

34–35 *turn him going* dispatch him

ACT IV

[Scene I. *A house in Rome.*]

Enter Antony, Octavius, and Lepidus.

Antony. These many then shall die; their names are
pricked.°

Octavius. Your brother too must die; consent you, Lepidus?

Lepidus. I do consent——

Octavius.　　　　　　　Prick him down, Antony.

Lepidus. Upon condition Publius shall not live,
5　Who is your sister's son, Mark Antony.

Antony. He shall not live; look, with a spot I damn him.°
But, Lepidus, go you to Caesar's house;
Fetch the will hither, and we shall determine
How to cut off some charge° in legacies.

10　*Lepidus.* What, shall I find you here?

Octavius. Or° here or at the Capitol.　　*Exit Lepidus.*

IV.i.1 *pricked* ticked off, marked on the list　6 *with a spot I damn him*
with a dot (on the wax tablet) I condemn him　9 *cut off some charge* re-
duce expenses (by altering the amount left in bequests)　11 *Or* either

Antony. This is a slight unmeritable° man,
    Meet° to be sent on errands; is it fit,
    The threefold world° divided, he should stand
    One of the three to share it?

Octavius.   So you thought him,   *15*
    And took his voice° who should be pricked to die
    In our black sentence° and proscription.°

Antony. Octavius, I have seen more days° than you;
    And though we lay these honors on this man,
    To ease ourselves of divers sland'rous loads,°   *20*
    He shall but bear them as the ass bears gold,
    To groan and sweat under the business,°
    Either led or driven, as we point the way;
    And having brought our treasure where we will,
    Then take we down his load, and turn him off,°   *25*
    (Like to the empty° ass) to shake his ears
    And graze in commons.°

Octavius.   You may do your will;
    But he's a tried and valiant soldier.°

Antony. So is my horse, Octavius, and for that
    I do appoint him store° of provender.   *30*
    It is a creature that I teach to fight,
    To wind,° to stop, to run directly on,
    His corporal° motion governed by my spirit.°
    And, in some taste,° is Lepidus but so.°
    He must be taught, and trained, and bid go forth.   *35*
    A barren-spirited° fellow; one that feeds

---

12 *slight unmeritable* insignificant and undeserving   13 *Meet* fit   14 *threefold world* three areas of the Roman empire, Europe, Asia, and Africa   16 *voice* vote   17 *black sentence* sentence of death   17 *proscription* condemnation to death or exile   18 *have seen more days* am older (and more experienced)   20 *divers sland'rous loads* blame which will be laid upon us for our various actions   22 *business* hard labor   25 *turn him off* drive him away   26 *empty* unburdened   27 *in commons* on public pasture   28 *soldier* (trisyllabic)   30 *appoint him store* allot him a supply   32 *wind* turn   33 *corporal* physical   33 *spirit* mind   34 *taste* measure   34 *so* the same   36 *barren-spirited* lacking initiative or ideas of his own

On objects, arts, and imitations,°
Which, out of use and staled° by other men,
Begin his fashion.° Do not talk of him
40 But as a property.° And now, Octavius,
Listen great things. Brutus and Cassius
Are levying powers;° we must straight make head.°
Therefore let our alliance be combined,
Our best friends made,° our means stretched;°
45 And let us presently° go sit in council
How covert matters may be best disclosed,
And open perils surest answerèd.°

Octavius. Let us do so; for we are at the stake,°
And bayed about with many enemies;
50 And some that smile have in their hearts, I fear,
Millions of mischiefs.°   *Exeunt.*

[Scene II. *Camp near Sardis.*]

*Drum. Enter Brutus, Lucilius, [Lucius,] and the Army.
Titinius and Pindarus meet them.*

Brutus. Stand ho!

Lucilius. Give the word, ho! and stand.

Brutus. What now, Lucilius, is Cassius near?

---

37 *objects, arts, and imitations* curiosities, artifices, and fashions (or
styles) 38 *staled* made common 39 *Begin his fashion* i.e., he is
always far behind the times 40 *property* mere tool (a thing rather
than a person) 42 *powers* armed forces 42 *straight make head* immediately gather troops 44 *Our best friends made* let our closest allies
be selected 44 *stretched* be used to the fullest advantage 45 *presently* immediately 46–47 *How . . . answerèd* to decide how hidden
dangers may best be discovered and open dangers most safely en-
countered 48 *at the stake* (metaphor derived from Elizabethan sport
of bearbaiting) i.e., like a bear tied to a stake and set upon by many
dogs 51 *mischiefs* plans to injure us

Lucilius. He is at hand, and Pindarus is come
  To do you salutation from his master.   *5*

Brutus. He greets me well.° Your master, Pindarus,
  In his own change, or by ill officers,°
  Hath given me some worthy° cause to wish
  Things done undone; but if he be at hand,
  I shall be satisfied.°

Pindarus.   I do not doubt   *10*
  But that my noble master will appear
  Such as he is, full of regard° and honor.

Brutus. He is not doubted. A word, Lucilius,
  How he received you; let me be resolved.°

Lucilius. With courtesy and with respect enough,   *15*
  But not with such familiar instances,°
  Nor with such free and friendly conference°
  As he hath used of old.

Brutus.   Thou hast described
  A hot friend cooling. Ever note, Lucilius,
  When love begins to sicken and decay   *20*
  It useth an enforcèd ceremony.°
  There are no tricks in plain and simple faith;
  But hollow° men, like horses hot at hand,°
  Make gallant show and promise of their mettle;°
                     Low march within.
  But when they should endure the bloody spur,   *25*
  They fall their crests,° and like deceitful jades°
  Sink in the trial.° Comes his army on?

Lucilius. They mean this night in Sardis to be quartered;

IV.ii.6 *He greets me well* he sends greetings by a very good man   7 *In his . . . officers* either from a change in his feelings toward me or through the actions of bad subordinates   8 *worthy* substantial   10 *be satisfied* receive a satisfactory explanation   12 *full of regard* worthy of respect   14 *resolved* fully informed   16 *familiar instances* marks of friendship   17 *conference* conversation   21 *enforcèd ceremony* strained formality   23 *hollow* insincere   23 *hot at hand* overspirited at the start   24 *mettle* quality, courage   26 *fall their crests* let fall the ridges of their necks   26 *jades* nags   27 *Sink in the trial* fail when put to the test

The greater part, the horse in general,°
Are come with Cassius.

Enter Cassius and his Powers.

30   *Brutus.*   Hark! He is arrived.
    March gently° on to meet him.

Cassius. Stand, ho!

Brutus. Stand, ho! Speak the word along.

[*First Soldier.*] Stand!

35   [*Second Soldier.*] Stand!

[*Third Soldier.*] Stand!

Cassius. Most noble brother, you have done me wrong.

Brutus. Judge me, you gods! Wrong I mine enemies?
    And if not so, how should I wrong a brother.

40   *Cassius.* Brutus, this sober form° of yours hides wrongs;
    And when you do them——

Brutus.   Cassius, be content.°
    Speak your griefs° softly; I do know you well.
    Before the eyes of both our armies here
    (Which should perceive nothing but love from us)
45   Let us not wrangle. Bid them move away;
    Then in my tent, Cassius, enlarge° your griefs,
    And I will give you audience.

Cassius.   Pindarus,
    Bid our commanders lead their charges° off
    A little from this ground.

50   *Brutus.* Lucilius, do you the like, and let no man
    Come to our tent till we have done our conference.
    Let Lucius and Titinius guard our door.
                    Exeunt. Mane[n]t Brutus and Cassius.

29 *the horse in general* all the cavalry   31 *gently* slowly   40 *sober form* staid manner   41 *be content* keep calm   42 *griefs* grievances   46 *enlarge* freely express   48 *charges* troops

[Scene III. *Brutus' tent.*]

Cassius. That you have wronged me doth appear in this:
　　You have condemned and noted° Lucius Pella
　　For taking bribes here of the Sardians;
　　Wherein my letters, praying on his side,°
　　Because I knew the man, was slighted off.°　　　　　　*5*

Brutus. You wronged yourself to write in such a case.

Cassius. In such a time as this it is not meet
　　That every nice offense should bear his comment.°

Brutus. Let me tell you, Cassius, you yourself
　　Are much condemned to have an itching palm,°　　　*10*
　　To sell and mart° your offices for gold
　　To undeservers.

Cassius.　　　　　　I an itching palm?
　　You know that you are Brutus that speaks this,
　　Or, by the gods, this speech were else your last.

Brutus. The name of Cassius honors° this corruption,　*15*
　　And chastisement doth therefore hide his head.

Cassius. Chastisement!

Brutus. Remember March, the ides of March remember.
　　Did not great Julius bleed for justice' sake?
　　What villain touched his body, that did stab,　　　　*20*
　　And not° for justice? What, shall one of us,
　　That struck the foremost man of all this world

IV.iii.2. *noted* publicly disgraced　4 *praying on his side* appealing on
his behalf　5 *was slighted off* was contemptuously disregarded ("letters" takes a singular verb because of its singular meaning)　8 *nice
. . . comment* trivial fault should receive criticism (*his* = its)　10
condemned . . . palm accused of being mercenary　11 *mart* traffic
in　15 *honors* lends an air of respectability　21 *And not* except

But for supporting robbers,° shall we now
Contaminate our fingers with base bribes,
25 And sell the mighty space of our large honors°
For so much trash° as may be graspèd thus?°
I had rather be a dog, and bay° the moon,
Than such a Roman.

Cassius.   Brutus, bait° not me;
I'll not endure it. You forget yourself
30 To hedge me in.° I am a soldier, I,
Older in practice, abler than yourself
To make conditions.°

Brutus.   Go to! You are not, Cassius.

Cassius. I am.

Brutus. I say you are not.

35 *Cassius.* Urge° me no more, I shall forget myself;
Have mind upon your health;° tempt° me no farther.

Brutus. Away, slight° man!

Cassius. Is't possible?

Brutus.   Hear me, for I will speak.
Must I give way and room to your rash choler?°
40 Shall I be frighted when a madman stares?°

Cassius. O ye gods, ye gods! Must I endure all this?

---

23 *supporting robbers* i.e., protecting dishonest officials (a point made
by Plutarch but mentioned only now by Shakespeare)   25 *mighty
. . . honors* vast capacity to be honorable and magnanimous (with sug-
gestion of potentiality for making other men free, and honorable in
office)   26 *trash* rubbish, i.e., money   26 *graspèd thus* (the small confined area of the closed fist contrasts with the "mighty space" gained
by their honorable deeds in abolishing injustice and corruption)
27 *bay* howl at   28 *bait* harass and worry (as a bear tied to a stake is
baited by dogs)   30 *hedge me in* limit my freedom of action   32 *make
conditions* manage practical matters   35 *Urge* drive, bully   36 *health*
safety   36 *tempt* provoke   37 *slight* insignificant   39 *give . . .
choler* let your hasty temper have free vent and run its course un-
checked   40 *stares* glares

Brutus. All this? Ay, more: fret till your proud heart
    break.
  Go show your slaves how choleric you are,
  And make your bondmen tremble. Must I budge?°
  Must I observe° you? Must I stand and crouch°   45
  Under your testy humor?° By the gods,
  You shall digest the venom° of your spleen,°
  Though it do split you; for, from this day forth,
  I'll use you for my mirth, yea, for my laughter,
  When you are waspish.

Cassius.   Is it come to this?   50

Brutus. You say you are a better soldier:
  Let it appear so; make your vaunting° true,
  And it shall please me well. For mine own part,
  I shall be glad to learn of° noble men.

Cassius. You wrong me every way; you wrong me,
    Brutus;   55
  I said, an elder soldier, not a better.
  Did I say, better?

Brutus.   If you did, I care not.

Cassius. When Caesar lived, he durst not thus have
    moved° me.

Brutus. Peace, peace, you durst not so have tempted°
    him.

Cassius. I durst not?   60

Brutus. No.

Cassius. What? Durst not tempt him?

Brutus.   For your life you durst not.

---

44 *budge* defer to it   45 *observe* wait on   45 *crouch* bow   46 *testy humor* irritability   47 *digest the venom* swallow the poison   47 *spleen* (considered the source of sudden passions) i.e., fiery temper   52 *vaunting* boasting   54 *learn of* (1) hear about the exploits of (2) take lessons from   58 *moved* exasperated   59 *tempted* provoked

Cassius. Do not presume too much upon my love;
I may do that I shall be sorry for.

65 *Brutus.* You have done that you should be sorry for.
There is no terror, Cassius, in your threats;
For I am armed so strong in honesty°
That they pass by me as the idle wind,
Which I respect° not. I did send to you
70 For certain sums of gold, which you denied me;
For I can raise no money by vile means.
By heaven, I had rather coin my heart
And drop my blood for drachmas than to wring
From the hard hands of peasants their vile trash
75 By any indirection.° I did send
To you for gold to pay my legions,
Which you denied me. Was that done like Cassius?
Should I have answered Caius Cassius so?
When Marcus Brutus grows so covetous
80 To lock such rascal counters° from his friends,
Be ready, gods, with all your thunderbolts,
Dash him to pieces!

Cassius.   I denied you not.

Brutus. You did.

Cassius.   I did not. He was but a fool
That brought my answer back. Brutus hath rived°
my heart.
85 A friend should bear his friend's infirmities;
But Brutus makes mine greater than they are.

Brutus. I do not, till you practice them on me.

Cassius. You love me not.

Brutus.   I do not like your faults.

Cassius. A friendly eye could never see such faults.

---

67 *honesty* integrity   69 *respect* heed   75 *indirection* irregular methods   80 *rascal counters* base (and worthless) coins   84 *rived* broken

Brutus. A flatterer's would not, though they do appear   *90*
  As huge as high Olympus.

Cassius. Come, Antony, and young Octavius, come,
  Revenge yourselves alone° on Cassius,
  For Cassius is aweary of the world:
  Hated by one he loves; braved° by his brother;   *95*
  Checked° like a bondman; all his faults observed,
  Set in a notebook, learned and conned by rote°
  To cast into my teeth.° O, I could weep
  My spirit from mine eyes! There is my dagger,
  And here my naked breast; within, a heart   *100*
  Dearer than Pluto's mine,° richer than gold;
  If that thou be'st a Roman, take it forth.
  I, that denied thee gold, will give my heart.
  Strike as thou didst at Caesar; for I know,
  When thou didst hate him worst, thou lovedst him better   *105*
  Than ever thou lovedst Cassius.

Brutus.   Sheathe your dagger.
  Be angry when you will, it shall have scope.°
  Do what you will, dishonor shall be humor.°
  O Cassius, you are yokèd with a lamb
  That carries anger as the flint bears fire,   *110*
  Who, much enforcèd,° shows a hasty spark,
  And straight° is cold again.

Cassius.   Hath Cassius lived
  To be but mirth and laughter to his Brutus
  When grief and blood ill-tempered° vexeth him?

Brutus. When I spoke that, I was ill-tempered too.   *115*

---

93 *alone* only   95 *braved* defied   96 *Checked* rebuked   97 *conned
by rote* learned by heart   98 *cast into my teeth* i.e., throw in my face
101 *Dearer than Pluto's mine* more precious than all the riches in the
earth (Pluto, god of the underworld, and Plutus, god of riches, were
frequently confused)   107 *shall have scope* (your anger) shall have
free play   108 *dishonor shall be humor* insults shall be regarded as
quirks of temperament   111 *much enforcèd* greatly provoked   112
straight immediately   114 *blood ill-tempered* i.e., a "black mood"

Cassius. Do you confess so much? Give me your hand.

Brutus. And my heart too.

Cassius.   O Brutus!

Brutus.   What's the matter?

Cassius. Have not you love enough to bear with me
When that rash humor° which my mother gave me
Makes me forgetful?

120 *Brutus.*   Yes, Cassius, and from henceforth,
When you are over-earnest with your Brutus,
He'll think your mother° chides, and leave you so.°

Enter a Poet, [followed by Lucilius, Titinius, and Lucius].

Poet. Let me go in to see the generals;
There is some grudge° between 'em; 'tis not meet
125 They be alone.

Lucilius. You shall not come to them.

Poet. Nothing but death shall stay me.

Cassius. How now. What's the matter?

Poet. For shame, you generals! What do you mean?
130 Love, and be friends, as two such men should be;
For I have seen more years, I'm sure, than ye.

Cassius. Ha, ha! How vilely doth this cynic° rhyme!

Brutus. Get you hence, sirrah! Saucy° fellow, hence!

Cassius. Bear with him, Brutus, 'tis his fashion.

135 *Brutus.* I'll know his humor when he knows his time.°
What should the wars do with these jigging° fools?
Companion,° hence!

119 *rash humor* hasty temperament   122 *your mother* i.e., your in-
herited temperament   122 *leave you so* leave it at that   124 *grudge*
bad feeling   132 *cynic* rude fellow   133 *Saucy* impertinent   135 *I'll
... time* I'll accept his eccentricity when he can judge the suitable time
for it   136 *jigging* doggerel-writing, rhyming   137 *Companion* base
fellow

Cassius.   Away, away, be gone!
                                        Exit Poet.

Brutus. Lucilius and Titinius, bid the commanders
    Prepare to lodge their companies tonight.

Cassius. And come yourselves, and bring Messala with
    you   *140*
    Immediately to us.   [*Exeunt Lucilius and Titinius.*]

Brutus.   Lucius, a bowl of wine.
                                        [*Exit Lucius.*]

Cassius. I did not think you could have been so angry.

Brutus. O Cassius, I am sick of many griefs.

Cassius. Of your philosophy you make no use,
    If you give place° to accidental evils.°   *145*

Brutus. No man bears sorrow better. Portia is dead.

Cassius. Ha? Portia?

Brutus. She is dead.

Cassius. How scaped I killing when I crossed° you so?
    O insupportable and touching° loss!   *150*
    Upon° what sickness?

Brutus.   Impatient of° my absence,
    And grief that young Octavius with Mark Antony
    Have made themselves so strong—for with her death
    That tidings came°—with this she fell distract,°
    And (her attendants absent) swallowed fire.°   *155*

Cassius. And died so?

Brutus.   Even so.

---

145 *place* way   145 *accidental evils* misfortunes brought on by chance
(Brutus seems not to be behaving as a Stoic philosopher should)
149 *crossed* contradicted   150 *touching* wounding, grievous   151
Upon as a result of   151 *Impatient of* unable to endure   153–54
for . . . came i.e., news of her death came at the same time as news
of their strength   154 *fell distract* became distraught   155 *swallowed
fire* (according to Plutarch she choked herself by putting hot coals into
her mouth)

Cassius.   O ye immortal gods!

Enter Boy [Lucius], with wine and tapers.

Brutus. Speak no more of her. Give me a bowl of wine.
In this I bury all unkindness, Cassius.   *Drinks.*

Cassius. My heart is thirsty for that noble pledge.
160 Fill, Lucius, till the wine o'erswell the cup;
I cannot drink too much of Brutus' love.
                              [*Drinks. Exit Lucius.*]

Enter Titinius and Messala.

Brutus. Come in, Titinius! Welcome, good Messala.
Now sit we close about this taper here,
And call in question° our necessities.

Cassius. Portia, art thou gone?

165 *Brutus.*   No more, I pray you.
Messala, I have here receivèd letters
That young Octavius and Mark Antony
Come down upon us with a mighty power,°
Bending their expedition° toward Philippi.

170 *Messala.* Myself have letters of the selfsame tenure.°

Brutus. With what addition?

Messala. That by proscription° and bills of outlawry°
Octavius, Antony, and Lepidus
Have put to death an hundred senators.

175 *Brutus.* Therein our letters do not well agree.
Mine speak of seventy senators that died
By their proscriptions, Cicero being one.

Cassius. Cicero one?

Messala.   Cicero is dead,
And by that order of proscription.
180 Had you your letters from your wife, my lord?

164 *call in question* consider 168 *power* army 169 *Bending their
expedition* directing their rapid march 170 *tenure* tenor, general
meaning 172 *proscription* proclamation of the death sentence 172
bills of outlawry lists of those proscribed

Brutus. No, Messala.

Messala. Nor nothing in your letters writ of her?

Brutus. Nothing, Messala.

Messala.   That methinks is strange.

Brutus. Why ask you? Hear you aught of her in yours?

Messala. No, my lord.   185

Brutus. Now as you are a Roman, tell me true.

Messala. Then like a Roman bear the truth I tell,
    For certain she is dead, and by strange manner.

Brutus. Why, farewell, Portia. We must die, Messala.
    With meditating that she must die once,°   190
    I have the patience to endure it now.

Messala. Even so great men great losses should endure.

Cassius. I have as much of this in art° as you,
    But yet my nature could not bear it so.°

Brutus. Well, to our work alive.° What do you think   195
    Of marching to Philippi presently?°

Cassius. I do not think it good.

Brutus.   Your reason?

Cassius.   This it is:
    'Tis better that the enemy seek us;
    So shall he waste his means, weary his soldiers,
    Doing himself offense,° whilst we, lying still,   200
    Are full of rest, defense, and nimbleness.

Brutus. Good reasons must of force° give place to better.
    The people 'twixt Philippi and this ground

190 *once* at some time   193 *this in art* i.e., this Stoicism in theory
180–94 *Had . . . so* (some editors suggest that this was the original
version of Shakespeare's account of Portia's death and that he later
deleted this and wrote in lines 142–57, preferring to demonstrate
Brutus' humanity rather than his Stoicism; the Folio printer then set
up both versions by mistake. Line 158 would follow 141—as 195 would
follow 179—neatly enough to make this an attractive theory)
195 *alive* as men still living   196 *presently* immediately   200 *offense*
harm   202 *force* necessity

Do stand but in a forced affection;°
205   For they have grudged us contribution.
The enemy, marching along by them,
By them shall make a fuller number up,
Come on refreshed, new-added° and encouraged;
From which advantage shall we cut him off
210   If at Philippi we do face him there,
These people at our back.

Cassius.   Hear me, good brother.

Brutus. Under your pardon.° You must note beside
That we have tried the utmost of our friends,
Our legions are brimful, our cause is ripe.
215   The enemy increaseth every day;
We, at the height, are ready to decline.
There is a tide in the affairs of men
Which, taken at the flood, leads on to fortune;
Omitted,° all the voyage of their life
220   Is bound in° shallows and in miseries.
On such a full sea are we now afloat,
And we must take the current when it serves,
Or lose our ventures.°

Cassius.   Then, with your will,° go on;
We'll along ourselves and meet them at Philippi.

225   *Brutus.* The deep of night is crept upon our talk,
And nature must obey necessity,
Which we will niggard with a little rest.°
There is no more to say?

Cassius.   No more. Good night.
Early tomorrow will we rise and hence.°

Enter Lucius.

---

204 *Do . . . affection* i.e., support us only under compulsion   208 *new-added* reinforced   212 *Under your pardon* excuse me   219 *Omitted* neglected   220 *bound in* limited to   223 *ventures* shipping trade, i.e., risks   223 *with your will* as you wish   227 *niggard with a little rest* i.e., put off with the shortest possible sleep   229 *hence* leave this place

Brutus. Lucius, my gown.°   *Exit Lucius.*
                    Farewell, good Messala.   230
   Good night, Titinius. Noble, noble Cassius,
   Good night, and good repose.

Cassius.   O my dear brother,
   This was an ill beginning of the night.
   Never come° such division 'tween our souls!
   Let it not, Brutus.

                Enter Lucius, with the gown.

Brutus.   Everything is well.   235

Cassius. Good night, my lord.

Brutus.   Good night, good brother.

Titinius, Messala. Good night, Lord Brutus.

Brutus.   Farewell, every one.
                                   Exeunt.
   Give me the gown. Where is thy instrument?°

Lucius. Here in the tent.

Brutus.   What, thou speak'st drowsily?
   Poor knave,° I blame thee not; thou art o'erwatched.° 240
   Call Claudius and some other of my men;
   I'll have them sleep on cushions in my tent.

Lucius. Varro and Claudius!

                Enter Varro and Claudius.

Varro. Calls my lord?

Brutus. I pray you, sirs, lie in my tent and sleep.   245
   It may be I shall raise° you by and by
   On business to my brother Cassius.

Varro. So please you, we will stand and watch your
      pleasure.°

230 *gown* dressing gown   234 *Never come* may there never again come
238 *instrument* (probably a lute)   240 *knave* boy   240 *o'erwatched*
tired out from lack of sleep   246 *raise* rouse   248 *watch your
pleasure* be on the watch for your command

Brutus. I will not have it so; lie down, good sirs;
250   It may be I shall otherwise bethink me.°

> [*Varro and Claudius lie down.*]

Look, Lucius, here's the book I sought for so;
I put it in the pocket of my gown.

Lucius. I was sure your lordship did not give it me.

Brutus. Bear with me, good boy, I am much forgetful.
255   Canst thou hold up thy heavy eyes awhile,
And touch° thy instrument a strain° or two?

Lucius. Ay, my lord, an't° please you.

Brutus.   It does, my boy.
I trouble thee too much, but thou art willing.

Lucius. It is my duty, sir.

260   *Brutus.* I should not urge thy duty past thy might;
I know young bloods° look for a time of rest.

Lucius. I have slept, my lord, already.

Brutus. It was well done, and thou shalt sleep again;
I will not hold thee long. If I do live,
265   I will be good to thee.

> *Music, and a song.*

This is a sleepy tune. O murd'rous° slumber!
Layest thou thy leaden° mace° upon my boy,
That plays thee music? Gentle knave, good night;
I will not do thee so much wrong to wake thee.
270   If thou dost nod, thou break'st thy instrument;
I'll take it from thee; and, good boy, good night.
Let me see, let me see; is not the leaf turned down
Where I left reading? Here it is, I think.

> *Enter the Ghost of Caesar.*

---

250 *otherwise bethink me* change my mind   256 *touch* play on   256
strain tune   257 *an't* if it   261 *young bloods* youthful constitutions
266 *murd'rous* deathlike   267 *leaden* heavy (association also with
death, for lead was used in coffinmaking)   267 *mace* staff of office
(with which a man was touched on the shoulder when arrested)

How ill this taper burns.° Ha! Who comes here?
I think it is the weakness of mine eyes   275
That shapes this monstrous apparition.
It comes upon° me. Art thou anything?
Art thou some god, some angel, or some devil,
That mak'st my blood cold, and my hair to stare?°
Speak to me what thou art.   280

Ghost. Thy evil spirit, Brutus.

Brutus.   Why com'st thou?

Ghost. To tell thee thou shalt see me at Philippi.

Brutus. Well; then I shall see thee again?

Ghost. Ay, at Philippi.

Brutus. Why, I will see thee at Philippi then.   285

                              [*Exit Ghost.*]
Now I have taken heart thou vanishest.
Ill spirit, I would hold more talk with thee.
Boy! Lucius! Varro! Claudius! Sirs, awake!
Claudius!

Lucius. The strings, my lord, are false.°   290

Brutus. He thinks he still is at his instrument.
Lucius, awake!

Lucius. My lord?

Brutus. Didst thou dream, Lucius, that thou so criedst
out?

Lucius. My lord, I do not know that I did cry.   295

Brutus. Yes, that thou didst. Didst thou see anything?

Lucius. Nothing, my lord.

Brutus. Sleep again, Lucius. Sirrah Claudius!
[*To Varro*] Fellow thou, awake!

274 *How . . . burns* (lights allegedly burned dimly or blue in the presence of a supernatural being) 277 *upon* toward 279 *stare* stand on end 290 *false* out of tune

300 *Varro.* My lord?

Claudius. My lord?

Brutus. Why did you so cry out, sirs, in your sleep?

Both. Did we, my lord?

Brutus.   Ay. Saw you anything?

Varro. No, my lord, I saw nothing.

Claudius.   Nor I, my lord.

305 *Brutus.* Go and commend me° to my brother Cassius;
        Bid him set on his pow'rs betimes before,°
        And we will follow.

Both.   It shall be done, my lord.

                                        Exeunt.

305 *commend me* give my greetings   306 *set . . . before* advance his
forces early in the morning before me

ACT V

[Scene I. *The plains of Philippi.*]

Enter Octavius, Antony, and their Army.

Octavius. Now, Antony, our hopes are answerèd;
You said the enemy would not come down,
But keep the hills and upper regions.
It proves not so; their battles° are at hand;
They mean to warn° us at Philippi here,   5
Answering before we do demand° of them.

Antony. Tut, I am in their bosoms,° and I know
Wherefore they do it. They could be content
To visit other places,° and come down
With fearful° bravery,° thinking by this face°   10
To fasten in our thoughts° that they have courage;
But 'tis not so.

                Enter a Messenger.

Messenger.   Prepare you, generals,
The enemy comes on in gallant show;
Their bloody sign° of battle is hung out,

V.i.4 *battles* armies   5 *warn* challenge   6 *Answering . . . demand* appearing in opposition before we force a meeting   7 *I am in their bosoms* I understand their inmost thoughts   8–9 *They could . . . places* they would prefer to be somewhere else   10 *fearful* (1) frightened (2) awe-inspiring   10 *bravery* bravado (and show of splendor)   10 *face* appearance   11 *fasten in our thoughts* persuade us   14 *bloody sign* red flag

119

15   And something to be done immediately.

Antony. Octavius, lead your battle softly° on
   Upon the left hand of the even° field.

Octavius. Upon the right hand I; keep thou the left.

Antony. Why do you cross° me in this exigent?°

20   *Octavius.* I do not cross you; but I will do so.   *March.*

Drum. Enter Brutus, Cassius, and their Army; [Lucilius,
    Titinius, Messala, and others].

Brutus. They stand, and would have parley.

Cassius. Stand fast, Titinius, we must out and talk.

Octavius. Mark Antony, shall we give sign of battle?

25   *Antony.* No, Caesar, we will answer on their charge.°
   Make forth;° the generals would have some words.

Octavius. Stir not until the signal.

Brutus. Words before blows; is it so, countrymen?

Octavius. Not that we love words better, as you do.

Brutus. Good words are better than bad strokes, Octavius.

Antony. In your bad strokes, Brutus, you give good
30   words;
   Witness the hole you made in Caesar's heart,
   Crying "Long live! Hail, Caesar!"

Cassius.   Antony,
   The posture° of your blows are yet unknown;
   But for your words, they rob the Hybla° bees,
   And leave them honeyless.

35   *Antony.*   Not stingless too.

16 *battle softly* army slowly   17 *even* level   19 *cross* oppose, con-
tradict   19 *exigent* crisis   24 *answer on their charge* meet them when
they attack   25 *Make forth* go forward   33 *posture* nature, quality
34 *Hybla* a Sicilian town famous for its sweet honey

Brutus. O, yes, and soundless too;
  For you have stol'n their buzzing, Antony,
  And very wisely threat before you sting.

Antony. Villains! You did not so, when your vile daggers
  Hacked one another in the sides of Caesar.   40
  You showed your teeth° like apes, and fawned like
    hounds,
  And bowed like bondmen, kissing Caesar's feet;
  Whilst damnèd Casca, like a cur, behind
  Struck Caesar on the neck. O you flatterers!

Cassius. Flatterers! Now, Brutus, thank yourself;   45
  This tongue had not offended so today,
  If Cassius might have ruled.°

Octavius. Come, come, the cause.° If arguing make us
    sweat,
  The proof° of it will turn to redder drops.
  Look,   50
  I draw a sword against conspirators.
  When think you that the sword goes up° again?
  Never, till Caesar's three and thirty wounds
  Be well avengèd; or till another Caesar°
  Have added slaughter to° the sword of traitors.   55

Brutus. Caesar, thou canst not die by traitors' hands,
  Unless thou bring'st them with thee.

Octavius.   So I hope.
  I was not born to die on Brutus' sword.

Brutus. O, if thou wert the noblest of thy strain,°
  Young man, thou couldst not die more honorable.   60

41 *showed your teeth* grinned   **47** *ruled* had his way (i.e., in urging that
Antony be slain)   **48** *cause* business at hand   **49** *proof* test   **52** *up*
into the sheath   **54** *another Caesar* i.e., Octavius himself   **55** *Have
added slaughter to* has also been killed by   **59** *strain* family, line of
descent

Cassius. A peevish° schoolboy, worthless° of such honor,
　　Joined with a masker and a reveler.°

Antony. Old Cassius still!

Octavius.　　　　　　Come, Antony; away!
　　Defiance, traitors, hurl we in your teeth.
65　If you dare fight today, come to the field;
　　If not, when you have stomachs.°
　　　　　　　　　　Exit Octavius, Antony, and Army.

Cassius. Why, now blow wind, swell billow, and swim
　　bark!
　　The storm is up, and all is on the hazard.°

Brutus. Ho, Lucilius, hark, a word with you.
　　　　　　　　　Lucilius and Messala stand forth.

Lucilius.　　　　　　　　　　My lord?
　　　　　　[*Brutus and Lucilius converse apart.*]

Cassius. Messala.

Messala.　　　What says my general?

70　*Cassius.*　　　　　　　　　　Messala,
　　This is my birthday; as this very day
　　Was Cassius born. Give me thy hand, Messala:
　　Be thou my witness that against my will
　　(As Pompey was)° am I compelled to set°
75　Upon one battle all our liberties.
　　You know that I held Epicurus strong,°
　　And his opinion; now I change my mind,
　　And partly credit things that do presage.°
　　Coming from Sardis, on our former° ensign

61 *peevish* childish (Octavius was 21) 61 *worthless* unworthy
62 *masker and a reveler* i.e., that dissipated Antony, who loved par-
ticipating in masques and wild parties (cf. I.ii.203–04, II.i.189,
II.ii.116) 66 *stomachs* inclination, appetite 68 *on the hazard* at
stake 74 *As Pompey was* (at Pharsalus where, having been persuaded to give battle against his will, he was decisively defeated and
later murdered) 74 *set* stake 76 *held Epicurus strong* believed
strongly in the philosophy of Epicurus (a materialist who believed that
because the gods were not interested in human affairs omens were to
be discounted) 78 *presage* foretell the future 79 *former* foremost

Two mighty eagles fell,° and there they perched,   80
Gorging and feeding from our soldiers' hands,
Who to Philippi here consorted° us.
This morning are they fled away and gone,
And in their steads do ravens, crows, and kites°
Fly o'er our heads and downward look on us   85
As we were sickly° prey; their shadows seem
A canopy most fatal,° under which
Our army lies, ready to give up the ghost.

Messala. Believe not so.

Cassius.   I but believe it partly,
For I am fresh of spirit and resolved   90
To meet all perils very constantly.°

Brutus. Even so, Lucilius.

Cassius.   Now, most noble Brutus,
The gods today stand friendly, that we may,
Lovers° in peace, lead on our days to age!
But since the affairs of men rests still incertain,°   95
Let's reason with the worst that may befall.°
If we do lose this battle, then is this
The very last time we shall speak together.
What are you then determinèd to do?

Brutus. Even by the rule of that philosophy°   100
By which I did blame Cato for the death
Which he did give himself; I know not how,
But I do find it cowardly and vile,
For fear of what might fall,° so to prevent°
The time° of life, arming myself with patience   105
To stay the providence° of some high powers
That govern us below.

80 *fell* swooped down   82 *consorted* accompanied   84 *ravens, crows,
and kites* (scavengers; traditionally, they know when a battle is pending
and accompany the armies)   86 *sickly* ready for death   87 *fatal*
presaging death   91 *constantly* resolutely   94 *Lovers* devoted friends
95 *rests still incertain* always stand in doubt   96 *reason . . . befall*
consider what must be done if the worst happens   100 *that philosophy*
i.e., Stoicism   104 *fall* befall   104 *prevent* anticipate   105 *time* term,
natural end   106 *stay the providence* await the ordained fate

Cassius.　　　　　　　　Then, if we lose this battle,
　　You are contented to be led in triumph°
　　Thorough the streets of Rome?

110 *Brutus.* No, Cassius, no; think not, thou noble Roman,
　　That ever Brutus will go bound to Rome;
　　He bears too great a mind. But this same day
　　Must end that work the ides of March begun;
　　And whether we shall meet again I know not.
115　Therefore our everlasting farewell take.
　　Forever, and forever, farewell, Cassius!
　　If we do meet again, why, we shall smile;
　　If not, why then this parting was well made.

Cassius. Forever, and forever, farewell, Brutus!
120　If we do meet again, we'll smile indeed;
　　If not, 'tis true this parting was well made.

Brutus. Why then, lead on. O, that a man might know
　　The end of this day's business ere it come!
　　But it sufficeth that the day will end,
125　And then the end is known. Come, ho! Away! *Exeunt.*

[Scene II. *The field of battle.*]

Alarum.° Enter Brutus and Messala.

Brutus. Ride, ride, Messala, ride, and give these bills°
　　Unto the legions on the other side.°　　*Loud alarum.*
　　Let them set on at once; for I perceive
　　But cold demeanor° in Octavius' wing,
5　And sudden push° gives them the overthrow.
　　Ride, ride, Messala! Let them all come down. *Exeunt.*

108 *in triumph* (as a captive) in the victor's procession　V.ii.1s.d. *Alarum*
call to arms (drums or trumpets)　1 *bills* written orders　2 *side* wing
(commanded by Cassius)　4 *But cold demeanor* marked lack of spirit
in fighting　5 *push* attack

[Scene III. *The field of battle.*]

Alarums. Enter Cassius and Titinius.

Cassius. O, look, Titinius, look, the villains° fly!
　Myself have to mine own° turned enemy.
　This ensign° here of mine was turning back;
　I slew the coward, and did take it° from him.

Titinius. O Cassius, Brutus gave the word too early,　　　5
　Who, having some advantage on Octavius,
　Took it too eagerly; his soldiers fell to spoil,°
　Whilst we by Antony are all enclosed.

Enter Pindarus.

Pindarus. Fly further off, my lord, fly further off!
　Mark Antony is in your tents, my lord.　　　　　　10
　Fly, therefore, noble Cassius, fly far° off!

Cassius. This hill is far enough. Look, look, Titinius!
　Are those my tents where I perceive the fire?

Titinius. They are, my lord.

Cassius.　　　　　　　　Titinius, if thou lovest me,
　Mount thou my horse and hide thy spurs in him　　　15
　Till he have brought thee up to yonder troops
　And here again, that I may rest assured
　Whether yond troops are friend or enemy.

Titinius. I will be here again even with a thought.°
　　　　　　　　　　　　　　　　Exit.

Cassius. Go, Pindarus, get higher on that hill;　　　20

V.iii.1 *villains* i.e., cowardly soldiers of his own side　2 *mine own* my
own men　3 *ensign* standard-bearer　4 *it* i.e., the standard　7 *spoil*
looting　11 *far* farther　19 *even with a thought* as quickly as thought

My sight was ever thick.° Regard Titinius,
And tell me what thou not'st about the field.

        [Exit Pindarus.]

This day I breathèd first. Time is come round,
And where I did begin, there shall I end.
25 My life is run his compass.° Sirrah, what news?

Pindarus. (Above)° O my lord!

Cassius. What news?

Pindarus. [Above] Titinius is enclosèd round about
With horsemen that make to him on the spur;°
30 Yet he spurs on. Now they are almost on him.
Now, Titinius! Now some light.° O, he lights too!
He's ta'en!° *(Shout.)* And, hark! They shout for joy.

Cassius. Come down; behold no more.
O, coward that I am, to live so long,
35 To see my best friend ta'en before my face!

      Enter Pindarus.

Come hither, sirrah.
In Parthia did I take thee prisoner;
And then I swore thee, saving of° thy life,
That whatsoever I did bid thee do,
40 Thou shouldst attempt it. Come now, keep thine oath.
Now be a freeman, and with this good sword,
That ran through Caesar's bowels, search° this bosom.
Stand° not to answer. Here, take thou the hilts,
And when my face is covered, as 'tis now,
45 Guide thou the sword—Caesar, thou art revenged,
Even with the sword that killed thee.   *[Dies.]*

Pindarus. So, I am free; yet would not so have been,
Durst I have done my will. O Cassius!
Far from this country Pindarus shall run,
50 Where never Roman shall take note of him. *[Exit.]*

---

21 *My . . . thick* I have always been nearsighted 25 *is run his compass*
has completed its circuit 26 s.d. *Above* on the upper stage 29 *make
. . . spur* ride toward him at top speed 31 *light* dismount 32 *ta'en*
taken, captured 38 *swore . . . of* made you swear, when I spared
42 *search* penetrate 43 *Stand* delay

Enter Titinius and Messala.

Messala. It is but change,° Titinius; for Octavius
  Is overthrown by noble Brutus' power,
  As Cassius' legions are by Antony.

Titinius. These tidings will well comfort Cassius.

Messala. Where did you leave him?

Titinius.   All disconsolate,   *55*
  With Pindarus his bondman, on this hill.

Messala. Is not that he that lies upon the ground?

Titinius. He lies not like the living. O my heart!

Messala. Is not that he?

Titinius.   No, this was he, Messala,
  But Cassius is no more. O setting sun,   *60*
  As in thy red rays thou dost sink to night,
  So in his red blood Cassius' day is set.
  The sun of Rome is set. Our day is gone;
  Clouds, dews,° and dangers come; our deeds are done!
  Mistrust of° my success hath done this deed.   *65*

Messala. Mistrust of good success hath done this deed.
  O hateful Error, Melancholy's child,°
  Why dost thou show to the apt° thoughts of men
  The things that are not? O Error, soon conceived,
  Thou never com'st unto a happy birth,   *70*
  But kill'st the mother° that engend'red thee!

Titinius. What, Pindarus! Where art thou, Pindarus?

Messala. Seek him, Titinius, whilst I go to meet
  The noble Brutus, thrusting this report
  Into his ears. I may say "thrusting" it;   *75*

---

51 *change* exchange (of fortune)   64 *dews* (considered unwholesome)
65 *Mistrust of* lack of confidence in   67 *Melancholy's child* (i.e., those
of despondent temperament are liable to be introspective and full of
imaginary fears)   68 *apt* easily impressed   71 *mother* i.e., the melancholy person, Cassius, who conceived the error

For piercing steel and darts envenomèd
Shall be as welcome to the ears of Brutus
As tidings of this sight.

Titinius.   Hie° you, Messala,
And I will seek for Pindarus the while.

                                        [*Exit Messala.*]

80   Why didst thou send me forth, brave° Cassius?
Did I not meet thy friends, and did not they
Put on my brows this wreath of victory,
And bid me give it thee? Didst thou not hear their
    shouts?
Alas, thou hast misconstrued everything!
85   But hold thee,° take this garland on thy brow;
Thy Brutus bid me give it thee, and I
Will do his bidding. Brutus, come apace,°
And see how I regarded° Caius Cassius.
By your leave,° gods. This is a Roman's part:°
90   Come, Cassius' sword, and find Titinius' heart. *Dies.*

*Alarum. Enter Brutus, Messala, young Cato, Strato,
Volumnius, and Lucilius.*

Brutus. Where, where, Messala, doth his body lie?

Messala. Lo, yonder, and Titinius mourning it.

Brutus. Titinius' face is upward.

Cato.   He is slain.

Brutus. O Julius Caesar, thou art mighty yet!
95   Thy spirit walks abroad, and turns our swords
In our own proper° entrails.   *Low alarums.*

Cato.   Brave° Titinius!
Look, whe'r° he have not crowned dead Cassius.

Brutus. Are yet two Romans living such as these?
The last of all the Romans, fare thee well!

78 *Hie* hasten   80 *brave* noble   85 *hold thee* wait a moment   87
apace quickly   88 *regarded* honored   89 *By your leave* with your
permission (because he is ending his life before the time appointed by
the gods)   89 *part* role, duty   96 *own proper* (emphatic) very own
96 *Brave* noble   97 *whe'r* whether

It is impossible that ever Rome   100
Should breed thy fellow.° Friends, I owe moe° tears
To this dead man than you shall see me pay.
I shall find time, Cassius; I shall find time.
Come, therefore, and to Thasos° send his body;
His funerals shall not be in our camp,   105
Lest it discomfort us.° Lucilius, come,
And come, young Cato; let us to the field.
Labeo and Flavius set our battles° on.
'Tis three o'clock; and, Romans, yet ere night
We shall try fortune in a second fight.   *Exeunt.*   110

[Scene IV. *The field of battle.*]

*Alarum. Enter Brutus, Messala, [young] Cato, Lucilius,
and Flavius.*

Brutus. Yet, countrymen, O, yet hold up your heads!
                          [*Exit, with followers.*]
Cato. What bastard° doth not? Who will go with me?
I will proclaim my name about the field.
I am the son of Marcus Cato,° ho!
A foe to tyrants, and my country's friend.   5
I am the son of Marcus Cato, ho!

Enter Soldiers and fight.

Lucilius.° And I am Brutus, Marcus Brutus, I;
Brutus, my country's friend; know me for Brutus!
                          [*Young Cato falls.*]

101 *fellow* equal   101 *moe* more   104 *Thasos* an island near Philippi
106 *discomfort us* dishearten our troops   108 *battles* armies   V.iv.2
What bastard who is such a low fellow that he   4 *son of Marcus
Cato* son of Cato of Utica, hence, brother of Brutus' wife   7 *Lucilius*
(the Folio fails to provide a speech prefix for lines 7–8, but because it is
clear from Plutarch and from line 14 that Lucilius impersonates Brutus
it is plausible to attribute 7–8 to Lucilius)

O young and noble Cato, art thou down?
10 Why, now thou diest as bravely as Titinius,
And mayst be honored, being Cato's son.

[*First*] *Soldier.* Yield, or thou diest.

Lucilius.   Only I yield to die°.
There is so much° that thou wilt kill me straight;°
Kill Brutus, and be honored in his death.

15 [*First*] *Soldier.* We must not. A noble prisoner!

Enter Antony.

Second Soldier. Room, ho! Tell Antony, Brutus is ta'en.

First Soldier. I'll tell thee news. Here comes the general.
Brutus is ta'en, Brutus is ta'en, my lord.

Antony. Where is he?

20 *Lucilius.* Safe, Antony; Brutus is safe enough.
I dare assure thee that no enemy
Shall ever take alive the noble Brutus.
The gods defend him from so great a shame!
When you do find him, or alive or dead,
25 He will be found like Brutus, like himself.°

Antony. This is not Brutus, friend, but, I assure you,
A prize no less in worth. Keep this man safe;
Give him all kindness. I had rather have
Such men my friends than enemies. Go on,
30 And see whe'r Brutus be alive or dead,
And bring us word unto Octavius' tent
How everything is chanced.°   *Exeunt.*

---

12 *Only I yield to die* I yield only to die   13 *so much* so great an induce-
ment, i.e., gaining great honor by killing Brutus (?), so much to be
blamed for(?), a sum of money (offered to the soldier) (?)   13 *straight*
immediately   25 *like himself* i.e., behaving in accordance with his
noble nature   32 *is chanced* has turned out

[Scene V. *The field of battle.*]

Enter Brutus, Dardanius, Clitus, Strato, and Volumnius.

Brutus. Come, poor remains° of friends, rest on this
  rock.

Clitus. Statilius showed the torchlight,° but, my lord,
  He came not back; he is or ta'en or slain.

Brutus. Sit thee down, Clitus. Slaying is the word;
  It is a deed in fashion. Hark thee, Clitus.   *5*
                                        [*Whispers.*]

Clitus. What, I, my lord? No, not for all the world!

Brutus. Peace then, no words.

Clitus.   I'll rather kill myself.

Brutus. Hark thee, Dardanius.   [*Whispers.*]

Dardanius.   Shall I do such a deed?

Clitus. O Dardanius!

Dardanius. O Clitus!   *10*

Clitus. What ill request did Brutus make to thee?

Dardanius. To kill him, Clitus. Look, he meditates.

Clitus. Now is that noble vessel° full of grief,
  That it runs over even at his eyes.

V.v.1 *poor remains* wretched survivors 2 *showed the torchlight*
(Statilius had volunteered to see if Cassius' camp was occupied by the
enemy; he signaled on arrival there but was obviously captured there-
after) 13 *vessel* (figurative for "human being." Also an allusion to
the small jars of tears offered to the dead)

15 *Brutus.* Come hither, good Volumnius; list° a word.

Volumnius. What says my lord?

Brutus.   Why, this, Volumnius:
The ghost of Caesar hath appeared to me
Two several° times by night; at Sardis once,
And this last night here in Philippi fields.
I know my hour is come.

20 *Volumnius.*   Not so, my lord.

Brutus. Nay, I am sure it is, Volumnius.
Thou seest the world, Volumnius, how it goes;
Our enemies have beat us to the pit.°   *Low alarums.*
It is more worthy to leap in ourselves
25 Than tarry till they push us. Good Volumnius,
Thou know'st that we two went to school together;
Even for that our love of old, I prithee
Hold thou my sword-hilts whilst I run on it.

Volumnius. That's not an office for a friend, my lord.
                                   Alarum still.°

30 *Clitus.* Fly, fly, my lord, there is no tarrying here.

Brutus. Farewell to you; and you; and you, Volumnius.
Strato, thou hast been all this while asleep;
Farewell to thee too, Strato. Countrymen,
My heart doth joy that yet in all my life
35 I found no man but he was true to me.
I shall have glory by this losing day
More than Octavius and Mark Antony
By this vile conquest° shall attain unto.
So fare you well at once,° for Brutus' tongue
40 Hath almost ended his life's history.
Night hangs upon mine eyes; my bones would rest,

---

15 *list* hear   18 *several* separate   23 *pit* (1) trap for capturing wild
animals (2) grave   29 s.d. *still* continuing   38 *vile conquest* i.e., overthrow of the revolution against tyranny   39 *at once* without further
delay

That have but labored to attain this hour.°
                    Alarum. Cry within, "Fly, fly, fly!"

Clitus. Fly, my lord, fly!

Brutus.   Hence! I will follow.
          [*Exeunt Clitus, Dardanius, and Volumnius.*]
I prithee, Strato, stay thou by thy lord,
Thou art a fellow of a good respect.°   45
Thy life hath had some smatch° of honor in it;
Hold then my sword, and turn away thy face,
While I do run upon it. Wilt thou, Strato?

Strato. Give me your hand first. Fare you well, my lord.

Brutus. Farewell, good Strato—Caesar, now be still;   50
I killed not thee with half so good a will.   *Dies.*

          Alarum. Retreat. Enter Antony, Octavius, Messala,
                    Lucilius, and the Army.

Octavius. What man is that?

Messala. My master's man.° Strato, where is thy master?

Strato. Free from the bondage you are in, Messala;
The conquerors can but make a fire of him.   55
For Brutus only overcame himself,°
And no man else hath honor by his death.

Lucilius. So Brutus should be found. I thank thee,
          Brutus,
That thou hast proved Lucilius' saying° true.

Octavius. All that served Brutus, I will entertain° them. 60
Fellow, wilt thou bestow° thy time with me?

Strato. Ay, if Messala will prefer° me to you.

Octavius. Do so, good Messala.

---

42 *but . . . hour* i.e., worked hard only to reach this goal of death
(which brings, for a Stoic, rest from life's trials)   45 *respect* reputation
46 *smatch* smack, taste   53 *man* servant   56 *Brutus only overcame
himself* only Brutus overcame Brutus   59 *saying* (see V.iv.21–25)
60 *entertain* take into service   61 *bestow* spend   62 *prefer* recommend

Messala. How died my master, Strato?

65   *Strato.* I held the sword, and he did run on it.

Messala. Octavius, then take him to follow thee,
    That did the latest° service to my master.

Antony. This was the noblest Roman of them all.
    All the conspirators save only he
70   Did that they did in envy of great Caesar;
    He, only in a general honest thought
    And common good to all, made one of them.°
    His life was gentle,° and the elements°
    So mixed° in him that Nature might stand up
75   And say to all the world, "This was a man!"

Octavius. According to his virtue,° let us use° him
    With all respect and rites of burial.
    Within my tent his bones tonight shall lie,
    Most like a soldier ordered honorably.°
80   So call the field° to rest, and let's away
    To part° the glories of this happy day.   *Exeunt omnes.*

FINIS

67 *latest* last   71–72 *He only . . . them* he, moved only by impersonal
motives directed to the good of the community, joined the conspirators   73 *gentle* noble   73 *elements* (the four opposed elements, of
which all nature was thought to be composed, were represented in the
human body by the four liquids, bile, phlegm, blood, and choler; the
dominance of one of these determined a man's temperament—melan-
cholic, phlegmatic, sanguine, or c oleric)   74 *So mixed* i.e., so well-
balanced   76 *virtue* excellence   76 *use* treat   79 *ordered honorably*
arrayed (and treated) with all honor   80 *field* army   81 *part* divide

Textual Note

The First Folio of 1623 provides us with the text for *Julius Caesar;* there are no early quarto editions. In setting this play for the press, the printer's compositors probably worked from the playhouse promptbook, for the Folio text contains remarkably few misprints, serious errors in punctuation, or misattribution of speeches. The stage directions, unusually numerous and detailed, also suggest a stage manager's prompt copy; stage directions like "Alarum still" and "Enter Boy with wine and tapers" are obviously closely connected with actual performance.

In the present edition, the names of characters have been normalized so that *Marullus* appears for the Folio Murellus (and Murrellus), *Casca* for Caska, *Lucilius* for Lucillius. Occasionally the Folio uses the forms "Antonio" (I.ii.3, 4, 6, 190; I.iii.37), "Claudio" (IV.iii.241, 243, 243 s.d., 288), "Flavio," "Labio" (V.iii.108), "Octavio" (III.i.275 s.d., V.ii.4), "Varrus" (IV.iii.243, 243 s.d., 288); these are standardized, appearing as *Antonius, Claudius, Flavius, Labeo, Octavius,* and *Varro*. The present edition modernizes spelling and punctuation, corrects a few obvious misprints, translates the act divisions from Latin into English, expands the speech prefixes, and alters the lineation of a few passages. The only other substantial departures from the Folio are listed below, the present reading in italics and then the Folio's reading in roman.

I.iii.129 *In favor's* Is Fauors
II.i.40. *ides* first   213 *eighth* eight

II.ii.19 *fought* fight   23 *did neigh* do neigh   46 *are* heare
III.i.39 *law* lane   113 *states* State   115 *lies* lye   283 *for* from
III.ii.106 *art* are
IV.iii.253 *not* it not
V.i.41 *teeth* teethes
V.iii.104 *Thasos* Tharsus
V.iv.7 *Lucilius* [F omits, and prints "Lucilius" as the prefix to line 9]

The Source of "Julius Caesar"

Shakespeare's main source for *Julius Caesar* was Sir Thomas North's translation of Plutarch's *The Lives of the Noble Grecians and Romans*, printed in 1579 and again in 1595. A classicist might be somewhat alarmed to learn that North translated not from the Greek of Plutarch but the French translation of Jacques Amyot. A student, unaware of the practice of Elizabethan dramatists, might be taken aback by Shakespeare's close adherence to various sources in writing his plays. Indeed, Shakespeare's use of Plutarch is detailed, literal, and incontrovertible. Sometimes he seems to versify directly from the book; at other times he selects, cuts, compresses, and amalgamates events from the full range of Plutarch's material dealing with the history of Julius Caesar. A complete understanding of his skill can be gained only by reading through Plutarch's comparisons of Demetrius and Antony, Dion and Brutus, and more particularly, the chapters on Julius Caesar, Brutus, and Antony, where we sometimes find three variant accounts of the same event, from each of which Shakespeare has taken some details to construct his own version.

Since it was impossible to give a complete selection of versions for each event of the play, let alone indicate all the historical events that Shakespeare does not use, we present one version of each happening—the one that seems closest to Shakespeare's own dramatization—and arrange these to read as a connected story. In addition, we add some brief selections to give a fuller view of each main character in the story. This use of extracts has inevitably led to some omissions and overlapping; however, we hope that readers will be stimulated to go to the sources themselves.

A number of other sources, besides Plutarch, have been suggested for this play, and those who are interested will find comprehensive discussions of this subject in the introduction to the New Arden edition of *Julius Caesar*, edited by T. S. Dorsch, and in Kenneth Muir's book, *Shakespeare's Sources* (Vol. I). Although Shakespeare must of course have used a sixteenth-century edition of North's Plutarch, because the 1612 edition—reprinted in modernized spelling by Walter W. Skeat, *Shakespeare's Plutarch* (Macmillan, 1875)—is the only one readily available to most readers, the selections below have been drawn from Skeat, and Skeat's page numbers have been given. In these selections the 1612 edition has no additions or subtractions in matters of substance; the only differences are trivial ones (e.g., "O Ligarius" vs. "Ligarius") that do not affect the study of Shakespeare's use of Plutarch.

Selections from *The Lives of the Noble Grecians and Romans*

CAESAR OVERCOMES THE SONS OF POMPEY

After all these things were ended, he was chosen Consul the fourth time, and went into Spain to make war with the sons of Pompey: who were yet but very young, but had notwithstanding raised a marvelous great army together and showed they had manhood and courage worthy to command such an army, insomuch as they put Caesar himself in great danger of his life. The greatest battle that was fought between them in all this war was by the city of Munda. For then Caesar, seeing his men sorely distressed, and having their hands full of their enemies, he ran into the press among his men that fought, and cried out unto them: "What, are ye not ashamed to be beaten and taken prisoners, yielding yourselves with your own hands to these young boys?" And so, with all the force he could make, having with much ado put his enemies to flight, he slew above thirty thousand of them in the field, and lost of his own men a thousand of the best he had. After this battle he went into his tent and told his friends that he had often before fought for victory, but, this last time now, that he had fought for the safety of his own life. He won this battle on the very feast day of the Bacchanalians, in the which men say that Pompey the Great went out of Rome, about

four years before, to begin this civil war. For his sons, the
younger scaped from the battle; but, within few days after,
Didius brought the head of the elder. This was the last war
that Caesar made. But the triumph he made into Rome for
the same did as much offend the Romans, and more, than
anything that ever he had done before: because he had not
overcome captains that were strangers, nor barbarous kings,
but had destroyed the sons of the noblest man of Rome,
whom fortune had overthrown. And because he had plucked
up his race by the roots, men did not think it meet for him
to triumph so for the calamities of his country, rejoicing at
a thing for the which he had but one excuse to allege in his
defense unto the gods and men, that he was compelled to do
that he did. And the rather they thought it not meet, because
he had never before sent letters nor messengers unto the
commonwealth at Rome, for any victory that he had ever
won in all the civil wars: but did always for shame refuse
the glory of it. [*The Life of Julius Caesar*, pp. 91–92.]

CAESAR IS GIVEN DICTATORIAL POWERS

This notwithstanding, the Romans, inclining to Caesar's
prosperity and taking the bit in the mouth, supposing that
to be ruled by one man alone, it would be a good mean for
them to take breath a little, after so many troubles and
miseries as they had abidden in these civil wars, they chose
him perpetual Dictator. This was a plain tyranny: for to
this absolute power of Dictator, they added this, never to
be afraid to be deposed. Cicero pronounced before the
Senate, that they should give him such honors as were meet
for a man: howbeit others afterwards added too honors
beyond all reason. For men striving who should most honor
him, they made him hateful and troublesome to themselves
that most favored him, by reason of the unmeasurable greatness and honors which they gave him. Thereupon it is
reported, that even they that most hated him were no less
favorers and furtherers of his honors than they that most
flattered him, because they might have greater occasions to
rise, and that it might appear they had just cause and color

to attempt that they did against him. And now for himself, after he had ended his civil wars, he did so honorably behave himself, that there was no fault to be found in him: and therefore methinks, amongst other honors they gave him, he rightly deserved this, that they should build him a temple of Clemency, to thank him for his courtesy he had used unto them in his victory. For he pardoned many of them that had borne arms against him, and furthermore, did prefer some of them to honor and office in the commonwealth: as, amongst others, Cassius and Brutus, both the which were made Praetors. And, where Pompey's images had been thrown down, he caused them to be set up again: whereupon Cicero said then, that, Caesar setting up Pompey's images again, he made his own to stand the surer. And when some of his friends did counsel him to have a guard for the safety of his person, and some also did offer themselves to serve him, he would never consent to it, but said: "It was better to die once than always to be afraid of death." [*The Life of Julius Caesar*, p. 92.]

CAESAR'S AMBITION

But the chiefest cause that made him mortally hated was the covetous desire he had to be called king: which first gave the people just cause, and next his secret enemies honest color, to bear him ill will. This notwithstanding, they that procured him this honor and dignity gave it out among the people that it was written in the Sibylline prophecies, "how the Romans might overcome the Parthians, if they made war with them and were led by a king, but otherwise that they were unconquerable." And furthermore they were so bold besides, that, Caesar returning to Rome from the city of Alba, when they came to salute him, they called him king. But the people being offended, and Caesar also angry, he said he was not called king, but Caesar. Then every man keeping silence, he went his way heavy and sorrowful. When they had decreed divers honors for him in the Senate, the Consuls and Praetors, accompanied with the whole assembly of the Senate, went unto him in the market place, where he was set by the pulpit for orations, to tell him what honors they had decreed for him in his absence. But he, sitting still in his majesty, disdaining to rise up unto them when they came in, as if they had been private men, answered them: "that his honors had more need to be cut off than enlarged." This did not only offend the Senate but the common people also, to see that he should so lightly esteem of the magistrates of the commonwealth: insomuch as every man that might lawfully go his way departed thence very sorrowfully. Thereupon also Caesar rising departed home to his house, and tearing open his doublet collar, making his neck bare, he cried out aloud to his friends, "that his throat was ready to offer to any man that would come and cut it." Notwithstanding it is reported that afterwards, to excuse his folly, he imputed it to his disease, saying, "that their wits are not perfect which have this disease of the falling evil, when standing on their feet they speak to the common people, but are soon troubled with a trembling of their body, and a sudden dimness and giddiness." But that was not true, for he would have risen up to the Senate, but Cornelius Balbus one of his friends (or rather a flatterer) would not let him, saying: "What, do you not remember that you are Caesar, and will you not let them reverence you and do their duties?" [*The Life of Julius Caesar*, pp. 94–95.]

CAESAR REFUSES THE CROWN

Besides these occasions and offenses, there followed also his shame and reproach, abusing the Tribunes of the people in this sort. At that time the feast *Lupercalia* was celebrated, the which in old time men say was the feast of shepherds or herdmen, and is much like unto the feast of the Lycaeans in Arcadia. But howsoever it is, that day there are divers noblemen's sons, young men (and some of them magistrates themselves that govern them), which run naked through the city, striking in sport them they meet in their way with leather thongs, hair and all on, to make them give place. And many noblewomen and gentlewomen also go of purpose to stand in their way, and do put forth their hands to be stricken, as scholars hold them out to their schoolmaster to be stricken with the ferula: persuading themselves that, being with child, they shall have good delivery; and so, being barren, that it will make them to conceive with child. Caesar sat to behold that sport upon the pulpit for orations, in a chair of gold, appareled in triumphant manner. Antonius, who was Consul at that time, was one of them that ran this holy course. So when he came into the market place, the people made a lane for him to run at liberty, and he came to Caesar, and presented him a diadem wreathed about with laurel. Whereupon there rose a certain cry of rejoicing, not very great, done only by a few appointed for the purpose. But when Caesar refused the diadem, then all the people together made an outcry of joy. [*The Life of Julius Caesar*, pp. 95–96.]

Antonius again did put it on his head: Caesar again refused it: and thus they were striving off and on a great while together. As oft as Antonius did put this laurel crown unto him, a few of his followers rejoiced at it: and as oft also as Caesar refused it, all the people together clapped their hands. And this was a wonderful thing, that they suffered all things subjects should do by commandment of their kings: and yet they could not abide the name of a king, detesting it as the utter destruction of their liberty. Caesar, in a rage, arose out of his seat, and plucking down the collar of his gown from his neck, he showed it naked, bidding any man strike off his head that would. This laurel crown was afterwards put upon the head of one of Caesar's statues or images, the which one of the tribunes plucked off. The people liked his doing therein so well that they waited on him home to his house, with great clapping of hands. Howbeit Caesar did turn them out of their offices for it. [*The Life of Marcus Antonius*, p. 164.]

Attempts to Turn Brutus Against Caesar

Hereupon the people went straight unto Marcus Brutus, who from his father came of the first Brutus, and by his mother of the house of the Servilians, a noble house as any

was in Rome, and was also nephew and son-in-law of
Marcus Cato. Notwithstanding, the great honors and favor
Caesar showed unto him kept him back that of himself
alone he did not conspire nor consent to depose him of his
kingdom. For Caesar did not only save his life after the
battle of Pharsalia, when Pompey fled, and did at his request
also save many mo of his friends besides: but furthermore,
he put a marvelous confidence in him. For he had already
preferred him to the Praetorship for that year, and furthermore was appointed to be Consul the fourth year after that,
having through Caesar's friendship obtained it before
Cassius, who likewise made suit for the same: and Caesar
also, as it is reported, said in this contention, "Indeed
Cassius hath alleged best reason, but yet shall he not be
chosen before Brutus." Some one day accusing Brutus while
he practiced this conspiracy, Caesar would not hear of it,
but, clapping his hand on his body, told them, "Brutus will
look for this skin": meaning thereby, that Brutus for his
virtue deserved to rule after him, but yet that, for ambition's
sake, he would not show himself unthankful or dishonorable.
Now they that desired change, and wished Brutus only their
prince and governor above all other, they durst not come to
him themselves to tell him what they would have him to do,
but in the night did cast sundry papers into the Praetor's
seat, where he gave audience, and the most of them to this
effect: "Thou sleepest, Brutus, and art not Brutus indeed."
Cassius, finding Brutus' ambition stirred up the more by
these seditious bills, did prick him forward and egg him on
the more, for a private quarrel he had conceived against
Caesar: the circumstance whereof we have set down more
at large in Brutus' life. Caesar also had Cassius in great
jealousy, and suspected him much: whereupon he said on
a time to his friends, "What will Cassius do, think ye? I like
not his pale looks." Another time when Caesar's friends
complained unto him of Antonius and Dolabella, that they
pretended some mischief towards him: he answered them
again, "As for those fat men and smooth-combed heads,"
quoth he, "I never reckon of them; but these pale-visaged
and carrion-lean people, I fear them most," meaning Brutus
and Cassius. [*The Life of Julius Caesar*, pp. 96–97.]

The Conspiracy Is Formed

Now when Cassius felt his friends, and did stir them up against Caesar: they all agreed, and promised to take part with him, so Brutus were the chief of their conspiracy. For they told him that so high an enterprise and attempt as that, did not so much require men of manhood and courage to draw their swords, as it stood them upon to have a man of such estimation as Brutus, to make every man boldly think, that by his only presence the fact were holy and just. If he took not this course, then that they should go to it with fainter hearts; and when they had done it, they should be more fearful: because every man would think that Brutus would not have refused to have made one with them, if the cause had been good and honest. Therefore Cassius, considering this matter with himself, did first of all speak to Brutus, since they grew strange together for the suit they had for the praetorship. So when he was reconciled to him again, and that they had embraced one another, Cassius asked him if he were determined to be in the Senate House the first day of the month of March, because he heard say that Caesar's friends should move the council that day, that Caesar should be called king by the Senate. Brutus answered him, he would not be there. "But if we be sent for," said Cassius, "how then?" "For myself then," said Brutus, "I mean not to hold my peace, but to withstand it, and rather die than lose my liberty."

Cassius being bold, and taking hold of this word: "Why," quoth he, "what Roman is he alive that will suffer thee to die for thy liberty? What? Knowest thou not that thou art Brutus? Thinkest thou that they be cobblers, tapsters, or suchlike base mechanical people, that write these bills and scrolls which are found daily in thy Praetor's chair, and not the noblest men and best citizens that do it? No; be thou well assured that of other Praetors they look for gifts, common distributions amongst the people, and for common plays, and to see fencers fight at the sharp, to show the people pastime: but at thy hands they specially require (as a due debt unto them) the taking away of the tyranny, being fully bent to suffer any extremity for thy sake, so that thou wilt show thyself to be the man thou art taken for, and that they hope thou art." Thereupon he kissed Brutus and embraced him: and so each taking leave of other, they went both to speak with their friends about it. Now amongst Pompey's friends, there was one called Caius Ligarius, who had been accused unto Caesar for taking part with Pompey, and Caesar discharged him. But Ligarius thanked not Caesar so much for his discharge, as he was offended with him for that he was brought in danger by his tyrannical power; and therefore in his heart he was always his mortal enemy, and was besides very familiar with Brutus, who went to see him being sick in his bed, and said unto him: "Ligarius, in what a time art thou sick?" Ligarius rising up in his bed, and taking him by the right hand, said unto him: "Brutus," said he, "if thou hast any great enterprise in hand worthy of thyself, I am whole."

After that time they began to feel all their acquaintance whom they trusted, and laid their heads together, consulting upon it, and did not only pick out their friends, but all those also whom they thought stout enough to attempt any desperate matter, and that were not afraid to lose their lives. For this cause they durst not acquaint Cicero with their conspiracy, although he was a man whom they loved dearly, and trusted best: for they were afraid that he being a coward by nature, and age also having increased his fear, he would quite turn and alter all their purpose, and quench the heat of their enterprise (the which specially required hot and earnest execution), seeking by persuasion to bring all things to such safety, as there should be no peril. Brutus also did let other of his friends alone, as Statilius Epicurian, and Faonius, that made profession to follow Marcus Cato: because that, having cast out words afar off, disputing together in philosophy to feel their minds, Faonius answered, "that civil war was worse than tyrannical government usurped against the law." [*The Life of Marcus Brutus*, pp. 112–14.]

Brutus and Porcia Are Troubled

Furthermore, the only name and great calling of Brutus did bring on the most of them to give consent to this conspiracy: who having never taken oaths together, nor taken or given any caution or assurance, nor binding themselves one to another by any religious oaths, they all kept the matter so secret to themselves, and could so cunningly handle it, that notwithstanding the gods did reveal it by manifest signs and tokens from above, and by predictions of sacrifices, yet all this would not be believed. Now Brutus, who knew very well that for his sake all the noblest, valiantest, and most courageous men of Rome did venture their lives, weighing with himself the greatness of the danger: when he was out of his house, he did so frame and fashion his countenance and looks that no man could discern he had anything to trouble his mind. But when night came that he was in his own house, then he was clean changed: for either care did wake him against his will when he would have slept, or else oftentimes of himself he fell into such deep thoughts of this enterprise, casting in his mind all the dangers that might happen: that his wife, lying by him, found that there was some marvelous great matter that troubled his mind, not being wont to be in that taking, and that he could not well determine with himself.

His wife Porcia (as we have told you before) was the daughter of Cato, whom Brutus married being his cousin, not a maiden, but a young widow after the death of her first husband Bibulus, by whom she had also a young son called Bibulus, who afterwards wrote a book of the acts and gests of Brutus, extant at this present day. This young lady, being excellently well seen in philosophy, loving her husband well, and being of a noble courage, as she was also wise: because she would not ask her husband what he ailed before she had made some proof by herself: she took a little razor, such as barbers occupy to pare men's nails, and, causing her maids and women to go out of her chamber, gave herself a great gash withal in her thigh, that she was straight all of a gore blood: and incontinently after a vehement fever took her, by reason of the pain of her wound. Then perceiving her husband was marvelously out of quiet, and that he could take no rest, even in her greatest pain of all she spoke in this sort unto him: "I being, O Brutus," said she, "the daughter of Cato, was married unto thee; not to be thy bedfellow and companion in bed and at board only, like a harlot, but to be partaker also with thee of thy good and evil fortune. Now for thyself, I can find no cause of fault in thee touching our match: but for my part, how may I show my duty towards thee and how much I would do for thy sake, if I cannot constantly bear a secret mischance or grief with thee, which requireth secrecy and fidelity? I confess that a woman's wit commonly is too weak to keep a secret safely: but yet, Brutus, good education and the company of virtuous men have some power to reform the defect of nature. And for myself, I have this benefit moreover, that I am the daughter of Cato, and wife of Brutus. This notwithstanding, I did not trust to any of these things before, until that now I have found by experience that no pain or grief whatsoever can overcome me." With those words she showed him her wound on her thigh, and told him what she had done to prove herself. Brutus was amazed to hear what she said unto him, and lifting up his hands to heaven, he besought the gods to give him the grace he might bring his enterprise to so good pass, that he might be found a husband worthy of so noble a wife as Porcia: so he then did comfort her the best he could. [*The Life of Marcus Brutus*, pp. 114–16.]

OMENS AND EVENTS PRECEDING THE MURDER

Certainly destiny may easier be foreseen than avoided, considering the strange and wonderful signs that were said to be seen before Caesar's death. For, touching the fires in the element, and spirits running up and down in the night, and also the solitary birds to be seen at noondays sitting in the great market place, are not all these signs perhaps worth the noting, in such a wonderful chance as happened? But

Strabo the philosopher writeth, that divers men were seen going up and down in fire: and furthermore, that there was a slave of the soldiers that did cast a marvelous burning flame out of his hand, insomuch as they that saw it thought he had been burnt; but when the fire was out, it was found he had no hurt. Caesar self also doing sacrifice unto the gods, found that one of the beasts which was sacrificed had no heart: and that was a strange thing in nature, how a beast could live without a heart. Furthermore there was a certain soothsayer that had given Caesar warning long time afore, to take heed of the day of the Ides of March (which is the fifteenth of the month), for on that day he should be in great danger. That day being come, Caesar going unto the Senate House, and speaking merrily unto the soothsayer, told him, "The Ides of March be come": "So they be," softly answered the soothsayer, "but yet are they not past." And the very day before, Caesar, supping with Marcus Lepidus, sealed certain letters, as he was wont to do, at the board: so, talk falling out amongst them, reasoning what death was best, he, preventing their opinions, cried out aloud, "Death unlooked for." Then going to bed the same night, as his manner was, and lying with his wife Calpurnia, all the windows and doors of his chamber flying open, the noise awoke him, and made him afraid when he saw such light: but more, when he heard his wife Calpurnia, being fast asleep, weep and sigh, and put forth many fumbling lamentable speeches: for she dreamed that Caesar was slain, and that she had him in her arms. Others also do deny that she had any such dream, as, amongst other, Titus Livius writeth that it was in this sort: the Senate having set upon the top of Caesar's house, for an ornament and setting forth of the same, a certain pinnacle, Calpurnia dreamed that she saw it broken down, and that she thought she lamented and wept for it. Insomuch that, Caesar rising in the morning, she prayed him, if it were possible, not to go out of the doors that day, but to adjourn the session of the Senate until another day. And if that he made no reckoning of her dream, yet that he would search further of the soothsayers by their sacrifices, to know what should happen him that day. Thereby it seemed that Caesar likewise did fear or suspect somewhat, because his wife Calpurnia until that time was never given to any fear and superstition: and that then he saw her so troubled in mind with this dream she had. But much more afterwards, when the soothsayers having sacrificed many beasts one after another, told him that none did like them: then he determined to send Antonius to adjourn the session of the Senate.

But in the meantime came Decius Brutus, surnamed Albinus, in whom Caesar put such confidence, that in his last will and testament he had appointed him to be his next heir, and yet was of the conspiracy with Cassius and Brutus: he, fearing that if Caesar did adjourn the session that day, the conspiracy would be betrayed, laughed at the sooth-sayers, and reproved Caesar, saying, "that he gave the Senate occasion to mislike with him, and that they might think he mocked them, considering that by his command-ment they were assembled, and that they were ready willingly to grant him all things, and to proclaim him king of all his provinces of the Empire of Rome out of Italy, and that he should wear his diadem in all other places both by sea and land. And furthermore, that if any man should tell them from him they should depart for that present time, and return again when Calpurnia should have better dreams, what would his enemies and ill-willers say, and how could they like of his friends' words? And who could persuade them otherwise, but that they would think his dominion a slavery unto them and tyrannical in himself? And yet if it be so," said he, "that you utterly mislike of this day, it is better that you go yourself in person, and, saluting the Senate, to dismiss them till another time." Therewithal he took Caesar by the hand, and brought him out of his house. Caesar was not gone far from his house, but a bond-man, a stranger, did what he could to speak with him: and when he saw he was put back by the great press and multi-tude of people that followed him, he went straight into his house, and put himself into Calpurnia's hands, to be kept till Caesar came back again, telling her that he had greater matters to impart unto him. And one Artemidorus also, born in the isle of Gnidos, a doctor of rhetoric in the Greek tongue, who by means of his profession was very familiar with certain of Brutus' confederates, and therefore knew the most part of all their practices against Caesar, came and brought him a little bill, written with his own hand, of all that he meant to tell him. He, marking how Caesar received all the supplications that were offered him, and that he gave them straight to his men that were about him, pressed nearer to him, and said: "Caesar, read this memorial to yourself, and that quickly, for they be matters of great weight, and touch you nearly." Caesar took it of him, but could never read it, though he many times attempted it, for the number of people that did salute him: but holding it still in his hand, keeping it to himself, went on withal into the Senate House. Howbeit others are of opinion, that it was some man else that gave him that memorial, and not Artemidorus, who did what he could all the way as he went to give it Caesar, but he was always repulsed by the people. For these things, they may seem to come by chance; but the place where the murder was prepared, and where the Senate were assembled, and where also there stood up an image of Pompey dedicated by himself amongst other ornaments which he gave unto the theater, all these were manifest proofs that it was the ordinance of some god that made this treason to be executed, specially in that very place. It is also reported that Cassius (though otherwise he did favor the doctrine of Epicurus) beholding the image of Pompey, before they entered into the action of their traitorous enterprise, he did softly call upon it to aid him: but the instant danger of the present time, taking away his former reason, did suddenly put him into a furious passion, and made him like a man half beside himself. [*The Life of Julius Caesar*, pp. 97–100.]

 . . . One came unto Casca being a conspirator, and taking him by the hand, said unto him: "O Casca, thou keptest it close from me, but Brutus hath told me all." Casca being amazed at it, the other went on with his tale, and said: "Why, how now, how cometh it to pass thou art thus rich, that thou dost sue to be Aedilis?" Thus Casca being deceived by the other's doubtful words, he told them it was a thousand to one, he blabbed not out all the conspiracy. Another Senator, called Popilius Laena, after he had saluted Brutus and Cassius more friendly than he was wont to do, he rounded softly in their ears, and told them: "I pray the gods you may go through with that you have taken in hand; but withal, dispatch, I read you, for your enterprise is betrayed." When he had said, he presently departed from them, and left them both afraid that their conspiracy would out.

Now in the meantime, there came one of Brutus' men posthaste unto him, and told him his wife was a-dying. For Porcia, being very careful and pensive for that which was to come, and being too weak to away with so great and inward grief of mind, she could hardly keep within, but was frighted with every little noise and cry she heard, as those that are taken and possessed with the fury of the Bacchantes; asking every man that came from the market place what Brutus did, and still sent messenger after messenger, to know what news. At length Caesar's coming being prolonged (as you have heard), Porcia's weakness was not able to hold out any longer, and thereupon she suddenly swooned, that she had no leisure to go to her chamber, but was taken in the midst of her house, where her speech and senses failed her. Howbeit she soon came to herself again, and so was laid in her bed and attended by her women. When Brutus heard these news, it grieved him, as it is to be presupposed: yet he left not off the care of his country and commonwealth, neither went home to his house for any news he heard. [*The Life of Marcus Brutus*, p. 117.]

When Caesar came out of his litter, Popilius Laena (that had talked before with Brutus and Cassius, and had prayed the gods they might bring this enterprise to pass) went unto Caesar and kept him a long time with a talk. Caesar gave good ear unto him: wherefore the conspirators (if so they should be called) not hearing what he said to Caesar, but conjecturing by that he had told them a little before that his talk was none other but the very discovery of their conspiracy, they were afraid, every man of them; and, one looking in another's face, it was easy to see that they all were of a mind, that it was no tarrying for them till they were apprehended, but rather that they should kill themselves with their own hands. And when Cassius and certain other clapped their hands on their swords under their gowns to draw them, Brutus, marking the countenance and gesture of Laena, and considering that he did use himself rather like an humble and earnest suitor than like an accuser, he said nothing to his companions (because there were many amongst them that were not of the conspiracy) but with a pleasant countenance encouraged Cassius. And immediately after Laena went from Caesar, and kissed his hand; which showed plainly that it was for some matter concerning himself that he had held him so long in talk. [*The Life of Marcus Brutus*, p. 118.]

THE ASSASSINATION

Now Antonius, that was a faithful friend to Caesar, and a valiant man besides of his hands, him Decius Brutus Albinus entertained out of the Senate House, having begun a long tale of set purpose. So Caesar coming into the house, all the Senate stood up on their feet to do him honor. Then part of Brutus' company and confederates stood round about Caesar's chair, and part of them also came towards him, as though they made suit with Metellus Cimber, to call home his brother again from banishment: and thus prosecuting still their suit, they followed Caesar till he was set in his chair. Who denying their petitions, and being offended with them one after another, because the more they were denied the more they pressed upon him and were the earnester with him, Metellus at length, taking his gown with both his hands, pulled it over his neck, which was the sign given the confederates to set upon him. Then Casca, behind him, struck him in the neck with his sword; howbeit the wound was not great nor mortal, because it seemed the fear of such a devilish attempt did amaze him and take his strength from him, that he killed him not at the first blow. But Caesar, turning straight unto him, caught hold of his sword and held it hard; and they both cried out, Caesar in Latin: "O vile traitor Casca, what doest thou?" and Casca, in Greek, to his brother: "Brother, help me." At the beginning of this stir, they that were present, not knowing of the conspiracy,

were so amazed with the horrible sight they saw, they had
no power to fly, neither to help him, nor so much as once
to make an outcry. They on the other side that had con-
spired his death compassed him in on every side with their
swords drawn in their hands, that Caesar turned him no-
where but he was stricken at by some, and still had naked
swords in his face, and was hackled and mangled among
them, as a wild beast taken of hunters. For it was agreed
among them that every man should give him a wound,
because all their parts should be in this murder: and then
Brutus himself gave him one wound about his privities.
Men report also, that Caesar did still defend himself against
the rest, running every way with his body: but when he saw
Brutus with his sword drawn in his hand, then he pulled his
gown over his head, and made no more resistance, and was
driven either casually or purposedly, by the counsel of the
conspirators, against the base whereupon Pompey's image
stood, which ran all of a gore blood till he was slain. Thus
it seemed that the image took just revenge of Pompey's
enemy, being thrown down on the ground at his feet, and
yielding up the ghost there, for the number of wounds he
had upon him. For it is reported, that he had three-and-
twenty wounds upon his body: and divers of the conspirators
did hurt themselves, striking one body with so many blows.
[*The Life of Julius Caesar*, pp.100–01.]

Caesar being slain in this manner, Brutus, standing in the
midst of the house, would have spoken and stayed the other
Senators that were not of the conspiracy, to have told them
the reason why they had done this fact. But they, as men
both afraid and amazed, fled one upon another's neck in
haste to get out at the door, and no man followed them. For
it was set down and agreed between them that they should
kill no man but Caesar only, and should entreat all the
rest to look to defend their liberty. All the conspirators,
but Brutus, determining upon this matter, thought it good
also to kill Antonius, because he was a wicked man, and
that in nature favored tyranny: besides also, for that he was
in great estimation with soldiers, having been conversant of
long time amongst them: and especially having a mind bent

to great enterprises, he was also of great authority at that time, being Consul with Caesar. But Brutus would not agree to it. First, for that he said it was not honest: secondly, because he told them there was hope of change in him. For he did not mistrust but that Antonius, being a noble-minded and courageous man (when he should know that Caesar was dead), would willingly help his country to recover her liberty, having them an example unto him to follow their courage and virtue. So Brutus by this means saved Antonius' life, who at that present time disguised himself and stole away: but Brutus and his consorts, having their swords bloody in their hands, went straight to the Capitol, persuading the Romans as they went to take their liberty again. Now at the first time, when the murder was newly done, there were sudden outcries of people that ran up and down the city, the which indeed did the more increase the fear and tumult. But when they saw they slew no man, neither did spoil or make havoc of anything, then certain of the Senators and many of the people, emboldening themselves, went to the Capitol unto them. [*The Life of Marcus Brutus*, pp. 119–20.]

PUBLIC REACTION; ANTONY GAINS CONTROL

There, a great number of men being assembled together one after another, Brutus made an oration unto them, to win the favor of the people, and to justify that they had done. All those that were by said they had done well, and cried unto them that they should boldly come down from the Capitol: whereupon Brutus and his companions came boldly down into the market place. The rest followed in troupe, but Brutus went foremost, very honorably compassed in round about with the noblest men of the city, which brought him from the Capitol, through the market place, to the pulpit for orations. When the people saw him in the pulpit, although they were a multitude of rakehells of all sorts, and had a good will to make some stir; yet, being ashamed to do it, for the reverence they bore unto Brutus, they kept silence to hear what he would say. When Brutus

began to speak, they gave him quiet audience: howbeit,
immediately after, they showed that they were not all contented with the murder. For when another, called Cinna,
would have spoken, and began to accuse Caesar, they fell
into a great uproar among them, and marvelously reviled
him; insomuch that the conspirators returned again into
the Capitol. There Brutus, being afraid to be besieged, sent
back again the noblemen that came thither with him, thinking it no reason that they, which were no partakers of the
murder, should be partakers of the danger. Then the next
morning, the Senate being assembled, and held within the
temple of the goddess Tellus, to wit, the Earth: and Antonius, Plancus, and Cicero, having made a motion to the
Senate in that assembly that they should take an order to
pardon and forget all that was past, and to establish friendship and peace again: it was decreed, that they should not
only be pardoned, but also that the Consuls should refer it
to the Senate, what honors should be appointed unto them.
This being agreed upon, the Senate broke up; and Antonius
the Consul, to put them in heart that were in the Capitol,
sent them his son for a pledge. Upon this assurance, Brutus
and his companions came down from the Capitol, where
every man saluted and embraced each other; among the
which Antonius himself did bid Cassius to supper to him,
and Lepidus also bade Brutus; and so one bade another, as
they had friendship and acquaintance together.

The next day following, the Senate, being called again to
council, did first of all commend Antonius, for that he had
wisely stayed and quenched the beginning of a civil war:
then they also gave Brutus and his consorts great praises;
and lastly they appointed them several governments of
provinces. For unto Brutus they appointed Crete; Africa
unto Cassius; Asia unto Trebonius; Bithynia unto Cimber;
and unto the other, Decius Brutus Albinus, Gaul on this
side of the Alps. When this was done, they came to talk of
Caesar's will and testament and of his funerals and tomb.
Then Antonius, thinking good his testament should be read
openly, and also that his body should be honorably buried,
and not in hugger-mugger, lest the people might thereby
take occasion to be worse offended if they did otherwise:

Cassius stoutly spoke against it. But Brutus went with the motion, and agreed unto it; wherein it seemeth he committed a second fault. For the first fault he did, was when he would not consent to his fellow conspirators, that Antonius should be slain; and therefore he was justly accused that thereby he had saved and strengthened a strong and grievous enemy of their conspiracy. The second fault was when he agreed that Caesar's funerals should be as Antonius would have them, the which indeed marred all. For first of all, when Caesar's testament was openly read among them, whereby it appeared that he bequeathed unto every citizen of Rome 75 drachmas a man; and that he left his gardens and arbors unto the people, which he had on this side of the river Tiber, in the place where now the temple of Fortune is built: the people then loved him, and were marvelous sorry for him. Afterwards, when Caesar's body was brought into the market place, Antonius making his funeral oration in praise of the dead, according to the ancient custom of Rome, and perceiving that his words moved the common people to compassion, he framed his eloquence to make their hearts yearn the more; and taking Caesar's gown all bloody in his hand, he laid it open to the sight of them all, showing what a number of cuts and holes it had upon it. Therewithal the people fell presently into such a rage and mutiny, that there was no more order kept amongst the common people. For some of them cried out, "Kill the murderers": others plucked up forms, tables, and stalls about the market place, as they had done before at the funerals of Clodius, and having laid them all on a heap together, they set them on fire, and thereupon did put the body of Caesar, and burnt it in the midst of the most holy places. And furthermore, when the fire was throughly kindled, some here, some there, took burning firebrands, and ran with them to the murderers' houses that killed him, to set them on fire. Howbeit the conspirators, foreseeing the danger before, had wisely provided for themselves and fled.

But there was a poet called Cinna, who had been no partaker of the conspiracy, but was always one of Caesar's chiefest friends: he dreamed, the night before, that Caesar bade him to supper with him, and that, he refusing to go,

Caesar was very importunate with him, and compelled him; so that at length he led him by the hand into a great dark place, where, being marvelously afraid, he was driven to follow him in spite of his heart. This dream put him all night into a fever; and yet notwithstanding, the next morning, when he heard that they carried Caesar's body to burial, being ashamed not to accompany his funerals, he went out of his house, and thrust himself into the press of the common people that were in a great uproar. And because someone called him by his name Cinna, the people, thinking he had been that Cinna who in an oration he made had spoken very evil of Caesar, they, falling upon him in their rage, slew him outright in the market place. This made Brutus and his companions more afraid than any other thing, next unto the change of Antonius. Wherefore they got them out of Rome, and kept at the first in the city of Antium, hoping to return again to Rome, when the fury of the people was a little assuaged. The which they hoped would be quickly, considering that they had to deal with a fickle and inconstant multitude, easy to be carried, and that the Senate stood for them: who notwithstanding made no enquiry for them that had torn poor Cinna the poet in pieces, but caused them to be sought for and apprehended that went with firebrands to set fire on the conspirators' houses. [*The Life of Marcus Brutus*, pp. 120–22.]

SUPERNATURAL EVENTS FOLLOW CAESAR'S DEATH

But his great prosperity and good fortune that favored him all his lifetime, did continue afterwards in the revenge of his death, pursuing the murderers both by sea and land, till they had not left a man more to be executed, of all them that were actors or counselers in the conspiracy of his death. Furthermore, of all the chances that happen unto men upon the earth, that which came to Cassius above all other, is most to be wondered at: for he, being overcome in battle at the journey of Philippi, slew himself with the same sword with the which he struck Caesar. Again, of signs in the element, the great comet, which seven nights together was seen very bright after Caesar's death, the eighth night after was never seen more. Also the brightness of the sun was darkened, the which all that year through rose very pale and shined not out, whereby it gave but small heat: therefore the air being very cloudy and dark, by the weakness of the heat that could not come forth, did cause the earth to bring forth but raw and unripe fruit, which rotted before it could ripe. [*The Life of Julius Caesar*, p. 103.]

THE TRIUMVIRATE

Now the state of Rome standing in these terms, there fell out another change and alteration, when the young man Octavius Caesar came to Rome. He was the son of Julius Caesar's niece, whom he had adopted for his son, and made his heir, by his last will and testament. But when Julius Caesar, his adopted father, was slain, he was in the city of Apollonia (where he studied) tarrying for him, because he was determined to make war with the Parthians: but when he heard the news of his death, he returned again to Rome. Where, to begin to curry favor with the common people, he first of all took upon him his adopted father's name, and made distribution among them of the money which his father had bequeathed unto them. By this means he troubled Antonius sorely, and by force of money got a great number of his father's soldiers together, that had served in the wars with him. [*The Life of Marcus Brutus*, p. 123.]

[After much political and military maneuvering, Octavius Caesar, Antonius, and Lepidus met] in an island environed round about with a little river, and there remained three days together. Now as touching all other matters they were easily agreed, and did divide all the Empire of Rome between them, as if it had been their own inheritance. But yet they could hardly agree whom they would put to death: for every one of them would kill their enemies, and save their kinsmen and friends. Yet at length, giving place to their greedy desire to be revenged of their enemies, they spurned all reverence of blood and holiness of friendship at their feet. For Caesar left Cicero to Antonius' will, Antonius also

forsook Lucius Caesar, who was his uncle by his mother:
and both of them together suffered Lepidus to kill his own
brother Paulus. Yet some writers affirm, that Caesar and
Antonius requested Paulus might be slain, and that Lepidus
was contented with it. In my opinion there was never a more
horrible, unnatural, and crueler change than this was. For
thus changing murder for murder, they did as well kill those
whom they did forsake and leave unto others, as those also
which others left unto them to kill: but so much more was
their wickedness and cruelty great unto their friends, for
that they put them to death being innocents, and having no
cause to hate them. [*The Life of Marcus Antonius*, p. 169.]

DISAGREEMENTS BETWEEN BRUTUS AND CASSIUS

Now whilst Brutus and Cassius were together in the city
of Smyrna, Brutus prayed Cassius to let him have some
part of his money whereof he had great store; because all
that he could rap and rend of his side, he had bestowed it
in making so great a number of ships, that by means of
them they should keep all the sea at their commandment.
Cassius' friends hindered this request and earnestly dis-
suaded him from it, persuading him, that it was no reason
that Brutus should have the money which Cassius had gotten
together by sparing and levied with great evil will of the
people their subjects, for him to bestow liberally upon his
soldiers, and by this means to win their good wills, by Cassius' charge. This notwithstanding, Cassius gave him the
third part of this total sum. [*The Life of Marcus Brutus*, pp.
130–31.]

. . . [Later] Brutus sent to pray Cassius to come to the
city of Sardis, and so he did. Brutus, understanding of his
coming, went to meet him with all his friends. There both
their armies being armed, they called them both *Emperors*.
Now as it commonly happened in great affairs between two
persons, both of them having many friends and so many
captains under them, there ran tales and complaints betwixt
them. Therefore, before they fell in hand with any other
matter, they went into a little chamber together, and bade

every man avoid, and did shut the doors to them. Then they began to pour out their complaints one to the other, and grew hot and loud, earnestly accusing one another, and at length fell both a-weeping. Their friends that were without the chamber, hearing them loud within, and angry between themselves, they were both amazed and afraid also, lest it would grow to further matter: but yet they were commanded that no man should come to them. Notwithstanding, one Marcus Faonius, that had been a friend and a follower of Cato while he lived, and took upon him to counterfeit a philosopher, not with wisdom and discretion, but with a certain bedlam and frantic motion: he would needs come into the chamber, though the men offered to keep him out. But it was no boot to let Faonius, when a mad mood or toy took him in the head: for he was a hot, hasty man, and sudden in all his doings, and cared for never a Senator of them all. Now, though he used this bold manner of speech after the profession of the Cynic philosophers (as who would say, *Dogs*), yet his boldness did no hurt many times, because they did but laugh at him to see him so mad. This Faonius at that time, in despite of the doorkeepers, came into the chamber, and with a certain scoffing and mocking gesture, which he counterfeited of purpose, he rehearsed the verses which old Nestor said in Homer:

> My lords, I pray you hearken both to me,
> For I have seen moe years than suchie three.

Cassius fell a-laughing at him: but Brutus thrust him out of the chamber, and called him dog, and counterfeit Cynic. Howbeit his coming in broke their strife at that time, and so they left each other. . . . The next day after, Brutus, upon complaint of the Sardians, did condemn and note Lucius Pella for a defamed person, that had been a praetor of the Romans, and whom Brutus had given charge unto: for that he was accused and convicted of robbery and pilfery in his office. This judgment much misliked Cassius, because he himself had secretly (not many days before) warned two of his friends, attainted and convicted of the like offenses, and

openly had cleared them: but yet he did not therefore leave
to employ them in any manner of service as he did before.
And therefore he greatly reproved Brutus, for that he would
show himself so straight and severe, in such a time as was
meeter to bear a little than to take things at the worst.
Brutus in contrary manner answered, that he should remember the Ides of March, at which time they slew Julius Caesar,
who neither pilled nor polled the country, but only was a
favorer and suborner of all them that did rob and spoil, by
his countenance and authority. And if there were any
occasion whereby they might honestly set aside justice and
equity, they should have had more reason to have suffered
Caesar's friends to have robbed and done what wrong and
injury they had would than to bear with their own men.
"For then," said he, "they could but have said we had been
cowards, but now they may accuse us of injustice, beside
the pains we take, and the danger we put ourselves into."
And thus may we see what Brutus' intent and purpose was.
[*The Life of Marcus Brutus*, pp. 134–35.]

THE GHOST OF CAESAR; OMENS OF
DEFEAT AND DECISIONS OF WAR

But as they both prepared to pass over again out of Asia
into Europe, there went a rumor that there appeared a
wonderful sign unto him. Brutus was a careful man, and
slept very little, both for that his diet was moderate, as also
because he was continually occupied. He never slept in the
daytime, and in the night no longer than the time he was
driven to be alone, and when everybody else took their rest.
But now whilst he was in war, and his head ever busily
occupied to think of his affairs and what would happen,
after he had slumbered a little after supper, he spent all the
rest of the night in dispatching of his weightiest causes; and
after he had taken order for them, if he had any leisure left
him, he would read some book till the third watch of the
night, at what time the captains, petty captains, and colonels,
did use to come to him. So, being ready to go into Europe,
one night very late (when all the camp took quiet rest) as

he was in his tent with a little light, thinking of weighty matters, he thought he heard one come in to him, and casting his eye towards the door of his tent, that he saw a wonderful strange and monstrous shape of a body coming towards him, and said never a word. So Brutus boldly asked what he was, a god or a man, and what cause brought him thither? The spirit answered him, "I am thy evil spirit, Brutus: and thou shalt see me by the city of Philippi." Brutus, being no otherwise afraid, replied again unto it: "Well, then I shall see thee again." The spirit presently vanished away: and Brutus called his men unto him, who told him that they heard no noise, nor saw anything at all. Thereupon Brutus returned again to think on his matters as he did before: and when the day broke, he went unto Cassius, to tell him what vision had appeared unto him in the night. Cassius being in opinion an Epicurean, and reasoning thereon with Brutus, spoke to him touching the vision thus. "In our sect, Brutus, we have an opinion, that we do not always feel or see that which we suppose we do both see and feel, but that our senses being credulous and therefore easily abused (when they are idle and unoccupied in their own objects) are induced to imagine they see and conjecture that which in truth they do not. . . ." With these words Cassius did somewhat comfort and quiet Brutus. When they raised their camp, there came two eagles that, flying with a marvelous force, lighted upon two of the foremost ensigns, and always followed the soldiers, which gave them meat and fed them, until they came near to the city of Philippi: and there, one day only before the battle, they both flew away. . . . The Romans called the valley between both camps, the Philippian fields: and there were never seen two so great armies of the Romans, one before the other, ready to fight. In truth, Brutus' army was inferior to Octavius Caesar's in number of men; but for bravery and rich furniture, Brutus' army far excelled Caesar's. For the most part of their armors were silver and gilt, which Brutus had bountifully given them: although, in all other things, he taught his captains to live in order without excess. . . . [*The Life of Marcus Brutus*, pp. 135–37.]

Brutus . . . mustered his army, and did purify it in the

fields, according to the manner of the Romans. . . . Notwithstanding, being busily occupied about the ceremonies of this purification, it is reported that there chanced certain unlucky signs unto Cassius. For one of his sergeants that carried the rods before him, brought him the garland of flowers turned backward, the which he should have worn on his head in the time of sacrificing. Moreover it is reported also, that another time before, in certain sports and triumph where they carried an image of Cassius' victory, of clean gold, it fell by chance, the man stumbling that carried it. And yet further, there was seen a marvelous number of fowls of prey, that feed upon dead carcasses: and beehives also were found, where bees were gathered together in a certain place within the trenches of the camp: the which place the soothsayers thought good to shut out of the precinct of the camp, for to take away the superstitious fear and mistrust men would have of it. The which began somewhat to alter Cassius' mind from Epicurus' opinions, and had put the soldiers also in a marvelous fear. Thereupon Cassius was of opinion not to try this war at one battle, but rather to delay time, and to draw it out in length, considering that they were the stronger in money, and the weaker in men and armor. But Brutus, in contrary manner, did alway before, and at that time also, desire nothing more than to put all to the hazard of battle, as soon as might be possible: to the end he might either quickly restore his country to her former liberty, or rid him forthwith of this miserable world, being still troubled in following and maintaining of such great armies together. But perceiving that, in the daily skirmishes and bickerings they made, his men were always the stronger and ever had the better, that yet quickened his spirits again, and did put him in better heart. And furthermore, because that some of their own men had already yielded themselves to their enemies, and that it was suspected moreover divers others would do the like, that made many of Cassius' friends which were of his mind before (when it came to be debated in council, whether the battle should be fought or not) that they were then of Brutus' mind. . . . Thereupon it was presently determined they should fight battle the next day. So Brutus, all supper time, looked with a cheerful countenance, like a man that had good hope, and talked very wisely of philosophy, and after supper went to bed. But touching Cassius, Messala reporteth that he supped by himself in his tent with a few of his friends, and that all supper time he looked very sadly, and was full of thoughts, although it was against his nature: and that after supper he took him by the hand, and holding him fast (in token of kindness, as his manner was) told him in Greek: "Messala, I protest unto thee, and make thee my witness, that I am compelled against my mind and will (as Pompey the Great was) to jeopard the liberty of our country to the hazard of a battle. And yet we must be lively, and of good courage, considering our good fortune, whom we should wrong too much to mistrust her, although we follow evil counsel." Messala writeth, that Cassius having spoken these last words unto him, he bade him farewell, and willed him to come to supper to him the next night following, because it was his birthday. The next morning, by break of day, the signal of battle was set out in Brutus' and Cassius' camp, which was an arming scarlet coat: and both the chieftains spoke together in the midst of their armies. There Cassius began to speak first, and said: "The gods grant us, O Brutus, that this day we may win the field, and ever after to live all the rest of our life quietly one with another. But sith the gods have so ordained it, that the greatest and chiefest things amongst men are most uncertain, and that if the battle fall out otherwise today than we wish or look for, we shall hardly meet again, what art thou then determined to do, to fly or die?" Brutus answered him, being yet but a young man and not over greatly experienced in the world: "I trust (I know not how) a certain rule of philosophy, by the which I did greatly blame and reprove Cato for killing himself, as being no lawful nor godly act, touching the gods: nor concerning men, valiant; not to give place and yield to divine providence, and not constantly and patiently to take whatsoever it pleaseth him to send us, but to draw back and fly: but being now in the midst of the danger, I am of a contrary mind. For if it be not the will of God that this battle fall out fortunate for us, I will look no more for hope, neither seek to make any new supply for war again,

but will rid me of this miserable world, and content me with
my fortune. For I gave up my life for my country in the
Ides of March, for the which I shall live in another more
glorious world." Cassius fell a-laughing to hear what he
said, and embracing him, "Come on then," said he, "let us
go and charge our enemies with this mind. For either we
shall conquer, or we shall not need to fear the conquerors."
After this talk, they fell to consultation among their friends
for the ordering of the battle. Then Brutus prayed Cassius
he might have the leading of the right wing, the which men
thought was far meeter for Cassius, both because he was
the elder man, and also for that he had the better experience.
But yet Cassius gave it him, and willed that Messala (who
had charge of one of the warlikest legions they had) should
be also in that wing with Brutus. So Brutus presently sent
out his horsemen, who were excellently well appointed, and
his footmen also were as willing and ready to give charge.
[*The Life of Marcus Brutus*, pp. 138–40.]

THE BATTLE

In the meantime Brutus, that led the right wing, sent little
bills to the colonels and captains of private bands, in the
which he wrote the word of the battle; and he himself,
riding a-horseback by all the troops, did speak to them, and
encouraged them to stick to it like men. So by this means
very few of them understood what was the word of the
battle, and besides, the most part of them never tarried to
have it told them, but ran with great fury to assail the enemies; whereby, through this disorder, the legions were
marvelously scattered and dispersed one from the other.
For first of all Messala's legion, and then the next unto them,
went beyond the left wing of the enemies and did nothing,
but glancing by them overthrew some as they went; and so
going on further, fell right upon Caesar's camp, out of the
which (as himself writeth in his commentaries) he had been
conveyed away a little before, through the counsel and
advice of one of his friends called Marcus Artorius: who,
dreaming in the night, had a vision appeared unto him, that

commanded Octavius Caesar should be carried out of his camp. Insomuch as it was thought he was slain, because his litter (which had nothing in it) was thrust through and through with pikes and darts. There was great slaughter in this camp. For amongst others, there were slain 2,000 Lacedaemonians, who were arrived but even a little before, coming to aid Caesar. The other also that had not glanced by, but had given a charge full upon Caesar's battle, they easily made them fly, because they were greatly troubled for the loss of their camp; and of them there were slain by hand three legions. Then, being very earnest to follow the chase of them that fled, they ran in amongst them hand over head into their camp, and Brutus among them. But that which the conquerors thought not of, occasion showed it unto them that were overcome; and that was, the left wing of their enemies left naked and unguarded of them of the right wing, who were strayed too far off, in following of them that were overthrown. So they gave a hot charge upon them. But, notwithstanding all the force they made, they could not break into the midst of their battle, where they found them that received them and valiantly made head against them. Howbeit they broke and overthrew the left wing where Cassius was, by reason of the great disorder among them, and also because they had no intelligence how the right wing had sped. So they chased them, beating them into their camp, the which they spoiled, none of both the chieftains being present there. For Antonius, as it is reported, to fly the fury of the first charge, was gotten into the next marsh: and no man could tell what became of Octavius Caesar after he was carried out of his camp. Insomuch that there were certain soldiers that showed their swords bloodied, and said that they had slain him, and did describe his face, and showed what age he was of. Furthermore, the voward and the midst of Brutus' battle had already put all their enemies to flight that withstood them, with great slaughter: so that Brutus had conquered all on his side and Cassius had lost all on the other side. For nothing undid them but that Brutus went not to help Cassius, thinking he had overcome them as himself had done; and Cassius on the other side tarried not for Brutus, thinking he had been overthrown

as himself was. And to prove that the victory fell on Brutus'
side, Messala confirmeth that they won three eagles and
divers other ensigns of the enemies, and their enemies won
never a one of theirs. Now Brutus returning from the chase,
after he had slain and sacked Caesar's men, he wondered
much that he could not see Cassius' tent standing up high
as it was wont, neither the other tents of his camp standing
as they were before, because all the whole camp had been
spoiled, and the tents thrown down, at the first coming of
their enemies. But they that were about Brutus, whose sight
served them better, told him that they saw a great glistering
of harness, and a number of silvered targets that went and
came into Cassius' camp, and were not (as they took it) the
armors nor the number of men that they had left there to
guard the camp; and yet that they saw not such a number of
dead bodies and great overthrow as there should have been,
if so many legions had been slain. This made Brutus at the
first mistrust that which had happened. So he appointed a
number of men to keep the camp of his enemy which he had
taken, and caused his men to be sent for that yet followed
the chase, and gathered them together, thinking to lead
them to aid Cassius, who was in this state as you shall hear.
[*The Life of Marcus Brutus*, pp. 140–42.]

THE DEATH OF CASSIUS

First of all, he was marvelous angry to see how Brutus'
men ran to give charge upon their enemies, and tarried not
for the word of the battle, nor commandment to give charge:
and it grieved him beside that after he had overcome them,
his men fell straight to spoil and were not careful to compass
in the rest of the enemies behind: but with tarrying too long
also, more than through the valiantness or foresight of the
captains his enemies, Cassius found himself compassed in
with the right wing of his enemies' army. Whereupon his
horsemen broke immediately, and fled for life towards the
sea. Furthermore perceiving his footmen to give ground, he
did what he could to keep them from flying, and took an

ensign from one of the ensign-bearers that fled, and stuck it fast at his feet: although with much ado he could scant keep his own guard together.

So Cassius himself was at length compelled to fly, with a few about him, unto a little hill, from whence they might easily see what was done in all the plain: howbeit Cassius himself saw nothing, for his sight was very bad, saving that he saw (and yet with much ado) how the enemies spoiled his camp before his eyes. He saw also a great troop of horsemen, whom Brutus sent to aid him, and thought that they were his enemies that followed him: but yet he sent Titinius, one of them that was with him, to go and know what they were. Brutus' horsemen saw him coming afar off, whom when they knew that he was one of Cassius' chiefest friends, they shouted out for joy; and they that were familiarly acquainted with him lighted from their horses, and went and embraced him. The rest compassed him in round about on horseback, with songs of victory and great rushing of their harness, so that they made all the field ring again for joy. But this marred all. For Cassius, thinking indeed that Titinius was taken of the enemies, he then spoke these words: "Desiring too much to live, I have lived to see one of my best friends taken, for my sake, before my face." After that, he got into a tent where nobody was, and took Pindarus with him, one of his bondsmen whom he reserved ever for such a pinch, since the cursed battle of the Parthians, where Crassus was slain, though he notwithstanding scaped from that over-throw: but then, casting his cloak over his head, and holding out his bare neck unto Pindarus, he gave him his head to be stricken off. So the head was found severed from the body: but after that time Pindarus was never seen more. Where-upon some took occasion to say that he had slain his master without his commandment. By and by they knew the horse-men that came towards them, and might see Titinius crowned with a garland of triumph, who came before with great speed unto Cassius. But when he perceived, by the cries and tears of his friends which tormented themselves, the mis-fortune that had chanced to his captain Cassius by mistak-ing, he drew out his sword, cursing himself a thousand times that he had tarried so long, and so slew himself presently in

the field. Brutus in the meantime came forward still, and
understood also that Cassius had been overthrown: but he
knew nothing of his death till he came very near to his camp.
So when he was come thither, after he had lamented the
death of Cassius, calling him the last of all the Romans,
being impossible that Rome should ever breed again so
noble and valiant a man as he, he caused his body to be
buried, and sent it to the city of Thasos, fearing lest his
funerals within his camp should cause great disorder. [*The
Life of Marcus Brutus*, pp. 142–44.]

THE EXPLOITS OF YOUNG CATO AND LUCILIUS

There was the son of Marcus Cato slain, valiantly fighting
among the lusty youths. For notwithstanding that he was
very weary and overharried, yet would he not therefore fly;
but manfully fighting and laying about him, telling aloud
his name and also his father's name, at length he was beaten
down amongst many other dead bodies of his enemies,
which he had slain round about him. So there were slain in
the field all the chiefest gentlemen and nobility that were in
his army, who valiantly ran into any danger to save Brutus'
life: amongst whom there was one of Brutus' friends called
Lucilius, who seeing a troop of barbarous men making no
reckoning of all men else they met in their way, but going
all together right against Brutus, he determined to stay them
with the hazard of his life; and being left behind, told them
that he was Brutus: and because they should believe him,
he prayed them to bring him to Antonius, for he said he
was afraid of Caesar, and that he did trust Antonius better.
These barbarous men, being very glad of this good hap, and
thinking themselves happy men, they carried him in the
night, and sent some before unto Antonius, to tell him of
their coming. He was marvelous glad of it, and went out to
meet them that brought him. Others also understanding
of it that they had brought Brutus prisoner, they came out of
all parts of the camp to see him, some pitying his hard
fortune and others saying that it was not done like himself,
so cowardly to be taken alive of the barbarous people for

fear of death. When they came near together, Antonius stayed a while bethinking himself how he should use Brutus. In the meantime Lucilius was brought to him, who stoutly with a bold countenance said: "Antonius, I dare assure thee, that no enemy hath taken nor shall take Marcus Brutus alive, and I beseech God keep him from that fortune: for wheresoever he be found, alive or dead, he will be found like himself. And now for myself, I am come unto thee, having deceived these men of arms here, bearing them down that I was Brutus, and do not refuse to suffer any torment thou wilt put me to." Lucilius' words made them all amazed that heard him. Antonius on the other side, looking upon all them that had brought him, said unto them: "My companions, I think ye are sorry you have failed of your purpose, and that you think this man hath done you great wrong: but I assure you, you have taken a better booty than that you followed. For instead of an enemy you have brought me a friend: and for my part, if you had brought me Brutus alive, truly I cannot tell what I should have done to him. For I had rather have such men my friends, as this man here, than mine enemies." Then he embraced Lucilius, and at that time delivered him to one of his friends in custody; and Lucilius ever after served him faithfully, even to his death. [*The Life of Marcus Brutus*, pp. 148–49.]

THE DEATH OF BRUTUS

Now Brutus having passed a little river, walled in on every side with high rocks and shadowed with great trees, being then dark night, he went no further, but stayed at the foot of a rock with certain of his captains and friends that followed him: and looking up to the firmament that was full of stars, sighing, he rehearsed two verses, of the which Volumnius wrote the one, to this effect:

> Let not the wight from whom this mischief went,
> O Jove, escape without due punishment:

and saith that he had forgotten the other. Within a little

while after, naming his friends that he had seen slain in battle before his eyes, he fetched a greater sigh than before, specially when he came to name Labeo and Flavius, of whom the one was his lieutenant, and the other captain of the pioneers of his camp. In the meantime one of the company being athirst, and seeing Brutus athirst also, he ran to the river for water and brought it in his sallet. At the same time they heard a noise on the other side of the river: whereupon Volumnius took Dardanus, Brutus' servant, with him, to see what it was: and returning straight again, asked if there were any water left. Brutus smiling, gently told him, "All is drunk, but they shall bring you some more." Thereupon he sent him again that went for water before, who was in great danger of being taken by the enemies, and hardly escaped, being sore hurt.

Furthermore, Brutus thought that there was no great number of men slain in battle: and to know the truth of it, there was one called Statilius that promised to go through his enemies, for otherwise it was impossible to go see their camp: and from thence, if all were well, that he would lift up a torchlight in the air and then return again with speed to him. The torchlight was lift up as he had promised, for Statilius went thither. Now Brutus seeing Statilius tarry long after that, and that he came not again, he said: "If Statilius be alive, he will come again." But his evil fortune was such that, as he came back, he lighted in his enemies' hands and was slain. Now the night being far spent, Brutus, as he sat, bowed towards Clitus, one of his men, and told him somewhat in his ear: the other answered him not, but fell a-weeping. Thereupon he proved Dardanus, and said somewhat also to him: at length he came to Volumnius himself, and speaking to him in Greek, prayed him for the studies' sake which brought them acquainted together that he would help him to put his hand to his sword, to thrust it in him to kill him. Volumnius denied his request, and so did many others: and amongst the rest, one of them said, there was no tarrying for them there, but that they must needs fly. Then Brutus, rising up, "We must fly indeed," said he, "but it must be with our hands, not with our feet." Then taking every man by the hand, he said these words unto them with a cheerful

countenance: "It rejoiceth my heart, that not one of my friends hath failed me at my need, and I do not complain of my fortune, but only for my country's sake: for as for me, I think myself happier than they that have overcome, considering that I leave a perpetual fame of virtue and honesty, the which our enemies the conquerors shall never attain unto by force or money; neither can let their posterity to say that they, being naughty and unjust men, have slain good men, to usurp tyrannical power not pertaining to them." Having so said, he prayed every man to shift for himself, and then he went a little aside with two or three only, among the which Strato was one, with whom he came first acquainted by the study of rhetoric. He came as near to him as he could, and taking his sword by the hilt with both his hands, and falling down upon the point of it, ran himself through. Others say that not he, but Strato (at his request) held the sword in his hand, and turned his head aside, and that Brutus fell down upon it, and so ran himself through, and died presently. Messala, that had been Brutus' great friend, became afterwards Octavius Caesar's friend: so, shortly after, Caesar being at good leisure, he brought Strato, Brutus' friend, unto him, and weeping said: "Caesar, behold, here is he that did the last service to my Brutus." Caesar welcomed him at that time, and afterwards he did him as faithful service in all his affairs as any Grecian else he had about him, until the battle of Actium. It is reported also that this Messala himself answered Caesar one day, when he gave him great praise before his face, that he had fought valiantly and with great affection for him at the battle of Actium (notwithstanding that he had been his cruel enemy before, at the battle of Philippi, for Brutus' sake): "I ever loved," said he, "to take the best and justest part."
[*The Life of Marcus Brutus*, pp. 149–51.]

Antonius having found Brutus' body after this battle, blaming him much for the murder of his brother Caius, whom he had put to death in Macedon for revenge of Cicero's cruel death, and yet laying the fault more in Hortensius than in him, he made Hortensius to be slain on his brother's tomb. Furthermore he cast his coat-armor

(which was wonderful rich and sumptuous) upon Brutus'
body, and gave commandment to one of his slaves enfranchised, to defray the charge of his burial. But afterwards
Antonius hearing that his enfranchised bondman had not
burnt his coat-armor with his body, because it was very rich
and worth a great sum of money, and that he had also kept
back much of the ready money appointed for his funeral
and tomb, he also put him to death. [*The Life of Marcus
Antonius*, p. 171.]

THE DEATH OF PORCIA

And for Porcia, Brutus' wife, Nicolaus the Philosopher
and Valerius Maximus do write that she, determining to kill
herself (her parents and friends carefully looking to her to
keep her from it), took hot burning coals and cast them into
her mouth, and kept her mouth so close that she choked
herself. There was a letter of Brutus found written to his
friends, complaining of their negligence, that his wife being
sick, they would not help her, but suffered her to kill herself;
choosing to die, rather than to languish in pain. Thus it
appeareth that Nicolaus knew not well that time, sith the
letter (at the least if it were Brutus' letter) doth plainly
declare the disease and love of this lady, and also the manner
of her death. [*The Life of Marcus Brutus*, pp. 151–52.]

THE CHARACTER OF CAESAR

Furthermore, they did not wonder so much at his valiantness in putting himself at every instant in such manifest
danger, and in taking so extreme pains as he did, knowing
that it was his greedy desire of honor that set him on fire,
and pricked him forward to do it: but that he always continued all labor and hardness, more than his body could
bear, that filled them all with admiration. For, concerning
the constitution of his body, he was lean, white, and soft-
skinned, and often subject to headache, and otherwhile to
the falling sickness (the which took him the first time, as it

is reported, in Corduba, a city of Spain) but yet therefore yielded not to the disease of his body, to make it a cloak to cherish him withal, but contrarily, took the pains of war as a medicine to cure his sick body, fighting always with his disease, traveling continually, living soberly, and commonly lying abroad in the field. [*The Life of Julius Caesar*, p. 57.]

Furthermore, Caesar being born to attempt all great enterprises, and having an ambitious desire besides to covet great honors, the prosperous good success he had of his former conquests bred no desire in him quietly to enjoy the fruits of his labors; but rather gave him the hope of things to come, still kindling more and more in him thoughts of greater enterprises and desire of new glory, as if that which he had present were stale and nothing worth. This humor of his was no other but an emulation with himself as with another man, and a certain contention to overcome the things he prepared to attempt. [*The Life of Julius Caesar*, p. 93.]

In this journey it is reported, that passing over the mountains of the Alps, they came through a little poor village that had not many households, and yet poor cottages. There his friends that did accompany him asked him merrily, if there were any contending for offices in that town, and whether there were any strife there amongst the noblemen for honor. Caesar, speaking in good earnest, answered: "I cannot tell that," said he, "but for my part I had rather be the chiefest man here than the second person in Rome." Another time also when he was in Spain, reading the history of Alexander's acts, when he had read it, he was sorrowful a good while after, and then burst out in weeping. His friends seeing that, marveled what should be the cause of his sorrow. He answered them, "Do ye not think," said he, "that I have good cause to be heavy, when King Alexander, being no elder than myself is now, had in old time won so many nations and countries: and that I hitherunto have done nothing worthy of myself?" [*The Life of Julius Caesar*, p. 52.]

But the time of the great armies and conquests he made afterwards, and of the war in the which he subdued all the

Gauls (entering into another course of life far contrary unto the first) made him to be known for as valiant a soldier and as excellent a captain to lead men, as those that afore him had been counted the wisest and most valiant generals that ever were, and that by their valiant deeds had achieved great honor. [*The Life of Julius Caesar*, p. 55.]

Now Caesar immediately won many men's good wills at Rome, through his eloquence in pleading of their causes, and the people loved him marvelously also, because of the courteous manner he had to speak to every man, and to use them gently, being more ceremonious therein than was looked for in one of his years. Furthermore, he ever kept a good board, and fared well at his table, and was very liberal besides: the which indeed did advance him forward, and brought him in estimation with the people. . . . Thereupon Cicero, like a wise shipmaster that feareth the calmness of the sea, was the first man that, mistrusting his manner of dealing in the commonwealth, found out his craft and malice, which he cunningly cloaked under the habit of outward courtesy and familiarity. "And yet," said he, "when I consider how finely he combeth his fair bush of hair, and how smooth it lieth, and that I see him scratch his head with one finger only, my mind gives me then, that such a kind of man should not have so wicked a thought in his head, as to overthrow the state of the commonwealth." But this was long time after that. [*The Life of Julius Caesar*, p. 45.]

THE CHARACTERS OF BRUTUS AND CASSIUS

Marcus Brutus came of that Junius Brutus, for whom the ancient Romans made his statue of brass to be set up in the Capitol, with the images of the kings, holding a naked sword in his hand: because he had valiantly put down the Tarquins from the kingdom of Rome. But that Junius Brutus, being of a sour, stern nature not softened by reason, being like unto sword blades of too hard a temper, was so subject to his choler and malice he bore unto the tyrants, that for their sakes he caused his own sons to be executed. But this Marcus Brutus in contrary manner, whose life we presently write, having framed his manners of life by the rules of virtue and study of philosophy, and having employed his wit, which was gentle and constant, in attempting of great things, methinks he was rightly made and framed unto virtue. So that his very enemies which wish him most hurt, because of his conspiracy against Julius Caesar, if there were any noble attempt done in all this conspiracy, they refer it wholly unto Brutus; and all the cruel and violent acts unto Cassius, who was Brutus' familiar friend, but not so well given and conditioned as he. [*The Life of Marcus Brutus*, pp. 105–06.]

He was properly learned in the Latin tongue, and was able to make long discourse in it: beside that he could also plead very well in Latin. But for the Greek tongue, they do note in some of his Epistles that he counterfeited that brief compendious manner of speech of the Lacedaemonians. As, when the war was begun, he wrote unto the Pergamenians in this sort: "I understand you have given Dolabella money: if you have done it willingly, you confess you have offended me; if against your wills, show it then by giving me willingly." Another time again unto the Samians: "Your councils be long, your doings be slow, consider the end." And in another Epistle he wrote unto the Patareians: "The Xanthians, despising my good will, have made their country a grave of despair; and the Patareians, that put themselves into my protection, have lost no jot of their liberty: and therefore, whilst you have liberty, either choose the judgment of the Patareians, or the fortune of the Xanthians." These were Brutus' manner of letters, which were honored for their briefness. [*The Life of Marcus Brutus*, p. 107.]

They say also that Caesar said, when he heard Brutus plead: "I know not," said he, "what this young man would; but what he would, he willeth it vehemently." For as Brutus' gravity and constant mind would not grant all men their requests that sued unto him, but, being moved with reason and discretion, did always incline to that which was good and honest: even so, when it was moved to follow any matter, he used a kind of forcible and vehement persuasion, that calmed not till he had obtained his desire. For by flattering of him a man could never obtain anything at his hands, nor make him to do that which was unjust. Further, he thought it not meet for a man of calling and estimation, to yield unto the requests and entreaties of a shameless and importunate suitor, requesting things unmeet: the which notwithstanding some men do for shame, because they dare deny nothing: and therefore he was wont to say, "that he thought them evil brought up in their youth, that could deny nothing." [*The Life of Marcus Brutus*, pp. 109–10.]

And surely (in my opinion), I am persuaded that Brutus might indeed have come to have been the chiefest man of Rome, if he could have contented himself for a time to have been next unto Caesar, and to have suffered his glory and authority, which he had gotten by his great victories, to consume with time. But Cassius, being a choleric man, and hating Caesar privately more than he did the tyranny openly, he incensed Brutus against him. It is also reported, that Brutus could evil away with the tyranny, and that Cassius hated the tyrant: making many complaints for the injuries he had done him; and amongst others, for that he had taken away his lions from him. Cassius had provided them for his sports when he should be aedilis; and they were found in the city of Megara, when it was won by Calenus: and Caesar kept them. The rumor went, that these lions did marvelous great hurt to the Megarians: for when the city was taken, they broke their cages where they were tied up and turned them loose, thinking they would have done great mischief to the enemies, and have kept them from setting upon them: but the lions (contrary to expectation) turned upon themselves that fled unarmed, and did so cruelly tear some in pieces, that it pitied their enemies to see them. And this was the cause (as some do report) that made Cassius conspire against Caesar. But this holdeth no water: for Cassius, even from his cradle, could not abide any manner of tyrants; as it appeared when he was but a boy, and went unto the same school that Faustus, the son of Sulla, did. And Faustus, bragging among other boys, highly boasted of his father's kingdom: Cassius rose up on his feet, and gave him two good wirts on the ear. Faustus' governors would have put this matter in suit against Cassius: but

Pompey would not suffer them, but caused the two boys to be brought before him and asked them how the matter came to pass. Then Cassius (as it is written of him) said unto the other: "Go to, Faustus, speak again, and thou darest, before this nobleman here, the same words that made me angry with thee, that my fists may walk once again about thine ears." Such was Cassius' hot stirring nature. [*The Life of Marcus Brutus*, pp.111–12.]

Now Cassius would have done Brutus much honor, as Brutus did unto him, but Brutus most commonly prevented him and went first unto him, both because he was the elder man as also for that he was sickly of body. And men reputed him commonly to be very skillful in wars, but otherwise marvelous choleric and cruel, who sought to rule men by fear rather than with lenity: and on the other side, he was too familar with his friends, and would jest too broadly with them. But Brutus, in contrary manner, for his virtue and valiantness, was well beloved of the people and his own, esteemed of noblemen, and hated of no man, not so much as of his enemies; because he was a marvelous lowly and gentle person, noble-minded, and would never be in any rage, nor carried away with pleasure and covetousness, but had ever an upright mind with him and would never yield to any wrong or injustice; the which was the chiefest cause of his fame, of his rising, and of the good will that every man bore him: for they were all persuaded that his intent was good. For they did not certainly believe that, if Pompey himself had overcome Caesar, he would have resigned his authority to the law, but rather they were of opinion that he would still keep the sovereignty and absolute government in his hands, taking only, to please the people, the title of Consul, or Dictator, or of some other more civil office. And as for Cassius, a hot, choleric, and cruel man, that would oftentimes be carried away from justice for gain, it was certainly thought that he made war and put himself into sundry dangers, more to have absolute power and authority than to defend the liberty of his country. For they that will also consider others that were elder men than they, as Cinna, Marinus, and Carbo, it is out of doubt that the end and hope of their victory was to be the lords of their country, and in manner they did all confess that they fought for the tyranny and to be lords of the Empire of Rome. And in contrary manner, his enemies themselves did never reprove Brutus for any such change or desire. For it was said that Antonius spoke it openly divers times, that he thought, that of all them that had slain Caesar, there was none but Brutus only that was moved to do it, as thinking the act commendable of itself: but that all the other conspirators did conspire his death for some private malice or envy that they otherwise did bear unto him. [*The Life of Marcus Brutus*, pp. 129–30.]

THE CHARACTER OF ANTONY

Now Antonius being a fair young man, and in the prime of his youth, he fell acquainted with Curio, whose friendship and acquaintance (as it is reported) was a plague unto him. For he was a dissolute man, given over to all lust and insolency, who, to have Antonius the better at his commandment, trained him on into great follies and vain expenses upon women, in rioting and banqueting: so that in short time he brought Antonius into a marvelous great debt, and too great for one of his years, to wit, of two hundred and fifty talents, for all which sum Curio was his surety. His father, hearing of it, did put his son from him and forbade him his house. Then he fell in with Clodius, one of the desperatest and most wicked tribunes at that time in Rome. Him he followed for a time in his desperate attempts, who bred great stir and mischief in Rome: but at length he forsook him, being weary of his rashness and folly, or else for that he was afraid of them that were bent against Clodius.

Thereupon he left Italy, and went into Greece, and there bestowed the most part of his time, sometime in wars, and otherwhile in the study of eloquence. He used a manner of phrase in his speech called "Asiatic," which carried the best grace and estimation at that time and was much like to his manners and life: for it was full of ostentation, foolish bravery, and vain ambition. [*The Life of Marcus Antonius*, pp. 154–55.]

So was his great courtesy also much commended of all, the which he showed unto Archelaus: for having been his very friend, he made war with him against his will while he lived; but after his death he fought for his body, and gave it honorable burial. For these respects he won himself great fame of them of Alexandria, and he was also thought a worthy man of all the soldiers in the Romans' camp. But besides all this, he had a noble presence, and showed a countenance of one of a noble house: he had a goodly thick beard, a broad forehead, crooked-nosed, and there appeared such a manly look in his countenance, as is commonly seen in Hercules' pictures, stamped or graven in metal. Now it had been a speech of old time, that the family of the Antonii were descended from one Anton, the son of Hercules, whereof the family took name. This opinion did Antonius seek to confirm in all his doings: not only resembling him in the likeness of his body, as we have said before, but also in the wearing of his garments. For when he would openly show himself abroad before many people, he would always wear his cassock girt down low upon his hips, with a great sword hanging by his side and upon that some ill-favored cloak. Furthermore, things that seem intolerable in other men, as to boast commonly, to jest with one or other, to drink like a good fellow with everybody, to sit with the soldiers when they dine, and to eat and drink with them soldierlike, it is incredible what wonderful love it won him amongst them. And furthermore, being given to love, that made him the more desired, and by that means he brought many to love him. For he would further every man's love, and also would not be angry that men should merrily tell him of those he loved. But besides all this, that which most procured his rising and advancement was his liberality, who gave all to the soldiers and kept nothing for himself: and when he was grown to great credit, then was his authority and power also very great, the which notwithstanding himself did overthrow by a thousand other faults he had. [*The Life of Marcus Antonius*, pp. 156–57.]

But then in contrary manner, he purchased divers other men's evil wills, because that through negligence he would not do them justice that were injured, and dealt very churlishly with them that had any suit unto him: and besides all this, he had an ill name to entice men's wives. [*The Life of Marcus Antonius*, p. 159.]

Now after that Caesar had gotten Rome at his commandment, and had driven Pompey out of Italy, he purposed first to go into Spain against the legions Pompey had there, and in the meantime to make provision for ships and marine preparation, to follow Pompey. In his absence, he left Lepidus, that was praetor, governor of Rome; and Antonius, that was tribune, he gave him charge of all the soldiers and of Italy. . . . To conclude, Caesar's friends, that governed under him, were cause why they hated Caesar's government (which indeed in respect of himself was no less than tyranny) by reason of the great insolencies and outrageous parts that were committed: amongst whom Antonius, that was of greatest power, and that also committed greatest faults, deserved most blame. But Caesar, notwithstanding, when he returned from the wars of Spain, made no reckoning of the complaints that were put up against him: but contrarily, because he found him a hardy man, and a valiant captain, he employed him in his chiefest affairs, and was no whit deceived in his opinion of him. [*The Life of Marcus Antonius*, pp. 158–59.]

Commentaries

LEONARD F. DEAN

"Julius Caesar" and Modern Criticism

Julius Caesar came into the curriculum in the days of elocution, formal rhetoric, the old school tie, and the British Empire. The Roman thing was presumably at home in that company, but the times now appear to be against it. "Strictly for the birds," says Holden Caulfield, contemplating a somewhat decayed exponent of the Roman thing, Pencey Prep, molder of men since 1888. "From Plutarch," says C. S. Lewis more suavely, "comes that almost oppressive crowd of generals, sages, courtesans, soothsayers, and noble dames. . . ." Mark Van Doren is more specific: "Brutus . . . the Roman conspirator has become an exemplary gentleman . . . the principal reason may be that Shakespeare has kept himself too conscious of a remote Roman grandeur. . . . *Julius Caesar* is more rhetoric than poetry, just as its persons are more orators than men . . . all its persons tend to talk alike . . . they are artists in declama-

From *The English Journal* (October, 1961), pp. 451–56. Reprinted by permission of the National Council of Teachers of English and Leonard F. Dean.

tion . . . Brutus addresses us through a wrapping of rhetoric, of public speech. . . . This is the noblest Roman of them all, and even in distress he keeps his distance. . . . The mistakes of Brutus are the mistakes of a man whose nobility muffles his intelligence . . . honesty in him is humorless and edgeless; it rings a little dully in our ears, and even a little smugly . . . it is virtue, it is true manhood demonstrating itself for the benefit of others." The play's nineteenth-century stage tradition, with its strong curtains, melodramatic tableaux, and its Roman Senate looking "like the cooling room of a Turkish bath," is in Harley Granville-Barker's mind when he asks: "Has not the vulgar modern conception of Rome, nourished in Latin lessons and the classic school of painting, become rather frigid? Are not our noble Romans, flinging their togas gracefully about them, slow-moving, consciously dignified, speaking with studied oratory and all past middle age, rather too like a schoolboy's vision of a congress of headmasters?"

Since there is no turning back to the days when schoolboys declaimed the famous orations to admiring audiences, but since the play remains a fixture of the high school program, teachers may properly ask if modern Shakespearean criticism has found anything in *Julius Caesar* which will appeal to the twentieth century. The answer, briefly, is that *Caesar* is now almost unanimously read as a problem play marked by political, ethical, and psychological ironies of a decidedly modern and painfully human kind.

THE CHARACTER OF BRUTUS

This modern interpretation appears first, as might be expected, in the analysis of the character of Brutus, and it takes form slowly through a progressive shift of critical tone and emphasis. This is clear if one takes his start at the beginning of the century with a still basic study of the play, Sir Mungo W. MacCallum's *Shakespeare's Roman Plays* (1910). A servant of the Empire, having gone out from Glasgow to Sidney, MacCallum writes firmly that in Brutus "Shakespeare wishes to portray a patriotic gentleman of the best Roman or the best English type ... very much in the form of a cultured and high-souled English nobleman, the heir of great traditions and their responsibilities, which he fulfills to the smallest jot and tittle. ..." After remarking Brutus' gentle qualities (his "winning courtesy," "affectionate nature," and "essential modesty"), MacCallum adds that they "are saved from all taint of weakness by an heroic strain, both high-spirited and public-spirited, both stoical and chivalrous." His only weakness, as MacCallum sees it, is a product of his virtue, and it comes out first through contrast with Caesar. Brutus is "recognized as no less preeminent in the sphere of ethics, than Caesar in the sphere of politics. ... And in each this leads to a kind of pose." In Brutus the pose appears when "the cult of perfection becomes the assumption and obtrusion of it ... a willingness to give a demonstration, so to speak, in Clinical Ethics." Furthermore, this "votary of duty cannot acknowledge a merely fugitive and cloistered virtue," and consequently "Brutus, who is so at home in his study with his book, who is so exemplary in all the relations of friend, master, and husband ... sweeps from his quiet anchorage to face the storms of political strife, which such as he are not born to master but which they think they must not avoid."

From these premises, MacCallum traces Brutus' career through disillusionment and defeat to heroic martyrdom. He is less of a philosopher than he thinks, and his attempts to impose the reason of the study on practical politics show him "so besotted by his own sophisms that he will listen to no warnings." He is "doubly duped, by his own subtlety and his own simplicity in league with his own conscientiousness. ..." The outstanding dramatization of Brutus' "education in disappointment" is the quarrel scene with Cassius, which "lays bare the significance of the story in its tragic pathos and its tragic irony." By the final act it is clear that Brutus' "attempt at remedy has resulted in a situation even more intolerable" for the reason that he has been "quite impractical and perverse, as every enthusiast for abstract justice must be, who lets himself be seduced into crime on the plea of duty, and yet shapes his course as though he were not a criminal." But at the end, according to Mac-

Callum, when Brutus' "life-failure stares him in the face, he does not allow it a wider scope than its due"; he regains his form, and in "inward and essential matters his character victoriously stands the test. . . ." It is not surprising that at the conclusion of his chapter, MacCallum brings Portia back on the stage for a strong curtain of his own invention: "at the side of this rare and lofty nature, we see the kindred figure of his wife. . . ." Though Brutus "is drawn by his political, and she by her domestic ideal into a position that overstrains the strength of each," the final weight of the play, as MacCallum feels it, is on the side of the noble character of the Victorian-Roman husband and wife.

Seventeen years after MacCallum, a shift of critical emphasis can be detected in Harley Granville-Barker's *Preface to Julius Caesar* (1927, slightly revised before 1946). Barker acknowledges the compelling power of the portrayal of Brutus, and the human appeal of the quarrel scene and his reaction to Portia's death, but he adds that Shakespeare, "having lifted his heroic Roman to this height, leaves him, we must own, rather stockishly upon it. . . . Now, when we expect nemesis approaching, some deeper revelation, some glimpse of the hero's very soul, this hero stays inarticulate, or, worse, turns oracular." In the final scenes, from Barker's view, Brutus "comes short of what we demand from the tragic hero" because his education is incomplete: "He is sent to his death, a figure of gracious dignity, the noblest Roman of them all, but with eyes averted from the issue still." Barker can only conclude that the Roman thing proved poetically indigestible for Shakespeare, that he could "in this last analysis *make* nothing of" Brutus.

BRUTUS AND IRONIC SATIRE

Twenty years after Granville-Barker, in John Palmer's *Political Characters of Shakespeare* (1948), the critical emphasis has shifted so far that Brutus is pictured as an object of ironic satire. The point and tone are established in Palmer's opening sentence: "Brutus has precisely the qualities which in every age have rendered the conscientious liberal ineffectual in public life." His career in brief is a "course of action which could only be justified by principles which had ceased to be valid for the society in which he lived and which entangle him in unforeseen consequences with which he was unable to cope." The details of this unsuccessful career are worked out through a series of contrasts: "Cassius, Antony, Caesar and the Roman crowd are in turn his foils." Cassius' initial attitude toward him is "just that blend of admiration and contempt felt by the practical man of affairs for the man of principle." Palmer asks us to "compare the candid simplicity with which Cassius sees and admits the truth about himself with the confused thinking of Brutus and his sharp divorce from political reality." Brutus on the one hand is too easily moved by the letters thrown in at his window, and on the other hand his recoil from the conspiracy illustrates that the "fastidious contempt of the shameful means necessary to achieve his ends is the constant mark of a political idealist."

Palmer admits that Brutus is never more likable than in his scenes with Portia, but he adds deflatingly that it "requires no Shakespeare to discover that an ineffectual politician can be happy and enlightened in his domestic relationships. . . ." Having taken the plunge from private to public life, Brutus is "now to be shown as the professed, self-conscious stoic in action," and Shakespeare, according to Palmer, "warns us not to be deceived by the front of brass which his hero is about to assume after the high Roman fashion." After the assassination, Antony replaces Cassius as the foil who brings out Brutus' deficiencies. Brutus characteristically underrates Antony because of the very un-Brutus-like qualities of sociability (his "ready tongue and coarse humanity," his "genius in adapting himself to the moods of men") that mark him out as a most dangerous enemy, and all of this is fully demonstrated in the orations and the scenes with the mob.

The quarrel scene is read by Palmer as an illustration of his conviction that the essential business of Shakespeare's political plays "is to show how the private person comes to terms with his political duties, offices or ambitions, and the dramatic climax is always to be found when the protagonists come before us stripped of their public pretensions." The "high Roman fashion" in which Brutus reacts publicly to the news of Portia's death is in keeping with his double nature as it has been revealed step by step to this point: "Brutus may be playing a part, but it is one which springs from the fundamental lie in his character, the lie that impels him to substitute a public figure for the natural man, that requires him to kill Caesar in order to live up to assumed principles, that drives him to play the statesman when he has no mind or quality for the vocation, that prompts him to offer reason to a mob with which he has no common ground of temper or understanding—the lie that sooner or later is imposed on any idealist who enters public life and must use means which he despises to achieve ends which have no true bearing on the political realities about him." Palmer sees Brutus and Cassius blundering through the remaining action to inevitable defeat, "weary and desperate men" who "desire a swift conclusion." The defeat, however, is a kind of therapeutic release for Brutus from the lie of the double private-public role. He "accepts his fate with a tired and wistful resignation," but as he sheds his unnatural political role, he regains the "assurance . . . of the man who can still be happy in the loyalty of his friends," and we see again, too late, the gentle, private Brutus. The final effect is therefore one of pathos.

THE CHARACTER OF CAESAR

Many other essays on Brutus could be placed along the line which runs from MacCallum's Victorian stoic to Palmer's ineffectual liberal, and the same movement in criticism is to be found in discussions of other characters and aspects of the play. The character of Caesar is an obvious example. MacCallum acknowledges that Shakespeare depicts Caesar's weaknesses (his physical disabilities, his credulity, his self-deception, and his posing), but he concludes that the impression Caesar "makes on the unsophisticated mind, on average audiences and the elder school of critics, is undoubtedly an heroic one. It is only a minute analysis that discovers his defects, and though the defects are certainly present and should be noted, they are far from sufficing to make the general effect absurd or contemptible." Caesar's childlessness is one of the defects which MacCallum would have thought discoverable only by minute analysis, but it is dramatically obvious to recent critics. Maynard Mack, for example, prepares us to respond to Caesar's first speech (I.ii) with this question and answer: "As he starts to speak, an expectant hush settles over the gathering: what does the great man have on his mind. . . . What the great man had on his mind, it appears, was to remind his wife, in this public place, that she is sterile; that there is an old superstition about how sterility can be removed; and that while of course he is much too sophisticated to accept such a superstition himself—it is 'our elders' who say it—still, Calpurnia had jolly well better get out there and get tagged, or else!"

This new emphasis on a pathetic or defective Caesar alongside the older and more simply heroic Caesar (like the dual public and private Brutus) is interpreted by Ernest Schanzer in the following typically modern way: "the polarity of critical estimates of the characters of the main *dramatis personae* . . . bears witness to Shakespeare's success in making *Julius Caesar* a problem play." In fact Schanzer goes so far as to suggest that there are more than two Caesars, that "we are given a series of images of Caesar none of which bear much mutual resemblance," and that this multiplicity of images interacting with multiple meanings elsewhere serves the aim of the play by breeding problems in a Pirandellian fashion.

THE STRUCTURE OF THE PLAY

When modern critics turn from the parts of *Julius Caesar* to the play as a whole, they tend to find a structure which in its ironic contrasts parallels and supports the ambiguous, problem-breeding nature of the characters. Brents Stirling, for example, looking beyond character and plot to the basic organization of the play, finds a series of analogous scenes which have in common "the bringing of serious ritual into

great prominence, and of subjecting it to satirical treatment."
The central scene of this kind is the assassination, which
Brutus sets out to dignify by "lifting it to a level of rite and
ceremony," but which is obviously a murder rather than a
pure sacrifice. The opening scenes have prepared us to take
this ironic view of the assassination, because in them, too,
ceremony is mocked. In the second scene, for example, "a
multiple emphasis on ceremony is capped by Casca's satire
which twists the crown ritual into imbecile mummery." And
after the assassination, we are reminded of its flawed nature
not only by events but also by Antony's insistence on the
real butchery of the act. Leo Kirschbaum had earlier argued
against the critical tradition which since the eighteenth
century has tried to remove the blood from the assassination
scene, and particularly from the noble hands of Brutus.
Kirschbaum reminds us that Shakespeare "invented the
blood-bath, deliberately gave the proposal for it to Brutus,
and followed it with the invention of the bloody handshaking
action with Antony." Shakespeare, according to Kirschbaum, deliberately shocks us into seeing that all "murder
is in the act savage and inhuman," and that "whether or
not killing ever justifies the doctrine of a bad means serving
a good end, the merciless rending of a man is an obscene
performance."

The interpretation of the political pattern and meaning
of *Julius Caesar* has also moved in the direction of the problem play, although topical one-sided productions are still
probably best known. The recording of Orson Welles' 1937
version of the play as an attack against dictatorship (in
which Welles of course played Brutus) will give one a striking
sample of the democratic slanting of the assassination which
runs back to Hazlitt and has been recently re-emphasized
by Dover Wilson. The 1956–1957 Stratford (England) production, as described by Roy Walker, illustrates the conserv-
ative, Caesar-centered interpretation of which MacCallum
is one of the early twentieth-century spokesmen: "Shakespeare makes it abundantly clear that the rule of the single
master-mind is the only admissible solution for the problem
of the time." Accepting this interpretation, Glen Byam
Shaw raised the curtain on his Stratford production to

show a "larger-than-life statue of Caesar, raised on a tall plinth in the center of the stage"; and he lowered his final curtain on a scene in which the "dead body of the tragically deluded liberator lay in the center of the stage, not in Rome but in the wilderness he had helped to make of Rome, and high above him shone out the star of whose true-fixed and resting quality there is no fellow in the firmament."

The balance characteristic of the problem play is maintained, however, in L. C. Knights' interpretation of the political meaning. He extends the idea of the dual Brutus and the dual Caesar into the play's structure by stressing the contrasts it offers between the public world of politics and the occasional glimpses of personal life. "The distance between these two worlds," he suggests, "is the measure of the distortion and falsity that takes place in the attempt to make 'politics' self-enclosed." The attempt, Knights adds, is common to both sides: "Caesar constantly assumes the public mask," and "Brutus, who loved Caesar, wrenches his mind to divorce policy from friendship." The play's political lesson, therefore, is not partisan, since it tells us "that human actuality is more important than *any* political abstraction" whether from the left or the right.

CRITICISM AND CULTURAL CHANGE

As one reviews the interpretations of *Julius Caesar* from late Victorian times to the present, he is struck by the responsiveness of criticism to cultural change. That *Caesar* should now be read as a problem play does not seem surprising given our strong sense today of the theatricality of politics, our knowingness about the images and the image-makers of public life, our feeling that the real person is the one behind the mask, and our experience with a cold war reality of mixed right and wrong and of patched-up measures which breed more dilemmas. All of this raises an awkward question: to what extent are the critics reacting to the play and to what extent to their times? In trying to answer that question, we are obliged, fortunately, to go back to the play and rely on our own taste and skill. We may very well conclude that the high Roman thing in the play is frequently no better than stereotyped writing calling for a stock response. And we may also conclude, on the other hand, that some of the problems which recent critics have found in the play are simply the product of Shakespeare's uncertain control of tone. Where the tone is firmly controlled and the writing is truly dramatic, as in the quarrel scene between Brutus and Cassius, critics from Samuel Johnson to the present have responded unanimously in praising those effects which are as old as drama and which we now associate with the so-called problem play.

REFERENCES

1. Granville-Barker, H. "Julius Caesar," *Prefaces to Shakespeare,* II. Princeton University Press: 1947.

2. Kirschbaum, L. "Shakespeare's Stage Blood and Its Critical Significance," *PMLA,* LXIV (1949), 517–29.

3. Knights, L. C. "Shakespeare and Political Wisdom: A Note on the Personalism of *Julius Caesar* and *Coriolanus,*" *Sewanee Review,* LXI (1953), 43–55.

4. MacCallum, M. W. *Shakespeare's Roman Plays.* London: Macmillan & Co., 1910.

5. Mack, Maynard. "Teaching Drama: *Julius Caesar,*" *Essays on the Teaching of English,* ed. E. J. Gordon and E. S. Noyes. New York: Appleton-Century-Crofts, in cooperation with NCTE, 1960.

6. Palmer, John. "Marcus Brutus," *Political Characters of Shakespeare.* London: Macmillan & Co., 1948.

7. Schanzer, Ernest. "The Problem of *Julius Caesar,*" *Shakespeare Quarterly,* VI (1955), 297–308.

8. Stirling, Brents. "Or else were this a savage spectacle," *PMLA,* LXVI (1951), 765–74; slightly revised in: *Unity in Shakespearian Tragedy* (Columbia University Press, 1956); reprinted in *Shakespeare: Modern Essays in Criticism,* ed. L. F. Dean (Oxford University Press, 1957; Galaxy Book 46).

9. Van Doren, Mark. *Shakespeare* (1939). New York: Doubleday, 1955; Anchor Book A11.

10. Walker, Roy. "Unto Caesar: A Review of Recent Productions," *Shakespeare Survey 11.* Cambridge University Press, 1958.

R. A. FOAKES

An Approach to "Julius Caesar"

Julius Caesar has often been regarded as a difficult or
unsatisfactory play, and two problems in particular seem
to demand a solution, problems that do not even arise in the
discussion of many other plays by Shakespeare. The first
concerns what the play is about and in what sense, if any, it
has unity. The answers are varied: to one critic the play
remains simply a puzzle; to another it can only be understood in terms of *Antony and Cleopatra*, as the first part of
a two-part play; to a third it is a tragedy with Brutus as a
tragic hero. It has been seen as a play about tyranny, a play
about Rome, a play about Brutus and as a play about Caesar
and Caesarism; Caesar has been seen as the villain, and, so,
perhaps more plausibly, has Brutus; both have also been
seen as the hero. This diversity of views indicates the
complexities of the central problem, and suggests how rash
it may be to offer yet another possible answer.

The way to a solution may lie through a consideration of
the second problem, which concerns style and imagery.
Some have praised the clarity of style and sparing use of
metaphor as giving a dignified and Roman simplicity to
the play; others have condemned what they saw as a stiffness and baldness of diction. The analysis has not been
taken much further; in particular, writers on imagery have

From *Shakespeare Quarterly*, V (Summer, 1954), pp. 259–70. Reprinted
by permission of *Shakespeare Quarterly* and R. A. Foakes.

had little to say of *Julius Caesar;* Caroline Spurgeon found no leading image in it, and fewer images than in any other play of Shakespeare's except *The Comedy of Errors.*[1] Marion Smith found still fewer images in the play, and because of their extreme bareness assigned the last two acts to an author other than Shakespeare.[2] W. H. Clemen almost ignores the play in *The Development of Shakespeare's Imagery;* only G. Wilson Knight has something constructive to say incidentally to his comparison between Brutus and Macbeth.[3]

Style and poetic imagery have usually been analyzed as aspects of *Julius Caesar* detachable from the rest of the play, and it may be for this reason that the study of them has been so unrewarding on the whole. Even the acute stylistic criticism of Mark Van Doren assumes from the simplicity of style that the play is "more rhetoric than poetry," so that the characters are for him simply "public men."[4] This is perhaps to ignore the dramatic functions of the use of oratory and rhetoric in the play, just as to concentrate on metaphors may be to ignore the dramatic means by which the powerful atmosphere of the play is created.

As is usual in Shakespeare's plays, language and action continually interfuse; what is a metaphor, a statement or a hint in the language at one point, is acted out or enters directly into the scene at another. So the rhetoric often noted throughout the play becomes at the peak of its stiffness and artificiality in the orations of Brutus and Antony, the very life and center of the action. To examine imagery and language from a dramatic viewpoint, is also to examine the action and structure; a more positive approach to the second problem may suggest a solution to, or illuminate the answers already given to the first.

One of the most notable features of the dramatic imagery is the way in which the various themes are all used to suggest a full circle of events. A striking theme is that of the super-

---

[1] *Shakespeare's Imagery and What it Tells Us* (Cambridge, 1935), pp. 346–47.

[2] *Marlowe's Imagery and the Marlowe Canon* (Philadelphia, 1940), pp. 189–91.

[3] *The Wheel of Fire* (London, 1930), pp. 120–39.

[4] *Shakespeare* (London, 1941), pp. 180–81.

stition and omens which surround the main figures, ennoble
Caesar and add grandeur to his downfall; soothsayers enter
on four occasions, and Caesar's death and the commotion
which follows are foreshadowed in the long list of portents
preceding his downfall:

> all the sway of earth
> Shakes like a thing unfirm.
>
> (I.iii.3–4)

> Either there is a civil strife in heaven,
> Or else the world, too saucy with the gods,
> Incenses them to send destruction.
>
> (I.iii.11–13)

All the strange happenings and prodigies prove indeed to be

> instruments of fear and warning
> Unto some monstrous state.
>
> (I.iii.70–71)

The cries of the soothsayer, the advice of the augurers Caesar
consults before deciding to go to the Capitol, the dream of
Calphurnia, the prophecy of war Antony makes (III.i.262–
64), all prove true. Cinna is led against his will to walk out,
although "things unluckily charge my fantasy" (III.iii.2),
and is torn in pieces. Men ignore omens, as Cassius walks
boldly out daring the gods, or reject them, as Caesar is led
to reject the warning of Calphurnia's dream, only as a mark
of evil or of foolishness. Caesar unwisely listens to the plea
of Decius and goes to his death. Cassius shows his evil in
defying the heavens before Caesar's death, but at the end,
when crows and ravens replace the eagles flying with the
rebels' army, he learns to reject Epicurus' opinion

> And partly credit things that do presage
>
> (V.i.78)

following the example of Caesar, who, before his downfall,
had

> superstitious grown of late
> Quite from the main opinion he held once
> Of fantasy, of dreams and ceremonies.
>
> (II.i.195–97)

The wheel is brought full circle from Cassius' defiance of the gods to his acceptance finally of omens. It is noteworthy that Brutus accepts false omens, such as the message thrown in at his window (II.i.45ff.) as philosophically as he accepts the true portent of Caesar's ghost (IV.iii.275ff.).

The full circle is also implied in the early creation of a warlike atmosphere. In the opening scene the tribunes ask why Caesar should receive the people's support, returning as he does not with conquest, but "in triumph over Pompey's blood" (I.i.54), victor in a civil war. The portents before Caesar's death tell of the civil war to come (I.iii.19–20), and the incitement of Brutus to join the conspirators is expressed in terms of war,

> ... poor Brutus, with himself at war
>
> (I.ii.46)

>   the man entire
> Upon the next encounter yields him ours.
>
> (I.iii.155–56)

>   the state of man
> Like to a little kingdom, suffers then
> The nature of an insurrection.
>
> (II.i.67–69)

Antony foresees the "domestic fury and fierce civil strife" (III.i.263) which engrosses the final part of the action. So the civil war which brought Caesar to power begins an action which culminates in another civil war, and Cassius, who had been ready in rebellion to "tempt the heavens" (I.iii.53), is driven to suicide on the sword that stabbed Caesar.

The portents are connected with dreams[5] and sleep, the conspiracy with darkness. Sleep is denied the plotters; Caesar desires "Sleek-headed men and such as sleep o' nights" about him (I.ii.193), not men like Cassius. The message

[5] See II.ii.76ff.; III.iii.1ff.; I.ii.24; II.i.65; IV.iii.294.

thrown into Brutus's window, "Brutus, thou sleep'st; awake!" (II.i.48) is ironical in relation to his inability to sleep in fact:[6]

> Since Cassius first did whet me against Caesar,
> I have not slept.
>
> (II.i.61–62)

Nor does the death of Caesar bring sleep or peace, for his spirit haunts Brutus, in contrast to the sound sleep enjoyed by his boy, the innocent Lucius. Only in death may he find rest, and put to rest Caesar;

> Night hangs upon mine eyes; my bones would rest
>
> (V.v.41)

> Caesar, now be still.
>
> (V.v.50)

The first of these lines points another way in which the circle of events has been completed; the conspirators, men who "hide their faces Even from darkness" (II.i.277–78), have their day, begun in darkness turning to dawn as Casca points his sword to the sunrise,

> Here, as I point my sword, the sun arises.
>
> (II.i.106)

and ended in the return of darkness at the close of the battle,

> O setting sun,
> As in thy red rays thou dost sink to-night,
> So in his red blood Cassius' day is set;
> The sun of Rome is set! Our day is gone.
>
> (V.iii.60–63)

This passage is a culmination of two other themes in the play, blood[7] and fire. In the opening scene we hear that Caesar has come to Rome, "in triumph over Pompey's blood" (I.i.54), and soon that he too must bleed (II.i.171).

---

[6] Cf. also II.i.4, 88, 252.

[7] Shakespeare's use of blood on the stage here and in *Coriolanus* has been discussed by Leo Kirschbaum, "Shakespeare's Stage Blood and Its Critical Significance," *PMLA*, LXIV (June 1949), 517–29.

The portents include "fierce fiery warriors" which drizzle "blood upon the Capitol" (II.ii.19–21), and the sky is "most bloody, fiery, and most terrible" (I.iii.130). In these, and in Calphurnia's dream of Caesar's statue spouting blood, the welter of blood in the third act is foreshadowed. Caesar is stabbed under Pompey's statue which "all the while ran blood" (III.ii.191); the conspirators bathe their arms in blood, and Antony enters to shake each by "his bloody hand" (III.i.184). The body, the "bleeding piece of earth" (III.i.254), remains on the stage for the bigger part of Act III, while Antony displays the wounds in it to the crowd, stirs up men's bloods to mutiny and prophesies future "blood and destruction" (III.i.265). Finally, as Caesar had paid with his blood for shedding Pompey's, so the conspirators pay with their blood for shedding Caesar's (V.iii.62). Fire, connected with blood in the portents and represented in lightning,[8] comes home to the conspirators when Antony incites the mob to "burn the house of Brutus ... fire the traitors' houses" (III.ii.233, 257). The fire,[9] which is really started by the conspirators, returns to plague them at the end also, when Portia kills herself by swallowing fire (IV.iii.155), and just before Cassius dies with the red rays of the setting sun, he sees his own tents burning,

> Are those my tents where I perceive the fire?
>
> (V.iii.13)

The idea of sickness functions in a similar way in relation to the conspirators, besides its use to point the contrast between the public ideal and private human being that are Caesar.[10] Brutus puts forward sickness as an excuse for staying up all night and ignoring Portia,

> Is Brutus sick? and is it physical
> To walk unbraced and suck up the humors
> Of the dank morning? What, is Brutus sick,
> And will he steal out of his wholesome bed ... ?
>
> (II.i.261–64)

[8] See also I.iii.10, 15–18, 25, 50–51, 63; II.i.44–45.
[9] For other references to fire see I.ii.175–77, 186; I.iii.57–58, 107–08; II.i.109–10, 120–21, 332; II.ii.31; III.iii.37; IV.iii.110–12.
[10] See I.ii.119, 127–28, 252–54.

and there is a fine irony in the entrance of Ligarius, a sick man, who joins the conspirators crying "I here discard my sickness" (II.i.321), for they are to do

> *Brutus.* A piece of work that will make sick men whole.

> *Ligarius.* But are not some whole that we must make sick?
> (II.i.327–28)

There are some indeed, the conspirators themselves, for Brutus finds his pretended sickness real, that he has a "sick offense" within his mind (II.i.268), and Portia notices his sickly appearance (II.iv.13–14). Instead of making sick men well, the deed of the conspirators only produces further griefs, leading to dissension even between Brutus and Cassius

> When love begins to sicken and decay
> It useth an enforced ceremony.
>
> (IV.ii.20–21)

> O Cassius, I am sick of many griefs.
>
> (IV.iii.143)

and before the final battle birds of ill-omen

> Fly o'er our heads and downward look on us,
> As we were sickly prey,
>
> (V.i.86–87)

which indeed they have shown themselves to be.

The use of noise may also be noted; sounds of battle, confusion and thunder occur in the portents foreshadowing Caesar's death, when the bird of night sits "Hooting and shrieking" (I.iii.28) in broad daylight, and

> The noise of battle hurtled in the air,
> Horses did neigh, and dying men did groan,
> And ghosts did shriek and squeal about the streets.
>
> (II.ii.22–24)

This noise of battle returns at the end of the play, and as

Calphurnia cries out in her sleep before the death of Caesar
(II.ii.2), so Brutus' servants cry out in their sleep before his
death (IV.iii.303). There is dramatic completeness also in
one other use of sound; Brutus and the conspirators had
sought to free a Rome "groaning underneath this age's
yoke" (I.ii.61), and immediately after the death of Caesar
had proclaimed liberty about the streets (III.i.79). At the
end of the play in their last despairing stand they have
nothing left but their own names to proclaim "about the
field" (V.iv.3) in defeat; now the name, the honor is all
they have to live, or rather die for,

> I am Brutus, Marcus Brutus, I;
> Brutus, my country's friend; know me for Brutus!
>   (V.iv.7–8)

These various themes in language and action all suggest
a full circle of events in the play, civil war leading to civil
war, blood to blood, imaged in the beginning and close of
a day. They form a large part of the play's imaginative
framework, and perhaps indicate that the structural unity
of *Julius Caesar* lies in the birth and completion of the
rebellion. If this view is taken, there is no need to go beyond
the play into *Antony and Cleopatra* in order to explain it, to
see the spirit of Caesar as a fate against which Brutus strives
in vain, or to see the play as a kind of revenge tragedy.[11]

At the same time this view of the play as being about
faction, and the waste and destruction that attends it, calls
for a reassessment of the main characters. For Caesar,
Brutus, and Cassius, in spite of their different natures and
functions, are equal participants. The conspirators stand
up against the spirit of Caesar, which only finds rest in their
deaths, so that in a sense the death of Brutus and Cassius
is the death of Caesar also. These three figures share the
main action of the play, which culminates in their destruction; Antony and Octavius are left to provide continuity,
to suggest the life that carries on. In this main action, the

11 See J. E. Phillips Jr., *The State in Shakespeare's Greek and Roman Plays*
(1940), p. 174; J. Dover Wilson (ed.), *Julius Caesar* (New Cambridge
Edition, 1949), p. xxii; J. A. K. Thomson, *Shakespeare and the Classics*
(1952), pp. 204–05.

rebellion, Brutus does not appear a tragic hero, as he is so often made out to be, nor does Caesar appear a villain, a tyrant-dictator.[12] Brutus believes in an ideal, honor, but confuses it with treachery; Caesar maintains an ideal vision of himself as necessary to his position; Cassius uses the various ideals posited in the play to sway Brutus, to engineer Caesar's murder, and yet himself shares the ideals of liberty and of being a Roman. Brutus and Caesar as men do not measure up to the ideal, and Cassius proves to be nobler than a manipulator, than a mere sketch for Iago.

Once again an examination of the use of language in relation to action amplifies this analysis. The use of rhetoric in the play has often been noticed; repetition, balanced phrasing, formal apostrophes and similes, give a "public" quality to much of the verse, culminating in the orations, which stand out from their context, yet are harmonious with it. By its nature the verse helps to point the contrast between the public figure and the private man. In addition it is hinted that the major characters are acting when in public, notably when Brutus tells the conspirators

> Let not our looks put on our purposes,
> But bear it as our Roman actors do,
> With untired spirits and formal constancy,
>
> (II.i.225–27)

and when, immediately after the murder, Cassius and Brutus in turn speak of the times "this our lofty scene" shall be "acted over" in the future, and Caesar shall "bleed in sport" (III.i.111ff.).

A more individual rhetorical feature is the device of speaking in the third person, as in Brutus's oration:

> Brutus' love to Caesar was no less than his. If then that friend demand why Brutus rose against Caesar. . . .
>
> (III.ii.19–21)

---

[12] J. Dover Wilson sought to prove that this was the traditional view of Caesar in his New Cambridge edition, but the arguments against have been well put by D. S. Brewer, " 'Brutus' Crime': A footnote to *Julius Caesar*," *R.E.S. New Series*, 111 (January 1952), 51–54.

This device puts a distance between the speaker and what he is saying, makes his words impersonal,[13] and it is a feature of Caesar's speeches that he speaks in this way:

> Speak; Caesar is turn'd to hear.
>
> (I.ii.17)

> Yet Caesar shall go forth; for these predictions
> Are to the world in general as to Caesar.
>
> (II.ii.28–29)

> Caesar should be a beast without a heart,
> If he should stay at home today for fear.
> No, Caesar shall not: danger knows full well
> That Caesar is more dangerous than he.
>
> (II.ii.42–45)

> Shall Caesar send a lie?
>
> (II.ii.65)

Caesar speaks in this way even in conversation with Calphurnia, but the contrast between the public figure, the name, the ideal, "know, Caesar doth not wrong" (III.i.47), Caesar on whose face "things that threaten'd" dare not look (II.ii.10), Caesar as "unshaked of motion" (III.i.70), constant as the northern star (III.i.60), and the private citizen, Caesar as deaf, subject to the falling-sickness, inclined to be superstitious, continually appears:

> I rather tell thee what is to be fear'd
> Than what I fear; for always I am Caesar.
>
> (I.ii.211–12)

The other important characters, especially Brutus and Cassius, speak sometimes in a similar way, as in the following examples:

13 It is notable that Brutus, who maintains his dignity and distance in his oration, uses the device, but Antony, who descends from the pulpit, mingles with the crowd, and pretends to be a "plain, blunt man" in contrast to the "orator" Brutus (III.ii.219–20), speaks in his own person. Professor Allardyce Nicoll, to whom I am indebted for his advice, points out that this device is used in other plays, as by Othello (III.iii.; V.ii.) and Hamlet (I.v.; V.ii.). In these plays it occurs infrequently and for special purposes, but emphasis on the worth of a name is by no means confined to *Julius Caesar*.

Brutus had rather be a villager ...

(I.ii.172)

You speak to Casca, and to such a man ...

(I.iii.116)

Cassius from bondage will deliver Cassius

(I.iii.90)

To see thy Antony making his peace ...

(III.i.197)

Revenge yourselves alone on Cassius,
For Cassius is aweary of the world

(IV.iii.93–94)

    think not, thou noble Roman,
That ever Brutus will go bound to Rome.

(V.i.110–11)

Names are thus important in themselves, being marks of
the lineage and standing of a character, and indicating the
qualities and virtues the character ought to have, though
not necessarily those he actually possesses. So Caesar does
not fear Cassius,

    Yet if my name were liable to fear,

(I.ii.199)

he would avoid no man sooner; Caesar may be afraid in
himself, but his name, his reputation must be impervious
to fear. Cassius incites Brutus by comparing his name with
Caesar's,

Brutus and Caesar: what should be in that Caesar?
Why should that name be sounded more than yours?
Write them together, yours is as fair a name;
Sound them, it doth become the mouth as well;
Weigh them, it is as heavy; conjure with 'em,
Brutus will start a spirit as soon as Caesar.

(I.ii.142–47)

and by throwing papers in at his window speaking of the
"great opinion That Rome holds of his name" (I.ii.318ff.).

Before the battle Brutus quarrels with Cassius over a question of bribery,

> The name of Cassius honors this corruption.
>
> (IV.iii.15)

The importance of a man's name is shown vividly when the plebeians seize Cinna the poet in spite of his protests,

> *Cinna.* I am not Cinna the conspirator.
>
> *4th Citizen.* It is no matter, his name's Cinna; pluck but his name out of his heart, and turn him going.
>
> (III.iii.32–35)

So the soldiers who capture Lucillius take the name he gives, Brutus, for the person; the name and the ideal, the reputation and the person, are identified in public, but the differences between them are clear to the audience; Caesar the man is less powerful than his name, and Brutus less honorable than his reputation, or his great ancestry,

> There was a Brutus once that would have brook'd
> The eternal devil to keep his state in Rome
>
> (I.ii.159–60)

> My ancestors did from the streets of Rome
> The Tarquin drive, when he was call'd a king,
>
> (II.i.53–54)

and the crowd's shout "Give him a statue with his ancestors" (III.ii.51) after Brutus's funeral speech carries irony. The contrast is apparent also in the character of Portia, who proudly calls herself

> A woman well reputed, Cato's daughter,
>
> (II.i.295)

yet has to confess in private that she is after all but a weak woman (II.iv.39).

The names of Caesar (211 times), Brutus (130 times), and to a much lesser degree Cassius (69 times) and Antony (68

times) echo through the play,[14] and are used frequently
where a pronoun would occur in the other tragedies. Besides
contributing to the formality and dignity of the play, the
names of Caesar and Brutus in particular have their own
special meanings. The word Caesar had long been in use to
signify an all-conquering, absolute monarch,[15] and is used
in the play with this implication:

> *3rd Citizen.* Let him be Caesar.
>
> *4th Citizen.*   Caesar's better parts
>   Shall be crown'd in Brutus.
>
> (III.ii.52–53)

Caesar is kingly: at the beginning of the play a crown is
offered to him three times, and later it is reported

>   The senators to-morrow
> Mean to establish Caesar as a king;
> And he shall wear his crown by sea and land.
>
> (I.iii.85–87)

>   The Senate have concluded
> To give this day a crown to mighty Caesar.
>
> (II.ii.93–94)

The main motive for Brutus' rebellion is that Caesar "would
be crown'd" (II.i.12ff.); Caesar is like a lion, the king of

---

[14] A comparison with other plays perhaps emphasizes this importance
of names; in *Hamlet*, a very much longer play, the hero's name occurs 85
times according to Bartlett's *Concordance*, in *Macbeth* 42 times, *Othello*
34 times, *Coriolanus* 43 times (30 as Coriolanus; 13 as Caius or Caius
Marcius). It may be significant also that in *Antony and Cleopatra*, where
the spirit of Caesar is again prominent, names are also prominent, the
name of Antony occurring in 116 passages, and that of Caesar (Octavius
and Julius) in 152 passages. This again is a much longer play than *Julius
Caesar*, and the repetition of names here seems to be a special feature.

[15] Especially in the form "kaiser," see *Oxford English Dictionary* "kaiser"
b, where uses are recorded from 1225 onwards, especially in the phrase
"king or kaiser"; see also *Oxford English Dictionary* "Caesar" 2 and 2b.
Shakespeare elsewhere uses "Caesar" in a generic sense, cf. *3 Henry VI*,
III.i., "No bending knee will call thee Caesar now," and *Merry Wives*, I.iii.

beasts, among the herd of Romans (I.iii.106) and more
dangerous than danger,[16]

> We are two lions litter'd in one day.
>
> (II.ii.46)

This "royal Caesar" (III.ii.246), whom Brutus had wished
to kill only in spirit, in name

> O that we then could come by Caesar's Spirit,
> And not dismember Caesar! But alas,
> Caesar must bleed for it!
>
> (II.i.169–71)

lives on in spirit after his death, and as Antony forecasts,

> Caesar's spirit, ranging for revenge,
> With Ate by his side come hot from hell,
> Shall in these confines with a monarch's voice
> Cry "Havoc," and let slip the dogs of war.
>
> (III.i.270–73)

Besides this linkage with royalty,[17] Caesar's name and the
presence of his dead body on the stage during much of Act
III, suggest the presence of Caesar's spirit, although the
character has only about 130 in a play of about 2,500 lines.
The conspirators "stand up against the spirit of Caesar"
(II.i.167) in order to kill him, but are vanquished by that
spirit, embodied in the ghost that visits Brutus, and represented in the iteration of the name,

> O Julius Caesar, thou art mighty yet!
> Thy spirit walks abroad, and turns our swords
> In our own proper entrails.
>
> (V.iii.94–96)

[16] It is notable that all the references to lions, in relation to Caesar, or as
portents, or in imagery, occur in the early part of the play, before Caesar's
death; see II.ii.17; I.iii.75; II.i.206. Perhaps it is not going too far to
associate Caesar with the "lion in the Capitol" (I.iii.75), and with Casca's
> Against the Capitol I met a lion
> Who glared upon me, and went surly by,
> Without annoying me (I.iii.20–22)

[17] The last ironical echo of crowning and kingliness comes in the final
scenes when a victor's wreath is placed upon the head of the dead Cassius
> Look, whether he have not crown'd dead Cassius! (V.iii.97)

Only on the death of Brutus may Caesar "now be still" (V.v.50).

The name of Brutus has connections already noticed with distinguished ancestors, and also, more prominently, with honor. This is particularly noticeable in the famous lines of Antony's funeral oration, the repeated "Brutus is an honorable man" (III.ii.84), but on his first appearance Brutus says

> Set honor in one eye and death i' the other,
> And I will look on both indifferently,
> For let the gods so speed me as I love
> The name of honor more than I fear death.

> (I.ii.86–89)

The "name of honor" is frequently attributed to him, not least by himself, as when he tells his audience in his oration, "Believe me for mine honor, and have respect to mine honor, that you may believe" (III.ii.14–16), blames Cassius for selling "the mighty space of our large honors" (IV.iii.25), and proudly tells Octavius that he could not die "more honorable" (V.i.60) than on the sword of Brutus. The name of Brutus is equated with honor, and it is appropriate and sufficient for Lucillius to say to the enemy

> When you do find him, or alive or dead,
> He will be found like Brutus, like himself.

> (V.iv.24–25)

The names of Caesar and Brutus thus have symbolic qualities, and represent a concept as well as an individual character. Two other names which have much importance are that of Rome and Roman (72 times in the play), and the name of liberty. The fact that he is a Roman should in itself indicate certain qualities in a man:

> those sparks of life
> That should be in a Roman you do want

> (I.iii.57–58)

> what other bond
> Than secret Romans, that have spoke the word,
> And will not palter?

> (II.i.124–26)

> every drop of blood
> That every Roman bears, and nobly bears,
> Is guilty of a several bastardy,
> If he do break the smallest particle
> Of any promise . . .

(II.i.136–40)

> . . . show yourselves true Romans

(II.i.223)

> Who is here so rude that would not be a Roman?

(III.ii.31–32)

> If that thou be'st a Roman, take it forth.

(IV.iii.102)

> *Brutus.* Now, as you are a Roman, tell me true.
> *Messenger.* Then like a Roman bear the truth I tell.

(IV.iii.186–87)

There is a contrast between the Roman ideal and Romans
in action, as is seen in the behavior of the conspirators and
the plebeians, similar to that between the ideal and the
living person represented in Caesar and Brutus. However,
it is in the Roman tradition ("this is a Roman's part,"
V.iii.89) that Brutus and Cassius commit suicide rather
than be taken prisoner, and it is significant that after the
end of Act III the words "Rome" and "Roman" occur only
in the mouths of the rebels until the final tribute of Antony
to Brutus

> This was the noblest Roman of them all.

(V.v.68)

The conspirators, especially Brutus and Cassius, associate
themselves with Rome as the home of truth, honor, liberty,
and manliness;[18] it is by suggesting that Romans are slaves

---

[18] The concept of manliness is enhanced by contrast with women as
characters and in imagery. So Calphurnia fears for Caesar and Portia, in
spite of her boast that she is "Cato's daughter," and stronger than her sex
(II.i.292ff.), has to confess later

> How weak a thing
> The heart of woman is! (II.iv.39–40)

Among the sights seen on the eve of Caesar's murder are women "transformed with their fear" (I.iii.22-24); for other references to the weakness,
rashness or "melting spirits" of women, cf. I.iii.83-84; II.i.120-22; IV.iii.
119-22.

that Cassius incites Brutus to rebel (I.ii.150ff.; I.iii.103ff.),
it is for Rome, "O Rome, I make thee promise" (II.i.56),
that Brutus joins the conspiracy, and he is conscious of the
duties of being a Roman,

> I had rather be a dog, and bay the moon,
> Than such a Roman.

(IV.iii.27–28)

Romans are free-men, to whom Pompey and Caesar bring
slaves, and whose servants are bond-men,

> What tributaries follow him to Rome
> To grace in captive bonds his chariot wheels?

(I.i.36–37)

> He hath brought many captives home to Rome

(III.ii.90)

> Who is here so base that would be a bondman?

(III.ii.29–30)

> Go show your slaves how choleric you are,
> And make your bondmen tremble.

(IV.iii.43–44)

It is in the name of freedom that Brutus is persuaded to join
the conspiracy against Caesar; Cassius speaks of "groaning
underneath this age's yoke" (I.ii.61), but he will deliver
himself from bondage, even by that last resort, suicide
(I.iii.90–95); the Romans are slaves, and Caesar would be
no tyrant, "no lion, were not Romans hinds" (I.iii.106). So
after the murder of Caesar the conspirators proclaim
"Liberty, freedom and enfranchisement" (III.i.78, 81, 110)
and in future ages they shall be called "the men that gave
our country liberty" (III.i.118). In his speech from the pulpit
Brutus pleads that the death of Caesar has brought liberty,

> Had you rather Caesar were living, and die all slaves, than
> that Caesar were dead, to live all free men?

(III.ii.23–24)

Yet just before they stab Caesar, the conspirators who so
eagerly stand up for freedom fawn upon him with "low-
crooked court'sies" (III.i.43), and as Antony later says,
"bow'd like bondmen, kissing Caesar's feet" (V.i.42). Instead of greater liberty, there are proscriptions and "bills
of outlawry" (IV.i; IV.iii.172ff.) in Rome, and Brutus and
his friends are forced to chance "upon one battle all our
liberties" (V.i.75). Finally Cassius is driven to seek freedom
in suicide; Brutus too, who had said he would never "go
bound to Rome" (V.i.111), kills himself, and Strato can
reply to Messala's question "Where is thy master?"

> Free from the bondage you are in, Messala.
>
> (V.v.54)

Through this emphasis on names and ideals a continual
contrast is drawn between belief and action. Caesar feels
he must act in accordance with his name, his royalty, the
public ideal, and goes to his death. Brutus believes it is in
accordance with his name of honor, and the reputation of
his great ancestor who drove Tarquin from Rome (II.i.53ff.)
that he should try to kill the name of Caesar, Caesar's
royalty, although he knows that

> the quarrel
> Will bear no color for the thing he is.
>
> (II.i.28–29)

He acts in the name of one ideal to destroy another, but the
action is dishonorable, and the ideal of liberty, an illusion.
Cassius too acts and incites Brutus in the name of liberty,
but in destroying Caesar the conspirators are not destroying
tyranny, for Caesar is no tyrant, but rather the force of
order in Rome. The murder is preceded by bodings of disorder in the portents, and followed by still greater disorder,
embodied dramatically in the mob that shouts and clamors
equally for Pompey, Caesar, Brutus, and Antony, and tears
Cinna to pieces simply because of his name; his death is the
first of many,

These many, then, shall die; their names are prick'd.

(IV.i.1)

The conspirators also believe in the name of Rome and Roman as indicating qualities of manliness, and the ability to control passion; and again, though they act in the name of Rome, action and ideal fail to correspond, as we see in the bickering of the quarrel scene, and as the behavior of the mob continually shows.

This study of the dramatic purposes for which language and imagery are used in *Julius Caesar* suggests solutions for the problems both of style and diction and of the nature and unity of the play. The imagery of words and action points to the imaginative and dramatic unity of the play as consisting in the completion of the circle of events beginning and ending the rebellion. The action of the play turns on the distance between the ideals and public symbols for which the names of Caesar, Brutus, and Cassius, stand, and their true nature and actions. The three main figures are all noble and yet weak; none has the stature of hero or villain. Brutus and Cassius kill the man Caesar and not his spirit, not what he stands for, what they aim to destroy; it is a treacherous and dishonorable act which brings disorder, loss of the liberty they had sought, and finally civil war. All they had hoped to gain they lose, until they have nothing left but their names, and the opportunity to die bravely, to find freedom in suicide;

I will proclaim my name about the field.

(V.iv.3)

Only by their deaths do they set at rest the spirit, the name of Caesar which they had sought to destroy. Their personal action is completed in this way, a tale of frustration and disorder which spreads outwards to involve the mob, the whole nation in civil destruction. All is the result of a self-deception, an obsession with names and an ignorance of reality, that could lead Brutus to think he was acting honorably in slaying his "best lover" (III.ii.46), and Cassius to think the death of one man would bring freedom.

ERNEST SCHANZER

The Problem of "Julius Caesar"

Julius Caesar is one of Shakespeare's most perplexing plays. Its stylistic simplicity, coupled with an absence of bawdy lines, has made it a favorite school text, and this has led some critics to believe that it ought to be a simple play, a belief which has easily ripened into the conviction that it *is* a simple play. Others have acknowledged its perplexities. Professor Allardyce Nicoll calls it one of Shakespeare's "most difficult plays rightly to assess,"[1] and Mr. Wilson Knight remarks that "to close analysis it reveals subtleties and complexities which render interpretation difficult."[2] There is widespread disagreement among critics about who is the play's principal character or whether it has a principal character, on whether it is a tragedy and if so whose, on whether Shakespeare wants us to consider the assassination as damnable or praiseworthy, while of all the chief characters in the play violently contradictory interpretations have been offered. To illustrate this polarity of views it will be sufficient to refer to two eminent critics. Professor Dover Wilson tells us that in this play Shakespeare adopted the traditional Renaissance view of Caesar, derived from Lucan, which regarded him as "a Roman Tamburlaine of illimitable ambition and ruthless irresistible genius; a monstrous tyrant

From *Shakespeare Quarterly*, VI (Summer, 1955), pp. 297–308. Reprinted by permission of *Shakespeare Quarterly* and Ernest Schanzer.
[1] Allardyce Nicoll, *Shakespeare*, p. 134.
[2] G. Wilson Knight, *The Imperial Theme*, p. 63.

who destroyed his country and ruined 'the mightiest and most flourishing commonwealth that the world will ever see.' "[3] "The play's theme is the single one, Liberty versus Tyranny" (p. xxi). The assassination is wholly laudable, the conspirators are unselfish champions of freedom, while Brutus' tragedy consists in his vain struggle against the destiny of Rome, which lies in the establishment of Caesarism (p. xxii).

When we turn from this to Sir Mark Hunter's interpretation of the play, we are told that "there can be no doubt that to Shakespeare's way of thinking, however much he extends sympathy to the perpetrators of the deed, the murder of Julius was the foulest crime in secular history." Of Caesar we learn, "When put to the test of the stage the personality of Julius 'moves before us as something right royal,' a character sufficiently great to render the impassioned eulogy of Antony and the calm tribute of Brutus not inconsistent with what we have actually heard and seen of the object of their praise." Of the conspirators we are told, "Brutus excepted, there is no sign anywhere that the enemies of the Dictator, though they have all the political catchwords at command—Liberty, Enfranchisement, etc.—care one jot for the welfare of anyone outside their own order." And of Brutus, "Noble-hearted and sincere beyond question, Brutus is intellectually dishonest," he is self-righteous, pathetically inconsistent, a "befogged and wholly mischievous politician."[4]

Thus, while Dover Wilson roots the play in the dominant literary tradition of the Renaissance, which is overwhelmingly hostile to Caesar, Sir Mark Hunter, with equal confidence, places it in the dominant medieval tradition, which is wholly eulogistic. In this he is supported by so great an authority as W. W. Fowler, who tells us that Shakespeare's idea of Caesar "was simply an inheritance from the education of the Middle Ages," when the textbook for Roman History was that of Orosius, who brings out the greatness and moderation of Caesar and the cruel injustice of the

[3] *Julius Caesar* (New Cambridge edition), p. xxv.
[4] *Trans. Royal Soc. Lit.*, X (1931), 136 ff.

assassination.[5] The reader of Shakespeare's play is thus faced with a difficult choice. Is he to throw in his lot with Professor Dover Wilson and Cassius, and regard Shakespeare's Caesar as a boastful tyrant, strutting blindly to his well-merited doom, and the assassination as a glorious act of liberation, or is he to follow Sir Mark Hunter and Mark Antony, and look at him as "the noblest man that ever lived in the tide of times," and at the assassination as a hideous crime? Fortunately for the less resolute spirits there is a third tradition in relation to which the play may be viewed, made up of writers whose reaction to Caesar and the conspiracy is not simple and undivided, like that of Lucan and Orosius, but of a complex and sometimes bafflingly contradictory nature.

Among these writers are above all Plutarch, Shakespeare's main source; Appian, with whose *Roman History* Shakespeare was probably acquainted in the 1578 translation; Suetonius; Dante; and a number of Renaissance writers, among them the author of the anonymous play entitled *Caesar's Revenge*, which, as I have argued elsewhere,[6] was probably one of the chief formative influences upon Shakespeare's play. The reasons for their divided attitude to the Caesar story vary, of course, a good deal among the different writers. With Plutarch it seems to result largely from a personal dislike of Caesar's character, coupled with a belief in him as the Man of Destiny "whom God had ordained of special grace to be Governor of the Empire of Rome, and to set all things again at quiet stay, the which required the counsel and authority of an absolute Prince."[7] And much the same seems to me to hold true of Dante's attitude. Plutarch's view of the conspirators is also complicated by a desire to show "his angel" Brutus as the only just man among the wicked, joined with a reluctance to accept the conclusion that Brutus chose other than honest men for his associates. Plutarch is thus driven to alternate between blackening and whitewashing the character of Brutus'

[5] W. W. Fowler, *Roman Essays and Interpretations*, p. 273.

[6] *Notes and Queries*, New Series, I, 5 (1954).

[7] *Tudor Translations*, ed. W. E. Henley, XII, 237. ("Comparison of Dion with Brutus.")

fellow conspirators. Appian's divided attitude seems to arise mainly from a mingling of admiration for Brutus and Cassius, "two most noble and illustrious Romans, and of incomparable virtue, but for one crime," and an abhorrence of their foul deed of murder. "Yet by these men the act against Caesar was done, contrary in all thing, being no simple work, nor in no small matter, for it was against their friend, contrary to reason, and against their well doer, unthankfully, whom he had saved in the war, and against the chief ruler, injustly in the Senate house, and against an holy man, having on an holy vesture; and such an officer, as never was the like, so profitable to all men and to his country and Empire. The which God did punish in them, and many times gave tokens of it."[8] (Had Shakespeare this passage at the back of his mind when he made Macbeth, contemplating the murder of Duncan, recoil at the threefold violation of sacred relationships, that of kinsman, subject, and host, and declare that Duncan had been "So clear in his great office, that his virtues/Will plead like angels, trumpet-tongued, against/The deep damnation of his taking-off"? [I.vii]) The divided attitude in *Caesar's Revenge* issues largely from the author's attempt to combine Appian's presentation of the Caesar story, which seems to have served as his chief source, with that of the French Senecan plays of Muret, Garnier, and Grévin, which makes him both depict Caesar as a thrasonical, infatuated world-conqueror, and show Brutus driven to despair and suicide through the burden of guilt incurred by having murdered his friend and benefactor.

It is to this tradition of a divided, complex, and often ambiguous response to the Caesar story that Shakespeare's play belongs. But with Shakespeare, as I hope to show, this ambiguity and divided response, however much it may also be a reflection of his own feelings, is used as a deliberate dramatic device, and is no mere accidental inheritance from his sources. It seems highly likely that Shakespeare's own attitude to the Caesar story underwent a complete change as a result of his reading of Plutarch. His earlier response

[8] Appian, *Roman History*, 1578 translation, p. 303.

appears to have been much like that of his medieval ancestors and was probably also that of the great mass of the people of England who had heard of Caesar at all. To them he was one of the Nine Worthies, the great warrior hero, and his murderers were damnable villains. This view is above all expressed in the *Henry VI* plays.

> A far more glorious star thy soul will make
> Than Julius Caesar or bright——

Bedford says of the dead Henry V (*1 Henry VI*, I.i)

> They that stabb'd Caesar shed no blood at all,
> Did not offend, nor were not worthy blame,
> If this foul deed were by to equal it

Queen Margaret exclaims at the murder of her son (*3 Henry VI*, V.v); while Suffolk tells his assassins:

> Great men oft die by vile besonians:
> A Roman sworder and banditto slave
> Murder'd sweet Tully; Brutus' bastard hand
> Stabb'd Julius Caesar.
>
> > (*2 Henry VI*, IV.i.)

Added to this popular view of Caesar we find the knowledge of him as the writer of commentaries, a man of learning and wit. "Kent, in the commentaries Caesar wrote,/Is term'd the civil'st place," we learn in *2 Henry VI*, IV.vii. And in *Richard III* Prince Edward admiringly exclaims,

> That Julius Caesar was a famous man;
> With what his valor did enrich his wit,
> His wit set down to make his valor live:
> Death makes no conquest of this conqueror;
> For now he lives in fame, though not in life.
>
> > (III.i.)

After this the tone and content of the Caesar references change. In *As You Like It* Rosalind speaks jestingly of

"Caesar's thrasonical brag of 'I came, saw, and overcame,'"
and Falstaff makes a similar allusion at his capture of
Coleville (2 *Henry IV*, IV.iii). Cloten speaks of "Caesar's
ambition/Which swell'd so much that it did almost stretch/
The sides o' the world" (*Cymbeline*, III.i). We hear no more
of Caesar's valor, glory, or wit, but a good deal of his
fabulous military skill (*All's Well*, III.vi; *Othello*, II.iii;
Cymbeline, III.i). The references to Caesar and Brutus in
the earlier plays are also of value in indicating what must
have been the attitude to the Caesar story of at least a
considerable portion of the audience. If the majority of the
spectators at the performance of *3 Henry VI* had in fact felt
that the murderers of Caesar "did not offend, nor were not
worthy blame," Queen Margaret's comparison would, to
say the least, be ill chosen. In the same way Bedford's
hyperbole would be a mere lapse into bathos unless a large
part of the audience were in sympathy with the medieval
apotheosis of Caesar. But there must have been other members of the audience, readers of Lucan and Plutarch, who,
a few years later, could respond to Shakespeare's sympathetic presentation of Brutus in *Julius Caesar*, without the
interference of preconceptions about Brutus' bastard hand
that stabbed his friend and benefactor. And there were
probably others, readers of Plutarch, Appian, and Suetonius,
who were divided in their attitude, and who had not made
up their minds. It is this variety and division of views
among his audience which, as it seems to me, Shakespeare
deliberately exploited.

I propose to begin with a discussion of Shakespeare's
presentment of the character of Caesar. Its nature will be
seen most clearly by being rapidly followed scene by scene,
from the opening of the play until Antony's funeral oration.

In Flavius and Marullus we get our first glimpses of the
republican opposition to Caesar's rule. Loyalty to Pompey's
memory as well as fear of future oppression seem their chief
motives. The metaphor which Flavius uses to justify their
"disrobing" of Caesar's images strikes an ominous note:

> These growing feathers plucked from Caesar's wing
> Will make him fly an ordinary pitch,

Who else would soar above the view of men
And keep us all in servile fearfulness.

(I.i.75–78)

It points forward to the image of the serpent's egg applied
to Caesar in Brutus' soliloquy. There a more drastic opera-
tion is advocated, but in both cases the action is thought of
as preventive, directed not against what Caesar is but what
he may become if not checked in time. Both images are
probably indebted to a passage in Plutarch's "Life of
Caesar," where his favorite equestrian metaphor is used to
convey the same thought: "But in fine, when they had thus
given him the bridle to grow to this greatness, and that they
could not then pull him back, though indeed in sight it
would turn one day to the destruction of the whole state
and commonwealth of Rome: too late they found, that
there is not so little a beginning of anything, but continuance
of time will soon make it strong, when through contempt
there is no impediment to hinder the greatness."[9] Immediately upon Flavius' words Caesar makes his first appearance,
and the imaginative impact of this short scene tends to bear
out rather than to discredit Flavius' fears. With the utmost
economy of words Shakespeare manages to create the
atmosphere of an oriental court with its cringing attendants
and fawning favorites. "Peace, ho! Caesar speaks." "When
Caesar says 'do this' it is performed." And into this atmosphere intrudes the first of the many warnings that come ever
thicker as the moment of the murder approaches, and like
all the others it is contemptuously brushed aside by Caesar.
"He is a dreamer, let us leave him: pass."

From this slow-moving and portentous scene we pass at
once to the rapid, feverish, and impassioned utterances of
Cassius in his great seduction scene. The contrast which
Cassius draws between Caesar's physical defects, which
make him succumb in a swimming match and shake when
suffering from a fever fit, and the greatness of his position,
is part of a general contrast, pervading the whole play,
between Caesar's frailties of body and character and the
strength of his spirit which has enabled him to become "the

9 P. 5. All page references in the article are to *Shakespeare's Plutarch*, ed.
Tucker Brooke, 2 vols., in the *Shakespeare's Library* series.

foremost man of all the world." Cassius is genuinely perplexed by this contrast. He is like a schoolboy who is puzzled and angry that someone whom he has always beaten at games should have become prefect and exact obedience from his physical equals and superiors.

> Now, in the names of all the gods at once,
> Upon what meat doth this our Caesar feed,
> That he is grown so great?

> (I.ii.148–50)

Contrary to his intention, Cassius does not throw doubt on Caesar's courage, but unwittingly testifies to it. It is the fever fit that makes Caesar shake, not the prospect of jumping into "the troubled Tiber chafing with her shores." The story of the swimming match epitomizes the triumph of Caesar's daring and resolution over his physical frailties.

It is significant that in this crucial scene, where Cassius can be expected to make the most of the opposition's case against Caesar, he makes no mention of any specific acts of oppression or tyrannical behavior. There is only the general assertion that Rome is "groaning underneath this age's yoke." But the yoke to Cassius lies in one man's usurpation of the honors and powers that previously belonged to many. To him the yoke is therefore very much an existing reality, whereas to Brutus the threat lies not in present but in impending conditions.

> Brutus had rather be a villager
> Than to repute himself a son of Rome
> Under these hard conditions as this time
> Is like to lay upon us

> (I.ii.172–75)

he tells Cassius in this scene. And in his soliloquy it is again not what Caesar *is* but what he may *become* that causes his fears.

What, then, is the effect of this scene upon our mental picture of Caesar? It heightens, rather than alters, our previous impression of him as an oriental monarch, a Colossus, and begins the process, continuing through much of the play, of disjoining and contrasting the human and the superhuman Caesar, the man with his physical and moral frailties and the God who is beyond human frailties. Caesar, by constantly putting himself outside the pale of humanity, collaborating, as Mr. John Palmer so well puts it,[10] in his own deification, yet reminding us of his frailties on each of his appearances, underlines this dissociation. In the very next episode we find him angry at the mob's opposition to his acceptance of the crown, afraid of Cassius, yet assuring Antony

> I rather tell thee what is to be feared
> Than what I fear; for always I am Caesar.

And at once follows the body-spirit contrast:

> Come on my right hand, for this ear is deaf
> And tell me truly what thou think'st of him.
>
> (I.ii.213–14)

As Dover Wilson points out (p. 113), the atmosphere is again that of the oriental court. When Caesar is angry "all the rest look like a chidden train." In his remarks about Cassius we get our chief glimpse of the Caesar we know from Plutarch, the shrewd politician, the keen observer of men, the Caesar of the Commentaries.

In Casca's narration of the day's events a new Caesar is revealed to us, again with Plutarchian traits, Caesar the play actor, skillfully exploiting the passions of the mob. While his fall in the market place is a sort of preview of his later fall in the Capitol, his adroit play upon the feelings of the mob adumbrates Antony's manipulation of them in his funeral oration. Casca's report ends on an ominous note, which, for the moment, makes the worst fears of the enemies of Caesar seem justified: "Marullus and Flavius, for pulling scarfs off Caesar's images, are put to silence." Not deprived of their tribuneship, as in Plutarch, but simply, cryptically, "put to silence."

Up to this point Shakespeare has tipped the balance in favor of the conspirators' view of Caesar and has made us

10 John Palmer, *Shakespeare's Political Characters*, p. 37.

share Brutus' apprehensions. Now, by making Cassius, in his soliloquy, so frankly impugn the integrity of his own motives and show us so clearly the personal nature of his opposition, we are brought to question the truth of our impression of Caesar, so much of which we have received through Cassius. And our doubts are strengthened by the play's next image of Caesar, again drawn by Cassius, this time for the terror-stricken Casca. For Cassius' picture of Caesar and his explanation of the portents is clearly part of an *argumentum ad hominem*. Cassius himself is an Epicurean and does not, at least not yet, "credit things that do presage." But to convince Casca, who does credit them, of the monstrosity of Caesar's rule, he is quite ready to put them to use to prop up his arguments. Against Cassius' explanation of the omens we have been indirectly warned just before by Cicero:

> But men may construe things, after their fashion,
> Clean from the purpose of the things themselves.
>
> (I.iii.34–35)

The groundwork of Cassius' indictment of Caesar here is much the same as in his scene with Brutus. There is again the contrast between what Caesar really is and what he has become, but what he has become is something slightly different, fitting the altered circumstances. It is no longer a God or a Colossus who dwarfs his fellowmen, and thus prevents them from achieving personal glory. This representation of Caesar seemed to Cassius suited to Brutus in whom he is trying to awake a sense of thwarted ambition. But upon the terrified Casca it is a sense of the fearfulness of Caesar that he tries to impress.

> Now could I, Casca, name to thee a man
> Most like this dreadful night,
> That thunders, lightens, opens graves, and roars
> As doth the lion in the Capitol;
> A man no mightier than thyself or me
> In personal action, yet prodigious grown
> And fearful, as these strange eruptions are.
>
> (I.iii.72–78)

But while the picture of Caesar as a God and a Colossus bore some semblance to the reality of which we have been allowed a few glimpses, the Caesar that "thunders, lightens, opens graves, and roars" is too obviously a fabrication of the moment for argumentative purposes to affect our mental image of the man. The ironic fact that Caesar later seems to bear out Cassius' description by referring to himself as a lion and Danger's elder twin brother does not alter this impression. For it is Caesar's most ludicrous utterance, and no more affrights us than Snug the joiner's impersonation of that "fearful wildfowl." Our image of Caesar receives its next modification in Brutus' soliloquy. Brutus' Caesar bears no resemblance either to Cassius' God and Colossus or to his roaring lion. He appears to Brutus in the image of a serpent's egg, someone yet harmless but potentially mischievous because of his desire for the crown. At the very moment when it is most in Brutus' interest to incriminate Caesar his intellectual honesty forces him to declare:

> And to speak truth of Caesar
> I have not known when his affections swayed
> More than his reason.
>
> (II.i.19–21)

It is an echo of Plutarch's "And now for himself, after he had ended his Civil Wars, he did so honorably behave himself, that there was no fault to be found in him" ("Caesar," p. 86). But are we to take this as a valid estimate of Caesar's character? Or is it as mistaken as Brutus' view of Antony and Cassius? His reference to Caesar's "lowliness" suggests this, for it is ludicrously inapposite to what we see of Caesar in this play. Thus Shakespeare calls in doubt the validity of Brutus' image of Caesar, just as he calls in doubt Cassius' image, and later Antony's, so that the nature of the real Caesar remains an enigma.

Nor is this enigma dispelled by what we see of Caesar in the following scenes. Even in the privacy of his home he is strenuously engaged in the creation of the legendary Caesar. There is never any real intimacy in his scene with Calpurnia, no momentary lifting of the mask in a soliloquy or an aside.

Here and in the Capitol Shakespeare gives us above all the thrasonical Caesar, who sees himself as outside and above humanity.

> Caesar shall forth: the things that threaten'd me
> Ne'er looked but on my back; when they shall see
> The face of Caesar, they are vanished. . . .
> Of all the wonders that I yet have heard,
> It seems to me most strange that men should fear.
> . . . .   Danger knows full well
> That Caesar is more dangerous than he:
> We are two lions littered in one day,
> And I the elder and more terrible.
>
> (II.ii.10–12, 34–35, 44–47)

Only upon the arrival of the conspirators does he unbend a little, for the first and last time in the play. For his bearing here Shakespeare is probably indebted to Plutarch's description of the youthful Caesar: "And the people loved him marvelously also because of the courteous manner he had to speak to every man, and to use them gently, being more ceremonious therein than was looked for in one of his years. Furthermore, he ever kept a good board, and fared well at his table, and was very liberal besides" ("Caesar," p. 5). Plutarch's coupling of Caesar's hospitality with his courtesy probably suggested to Shakespeare his

> Good friends, go in and taste some wine with me;
> And we, like friends, will straightway go together.
>
> (II.ii.126–27)

But these lines also call up memories of the ceremonial sharing of wine before another betrayal, memories which are strengthened by the kiss which Brutus gives to Caesar in the Capitol ("I kiss thy hand, but not in flattery, Caesar"), and later by Antony's reproach of Brutus at Philippi:

> In your bad strokes, Brutus, you give good words.
> Witness the hole you made in Caesar's heart
> Crying "Long live! hail Caesar!"
>
> (V.i.30–32)

("And forthwith he came to Jesus, and said, Hail master; and kissed him," Matthew 26:49).

We are next given another estimation of Caesar and the conspiracy in Artemidorus'

> My heart laments that virtue cannot live
> Out of the teeth of emulation.
> If thou read this, O Caesar, thou mayst live;
> If not, the Fates with traitors do contrive.
>
> (II.iii.12–15)

Having engaged our sympathies for Caesar more fully than at any previous point in the play, Shakespeare loses little time to alienate them again, so that by the moment of the assassination our antipathies are more strongly aroused than ever before. In his two short speeches in the Capitol Shakespeare gives us a compendium of Caesar's most un-amiable qualities: the cold, glittering hardness, the supreme arrogance, and again the dissociation of himself from the rest of mankind. A note of irony intrudes in his reference to his constancy:

> But I am constant as the northern star,
> Of whose true-fixed and resting quality
> There is no fellow in the firmament.
>
> (III.i.60–62)

The whole speech is ironic both in view of the mental vacillation which we have just witnessed, and his impending fall. It anticipates Othello's similarly ironic comparison of himself to the Pontic sea, which is equally belied by succeed-ing events. Shakespeare adds a final somewhat ludicrous touch in Caesar's "Hence! Wilt thou lift up Olympus?", which, juxtaposed with the immediately succeeding spectacle of his lifeless body lying at the foot of Pompey's statue, crystallizes the contrast between the corporeal and spiritual Caesar, which is summed up a little later by Antony's

> O mighty Caesar! dost thou lie so low?
> Are all thy conquests, glories, triumphs, spoils
> Shrunk to this little measure?
>
> (III.i.148–50)

From Antony we now receive our last image of Caesar. His is the Caesar of popular medieval tradition, the great warrior, the Mirror of Knighthood, the noble Emperor. There is Caesar's nobility,

> Thou art the ruins of the noblest man
> That ever lived in the tide of times;
>
> (III.i.256–57)

his fidelity,

> He was my friend, faithful and just to me;

his largesse,

> To every Roman citizen he gives,
> To every several man, seventy-five drachmas;

his military prowess,

> He hath brought many captives home to Rome;

his compassionate nature,

> When that the poor have cried, Caesar hath wept.
> (III.ii.87, 243–44, 90, 93)

Yet though we are not made to doubt the sincerity of Antony's tribute to Caesar in his soliloquy, the image of him created by Antony in his funeral oration is called into question by its forming a part of Antony's consummate and carefully contrived play upon the emotions of the crowd. As with Cassius' and Brutus' image of Caesar, we cannot accept it as a simple presentment of facts.

Throughout the first half of the play, then, we are given a series of images of Caesar none of which bear much mutual resemblance, though some of them are not irreconcilable with each other. There are the two Caesar's of Cassius, there is Casca's Caesar, Brutus' Caesar, Artemidorus' Caesar, and finally Antony's Caesar. But doubt is thrown in one way or another on the validity of most of these images. And to these Shakespeare adds his own presentation of Caesar, a presentation so enigmatic and ambiguous that none of the other images are really dispelled by it. It is a Pirandellian presentation of the Caesar figure. "Which of all these is the real Caesar?" Shakespeare seems to ask. And he takes care not to provide an answer. But does not Shakespeare further anticipate Pirandello by making us feel that perhaps there *is* no real Caesar, that he merely exists as a set of images in other men's minds and his own? For Shakespeare's Caesar is continuously engaged in what Pirandello calls *costruirsi*, "building himself up," creating his own image of Caesar, until we are left to wonder whether a lifting of the mask would reveal to us any face at all.

What reasons lie behind Shakespeare's peculiar presentation of the figure of Caesar? The usual answer given by critics, that Shakespeare draws Caesar unsympathetically in order to preserve our regard for the conspirators, or, as Bernard Shaw more bluntly put it, that he writes "Caesar down for the mere technical purpose of writing Brutus up,"[11] will not do. For, as we have seen, what is involved in Shakespeare's presentation is something quite different from a mere writing down of the character. Another explanation is provided by Mr. H. M. Ayres who, as long ago as 1910, argued that, ever since Muret modeled his Caesar on the braggart Hercules of Seneca, the typical stage Caesar in the Renaissance was the vainglorious, hubristic figure of the French Senecans, and that Shakespeare had to endow his Caesar with these characteristics to fulfill the expectations of his audience.[12] However, there is no indication that any of the Elizabethan Caesar plays that were performed in the public theaters were influenced by the French Senecans. Muret, Grévin, and Garnier wrote only for academic audiences, and even a more popular play, like the anonymous *Caesar's Revenge*, may never have reached the public stage, for on its title page appears the note, "Privately acted by the Studentes of Trinity Colledge in Oxford." If Shakespeare endowed his Caesar with traits ultimately derived

[11] G. B. Shaw, *Three Plays for Puritans* (Constable, 1925), p. xxx.
[12] *PMLA*, XXV, 183ff.

from the French Senecan Caesar plays he must have done so for other reasons than those suggested by Mr. Ayres.

Partly Shakespeare's presentment of Caesar was probably done in the interest of dramatic suspense. Shakespeare appears to be playing on the audience's divided attitude to the Caesar story, giving encouragement in turn to each man's preconceived ideas. And since on our estimate of Caesar depends to a large extent our view of the justification of the entire conspiracy, the whole drama is thus kept within the area of the problem play. For though, as it seems to me, Shakespeare makes abundantly clear the catastrophic consequences of the murder, he does not, I think, make wholly clear its moral indefensibility. His ambiguous presentment of the Caesar figure allows responses like that of Professor Dover Wilson to be formulated, and I see no reason to doubt that there were also Dover Wilsons in Shakespeare's audience. In fact, the polarity of critical estimates of the character of the main *dramatis personae* and of the poet's attitude to the conspiracy bears witness to Shakespeare's success in making *Julius Caesar* a problem play. It is a problem play in much the same way as the *Wild Duck*, which has a very similar theme: the tragic mischief created by the actions of a young idealist in fulfillment of the highest principles, partly through his utter blindness to what people are really like. In both cases the question is put to the audience: "Was he or was he not morally justified in doing what he did?", and in both cases the dramatist's answer seems to me an insistent but not a compelling "No."

The main purpose of Shakespeare's dissociation of the corporeal and the spiritual Caesar throughout the play is, no doubt, to show up the futility and foolishness of the assassination. The whole second part of the play is an ironic comment on Brutus'

> We all stand up against the spirit of Caesar,
> And in the spirit of men there is no blood;
> O, that we then could come by Caesar's spirit,
> And not dismember Caesar!

(II.i.167–70)

What is involved in the second half of the play is more than a grim pun, which makes the conspirators find that, while they have dismembered Caesar's body, his spirit, i.e. his ghost, still walks abroad, and exacts his revenge. For the spirit of Caesar is also that legendary figure, that God and Colossus, whom Cassius deplores, and whom Caesar seeks to impose upon the imagination of his countrymen and, it would seem, upon his own. In this he is handicapped by physical and moral frailties from which the murder frees him, and allows the legendary Caesar to come into his own, assisted by Antony's rhetoric, just as Antony later assists that other "spirit" of Caesar, his ghost, in executing his revenge.

That the spirit of Caesar in the sense of "Caesarism," the absolute rule of a single man, informs the second part of the play, as MacCallum, Dover Wilson, and others maintain, seems to me unsupported by anything in the text. Dover Wilson writes: "When Brutus exclaims 'We all stand up against the spirit of Caesar' he sums up the play in one line. For the spirit of Caesar, which was the destiny of Rome, is the fate against which Brutus struggles in vain" (p. xxii). And MacCallum, in a rather different spirit, tells us that "Shakespeare makes it abundantly clear that the rule of the single master-mind is the only admissible solution for the problem of the time."[13] Both these critics, and the many others who have expressed similar opinions, seem to me to be reading Plutarch's view into Shakespeare's play. Nothing in the play suggests to me that Caesar is to be thought of as the Man of Destiny or that the establishment of one man's rule is the inevitable outcome of the Civil War. As in Plutarch, the people are shown to be strongly opposed to Caesar's assumption of the crown, as the Lupercal scene makes clear. Over against this can only be set the plebeians' shouts after Brutus' speech, "Let him be Caesar," "Caesar's better parts shall be crowned in Brutus," but to take these as evidence of strong monarchic feelings among the Roman people is surely to miss their function in the scene's context. At Philippi it is not Caesarism or the providential scheme of Plutarch and Dante which defeats Brutus and Cassius, but their flaws of soldiership and character, which make

13 Sir Mungo MacCallum, *Shakespeare's Roman Plays*, p. 214.

Brutus give the word for attack too early, and Cassius slay himself rashly, in premature despair. As far as the super-natural interferes in the affairs of men, it is Caesar's ghost rather than the hand of God that contributes to the defeat of the conspirators. Nor are we anywhere made to feel, as we are in Plutarch and Appian, that the Roman Republic has sunk into a state of corruption which only the establish-ment of one man's rule can cure.

Kittredge was undoubtedly right when, first among critics, he pointed to the element of "hubris" and ἄτη that pervades Shakespeare's portrayal of Caesar.[14] His infatuation, which makes him disregard all warnings, is repeatedly emphasized, from his first contemptuous dismissal of the soothsayer until his refusal to read Artemidorus' petition, and is pointed out by Calpurnia: "Alas, my lord, Your wisdom is consumed in confidence." His "hubris" is heightened with each appearance until it reaches its climax in his last speech in the Capitol. It is not difficult to trace the pedigree of this tragedy of "hubris," which is one of the several tragedies imbedded in the play. It is in a direct line of descent from Greek tragedy by way of Seneca, the adaptation of Senecan tragedy to the Caesar story by Muret and his imitators, and its adoption in the *Caesar's Revenge* play. But while the theme of "hubris" is dominant in all the plays in the Muret tradition, that of blind infatuation is only developed by Shakespeare.

We have seen, then, that in *Julius Caesar* Shakespeare puts a twofold problem before his audience: There is the psychological problem of the nature of the real Caesar; and hinging upon it there is the ethical problem of the moral defensibility of the murder. Looked at in this way *Julius Caesar* reveals an unobtrusive kinship with Shakespeare's other chief problem play, *Measure for Measure*. Central to both is a moral choice imposed upon the protagonists, Brutus and Isabel. And in both cases Shakespeare, while, as it seems to me, strongly suggesting by the orientation of his dramatic material the wrongfulness of their choice, makes it remain sufficiently problematic to allow his audience to form varying views about it.

[14] *Julius Caesar*, ed. Kittredge, *Introduction*.

ROY WALKER

from *Unto Caesar: A Review of Recent Productions*

No major play of Shakespeare's has suffered more from democratic distortion than *Julius Caesar*. It seems improbable that the sympathies of the Elizabethan poet and his audience would be hostile to the aging, sick and childless personal ruler, brutally and treacherously assassinated by professed friends who then plunge their country into the dread cycle of civil wars that ends only with the disruption and downfall of the Republic. Although Hazlitt supposed that Shakespeare painted an entirely antipathetic portrait of Caesar, it was still possible, before two world wars darkened the scene, to recognize, as MacCallum did in 1910, that "Shakespeare makes it abundantly clear that the rule of the single master-mind is the only admissible solution for the problem of the time".[1] The Hazlitt tradition reached its patriotic peak in Dover Wilson's 1949 edition of the play. Meanwhile it had spread to the stage. After Orson Welles' 1937 modern-dress production (in which, of course, this powerful actor elected to play Brutus), other modern-dress *Caesars* in this country, and most costume productions too, presented the drama as the democratic doing-in of a diabolical dictator. They could therefore make nothing of the celestial portents and still less of the fifth act in which the spirit of the dead dictator inconveniently triumphs.

From *Shakespeare Survey*, XI (1958), pp. 132–35. Reprinted by permission of The Cambridge University Press.
[1] M. W. MacCallum, *Shakespeare's Roman Plays* (1910), p. 214.

Now that the dogs of war are on the leash again there are signs of scholarly reaction on both sides of the Atlantic. In 1953 Virgil Whitaker argued that Shakespeare meant Caesar to seem "a great and good ruler"[2] and in the new Arden edition two years later T. S. Dorsch agreed that "Shakespeare wishes us to admire his Caesar."[3] A similar rehabilitation on the stage was overdue. It was peculiarly appropriate that this should be achieved in the year of the 2000th anniversary of the assassination, and in the Shakespeare Memorial Theatre at Stratford-upon-Avon, where Glen Byam Shaw produced the play. The main interest of this production lay in its bold centralization of Caesar, who became the real as well as the nominal protagonist, and in the means employed to keep this presence dramatically alive on the stage after the actual murder, with a consequent gain in coherency and in the significance of the last act.

Glen Byam Shaw's interpretation began at the beginning of the play. The curtain rose on a stage dominated by a larger-than-life statue of Caesar, raised on a tall plinth in the center of the stage. After the disrobing of this image by the envious tribunes, this statue pivoted backwards out of sight, the two walls of grey stone parted and against the blue sky at the back the living Caesar was acclaimed. The statue might easily have dwarfed the human figure, but the magnificence of the gold-embroidered crimson toga and the majesty of Cyril Luckham's bearing made him the incarnation of an immutable and pivotal principle of order. This ordered Rome was visible in the massive fluted monoliths of light grey stone, ranged outwards from Caesar as their personal center in two symmetrical lines, continued in the tall stone portals flanking the forestage. Here was the wide perspective of Caesar's Rome with Caesar himself the keystone.

When the procession had passed, that center was unfilled while Cassius, effectively played as a "little Caesar," a Corsican upstart, by Geoffrey Keen, maneuvered for the advantage of height with a Brutus (Alec Clunes) who was every inch Caesar's angel in presence and noble innocence.

[2] Virgil K. Whitaker, *Shakespeare's Use of Learning* (1953), p. 234.
[3] T. S. Dorsch (ed.), *Julius Caesar* (1955), p. xxxviii.

At the end of this scene of lurking disorder, the sky darkened with supernatural speed and an ominous patch of crimson appeared above the place where Caesar had stood. Cassius' defiance of the lightning was posed at stage center and met with a crackling blaze of white light from heaven, a warning which went unheeded by the arch-plotter.

The foremost monoliths converged again to close the main stage and leave the forestage for Brutus' orchard, but the central niche where Caesar's image had been was now eloquently empty while Brutus struggled to put away loyalty and friendship. When this orchard wall parted to reveal the interior of Caesar's house, the central entrance was hung with a divided crimson curtain, behind which was visible a head of Caesar, now isolated on a pedestal of his own height. The front walls converged again and Artemidorus paused before the empty niche to read over his warning to Caesar. They reopened on the Senate, with a raised central throne, its back a solid sheet of gleaming gold, on which Caesar took his place with his head high against the blue sky beyond. As he fell to the assassins' swords there was a fierce crackle of lightning from the clear sky, which was then rapidly overcast.

When the scene changed to the Forum, the two lines of monoliths had fallen back in disorder, leaving a wider gap in the center. Caesar's central throne had now given place to the popular pulpit from which successive demagogues harangued the changeable many who lined the front of the stage in dark silhouette, as though under a sinister shadow that had fallen on all Rome. Caesar's catafalque, the body shrouded with the crimson, gold-ornamented robe, was laid on the center of the forestage, below the pulpit. As Antony (Richard Johnson) passionately roused the mob to blood, the sky reddened, and at the climactic cry "Here was Caesar! when comes such another?" he was standing a little off-center in front of the now empty pulpit, his right arm thrust straight up to heaven; and suddenly in the true center of the sky the northern star shone out alone. After the tumultuous exit the stage was empty and silent for a moment with the star shining distantly down. The poet Cinna half turned his head towards it as he entered saying "I dreamt tonight that I did feast with Caesar." Back surged the mob, now bearing lighted torches, bobbing and blazing symbols of disorder, the wandering fires of an earth from which the unmoved mover had been withdrawn. The interval arrived with an unforgettable stage picture of the murdered poet, flopped brokenly over the front of the pulpit like a discarded glove-puppet, and the star, blazing brighter in a sky that turned from blue to black, shining down in silent comment on the grim scene of chaos come again.

The second half opened with the triumvirate standing apart with their backs to a huge suspended map of the Mediterranean. Antony was in front of Italy, Octavius before the Balkans, Lepidus over against Asia Minor; the stretches of sea between the actors subtly suggested the space that always separated them, and the pattern of civil wars to come. Rome was now gone without a trace, and it was in a blood-red tent near Sardis that Brutus contended with Cassius and saw Caesar's ghost, which materialized in the open mouth of the tent, against the sky. When this tent was struck the bare stage was broken only by a low ridge of fissured rock which rose to a slight eminence a little off-center. It was from here that Octavius and Antony, with their troops and standards, saw Brutus and Cassius coming down to battle in the plains where dusty death awaits them. Cassius fell, then Brutus, their own swords turned against them by friendly hands, in the same central area and general posture as Caesar was, but further downstage, on a lower level. When Brutus came upon Cassius' body and exclaimed "O Julius Caesar, thou art mighty yet!", the northern star suddenly appeared again. There it remained, so that the final curtain recalled and resolved the first-half curtain. The dead body of the tragically deluded liberator lay in the center of the stage, not in Rome but in the wilderness he had helped to make of Rome, and high above him shone out the star of whose true-fixed and resting quality there is no fellow in the firmament.[4]

[4] It is necessary for the reviewer to disclose an interest. The present writer suggested to Mr. Byam Shaw the parallel between "that bright Occidental star," as the Jacobean translators of the Bible called the Queen, and the Caesar whose soul was taken up and made a star in the climax of Ovid's *Metamorphoses*, an episode to which Shakespeare refers in the opening

scene of *1 Henry VI*. He also suggested that the northern star speech in *Julius Caesar* draws poetically on that Ovidian climax, and that the promise that the ghost will appear again at Philippi may have been kept by displaying an emblematic star in "the heavens." (For a more elaborate staging of the transfiguration of a soul into a star on the stage, see the stage direction for the death of Hercules in Thomas Heywood's *The Brazen Age*.) Ways in which a comparable effect might be provided for modern audiences with present-day lighting equipment were also discussed. But a suggested interpretation is one thing; imaginative transformation is another. Mr. Byam Shaw transmuted the argument into his own art. If I am open to suspicion of being prejudiced in favor of the result, I may at least point out that the general opinion of responsible critics was that the production was conspicuously successful in its rendering of the true values of the play.

Suggested References

The number of possible references is vast and grows alarmingly. (The *Shakespeare Quarterly* devotes a substantial part of one issue each year to a list of the previous year's work, and *Shakespeare Survey*—an annual publication—includes a substantial review of recent scholarship, as well as an occasional essay surveying a few decades of scholarship on a chosen topic.) Though no works are indispensable, those listed below have been found helpful.

1. Shakespeare's Times

Byrne, M. St. Clare. *Elizabethan Life in Town and Country*. Rev. ed. New York: Barnes & Noble, Inc., 1961. Chapters on manners, beliefs, education, etc., with illustrations.

Craig, Hardin. *The Enchanted Glass: the Elizabethan Mind in Literature*. New York and London: Oxford University Press, 1936. The Elizabethan intellectual climate.

Nicoll, Allardyce (ed.). *The Elizabethans*. London: Cambridge University Press, 1957. An anthology of Elizabethan writings, especially valuable for its illustrations from paintings, title pages, etc.

Shakespeare's England. 2 vols. Oxford: The Clarendon Press, 1916. A large collection of scholarly essays on a wide variety of topics (e.g., astrology, costume, gardening, horsemanship), with special attention to Shakespeare's references to these topics.

Tillyard, E. M. W. *The Elizabethan World Picture*. London: Chatto & Windus, 1943; New York: The Macmillan Company, 1944. A brief account of some Elizabethan ideas of the universe.

Wilson, John Dover (ed.). *Life in Shakespeare's England.* 2nd ed. New York: The Macmillan Company, 1913. An anthology of Elizabethan writings on the countryside, superstition, education, the court, etc.

2. Shakespeare

Bentley, Gerald E. *Shakespeare: A Biographical Handbook.* New Haven, Conn.: Yale University Press, 1961. The facts about Shakespeare, with virtually no conjecture intermingled.

Bradby, Anne (ed.). *Shakespeare Criticism, 1919–1935.* London: Oxford University Press, 1936. A small anthology of excellent essays on the plays.

Bush, Geoffrey Douglas. *Shakespeare and the Natural Condition.* Cambridge, Mass.: Harvard University Press; London: Oxford University Press, 1956. A short, sensitive account of Shakespeare's view of "Nature," touching most of the works.

Chambers, E. K. *William Shakespeare: A Study of Facts and Problems.* 2 vols. London: Oxford University Press, 1930. An invaluable, detailed reference work; not for the casual reader.

Chute, Marchette. *Shakespeare of London.* New York: E. P. Dutton & Co., Inc., 1949. A readable biography fused with portraits of Stratford and London life.

Clemen, Wolfgang H. *The Development of Shakespeare's Imagery.* Cambridge, Mass.: Harvard University Press, 1951. (Originally published in German, 1936.) A temperate account of a subject often abused.

Craig, Hardin. *An Interpretation of Shakespeare.* New York: Citadel Press, 1948. A scholar's book designed for the layman. Comments on all the works.

Dean, Leonard F. (ed.). *Shakespeare: Modern Essays in Criticism.* New York: Oxford University Press, 1957. Mostly mid-twentieth-century critical studies, covering Shakespeare's artistry.

Granville-Barker, Harley. *Prefaces to Shakespeare*. 2 vols. Princeton, N.J.: Princeton University Press, 1946–47. Essays on ten plays by a scholarly man of the theater.

Harbage, Alfred. *As They Liked It*. New York: The Macmillan Company, 1947. A sensitive, long essay on Shakespeare, morality, and the audience's expectations.

Smith, D. Nichol (ed.). *Shakespeare Criticism*. New York: Oxford University Press, 1916. A selection of criticism from 1623 to 1840, ranging from Ben Jonson to Thomas Carlyle.

Spencer, Theodore. *Shakespeare and the Nature of Man*. New York: The Macmillan Company, 1942. Shakespeare's plays in relation to Elizabethan thought.

Stoll, Elmer Edgar. *Shakespeare and Other Masters*. Cambridge, Mass.: Harvard University Press; London: Oxford University Press, 1940. Essays on tragedy, comedy, and aspects of dramaturgy, with special reference to some of Shakespeare's plays.

Traversi, D. A. *An Approach to Shakespeare*. Rev. ed. New York: Doubleday & Co., Inc., 1956. An analysis of the plays, beginning with words, images, and themes, rather than with characters.

Van Doren, Mark. *Shakespeare*. New York: Henry Holt & Company, Inc., 1939. Brief, perceptive readings of all of the plays.

Whitaker, Virgil K. *Shakespeare's Use of Learning*. San Marino, Calif.: Huntington Library, 1953. A study of the relation of Shakespeare's reading to his development as a dramatist.

3. Shakespeare's Theater

Adams, John Cranford. *The Globe Playhouse*. Rev. ed. New York: Barnes & Noble, Inc., 1961. A detailed conjecture about the physical characteristics of the theater Shakespeare often wrote for.

Beckerman, Bernard. *Shakespeare at the Globe, 1599–1609*. New York: The Macmillan Company, 1962. On the playhouse and on Elizabethan dramaturgy, acting, and staging.

Chambers, E. K. *The Elizabethan Stage.* 4 vols. New York: Oxford University Press, 1923. Reprinted with corrections, 1945. An indispensable reference work on theaters, theatrical companies, and staging at court.

Harbage, Alfred. *Shakespeare's Audience.* New York: Columbia University Press; London: Oxford University Press, 1941. A study of the size and nature of the theatrical public.

Hodges, C. Walter. *The Globe Restored.* London: Ernest Benn, Ltd., 1953; New York: Coward-McCann, Inc., 1954. A well-illustrated and readable attempt to reconstruct the Globe Theatre.

Nagler, A. M. *Shakespeare's Stage.* Tr. by Ralph Manheim. New Haven, Conn.: Yale University Press, 1958. An excellent brief introduction to the physical aspect of the playhouse.

Smith, Irwin. *Shakespeare's Globe Playhouse.* New York: Charles Scribner's Sons, 1957. Chiefly indebted to J. C. Adams' controversial book, with additional material and scale drawings for model-builders.

Venezky, Alice S. *Pageantry on the Shakespearean Stage.* New York: Twayne Publishers, Inc., 1951. An examination of spectacle in Elizabethan drama.

4. Miscellaneous Reference Works

Abbott, E. A. *A Shakespearean Grammar.* New edition. New York: The Macmillan Company, 1877. An examination of differences between Elizabethan and modern grammar.

Bartlett, John. *A New and Complete Concordance . . . to . . . Shakespeare.* New York: The Macmillan Company, 1894. An index to most of Shakespeare's words.

Bullough, Geoffrey. *Narrative and Dramatic Sources of Shakespeare.* 4 vols. Vols. 5 and 6 in preparation. New York: Columbia University Press; London: Routledge & Kegan Paul, Ltd., 1957–. A collection of many of the books Shakespeare drew upon.

Greg, W. W. *The Shakespeare First Folio*. New York and London: Oxford University Press, 1955. A detailed yet readable history of the first collection (1623) of Shakespeare's plays.

Kökeritz, Helge. *Shakespeare's Names*. New Haven, Conn.: Yale University Press, 1959; London: Oxford University Press, 1960. A guide to the pronunciation of some 1,800 names appearing in Shakespeare.

————. *Shakespeare's Pronunciation*. New Haven, Conn.: Yale University Press; London: Oxford University Press, 1953. Contains much information about puns and rhymes.

Linthicum, Marie C. *Costume in the Drama of Shakespeare and His Contemporaries*. New York and London: Oxford University Press, 1936. On the fabrics and dress of the age, and references to them in the plays.

Muir, Kenneth. *Shakespeare's Sources*. London: Methuen & Co., Ltd., 1957. Vol. 2 in preparation. The first volume, on the comedies and tragedies, attempts to ascertain what books were Shakespeare's sources, and what use he made of them.

Onions, C. T. *A Shakespeare Glossary*. London: Oxford University Press, 1911; 2nd ed., rev., with enlarged addenda, 1953. Definitions of words (or senses of words) now obsolete.

Partridge, Eric. *Shakespeare's Bawdy*. Rev. ed. New York: E. P. Dutton & Co., Inc.; London: Routledge & Kegan Paul, Ltd., 1955. A glossary of bawdy words and phrases.

Shakespeare Quarterly. See headnote to Suggested References.

Shakespeare Survey. See headnote to Suggested References.

5. *Julius Caesar*

Ayres, H. M. "Shakespeare's *Julius Caesar* in the Light of Some Other Versions," *Publications of the Modern Language Association*, XXV (1910), 183–227.

Bonjour, Adrien. *The Structure of "Julius Caesar."* Liverpool, Eng.: University Press of Liverpool, 1958.

Charlton, H. B. *Shakespearian Tragedy*. New York and London: Cambridge University Press, 1948.

Charney, Maurice. *Shakespeare's Roman Plays*. Cambridge, Mass.: Harvard University Press, 1961.

Dorsch, T. S. (ed.). *Julius Caesar*. Cambridge, Mass.: Harvard University Press, 1955.

Granville-Barker, Harley. *Prefaces to Shakespeare*. Vol. II. Princeton, N.J.: Princeton University Press, 1947.

Knight, G. Wilson. *The Imperial Theme*. New York: British Book Centre, Inc.; London: Methuen & Co., Ltd., 1951.

MacCallum, M. W. *Shakespeare's Roman Plays and Their Background*. New York and London: The Macmillan Company, 1910.

Muir, Kenneth. *Shakespeare's Sources*. Vol. I. London: Methuen & Co., Ltd., 1957.

Palmer, John. *Political Characters of Shakespeare*. London and New York: The Macmillan Company, 1945, 1946.

Schanzer, Ernest. *The Problem Plays of Shakespeare*. New York: Schocken Books, Inc.; London: Routledge & Kegan Paul, Ltd., 1963.

Smith, Gordon Ross. "Brutus, Virtue, and Will," *Shakespeare Quarterly*, X (1959), 367–79.

Smith, Warren D. "The Duplicate Revelation of Portia's Death," *Shakespeare Quarterly*, IV (1953), 153–61.

Stewart, J. I. M. *Character and Motive in Shakespeare*. New York: Longmans, Green & Co., Inc., 1949.

Stirling, Brents. *Unity in Shakespearian Tragedy*. New York: Columbia University Press; London: Oxford University Press, 1956.

Whitaker, Virgil K. *Shakespeare's Use of Learning*. San Marino, Calif.: Huntington Library, 1953.